Freedom of Association

OXFORD LABOUR LAW

The *Oxford Labour Law* series (formerly known as the *Oxford Monographs on Labour Law* series) has come to represent a significant contribution to the literature of British, European, and international labour law. The series recognizes the arrival not only of a renewed interest in labour law generally, but also the need for fresh approaches to the study of labour law following a period of momentous change in the UK, Europe, and the common law world. The series is concerned with all aspects of labour law, including traditional subjects of study such as collective labour law and individual employment law. It also includes works that concentrate on the growing role of human rights and the combating of discrimination in employment. Other works in the series have examined the law and economics of the labour market and the impact of social security law. The series includes national, comparative and international perspectives on all of these topics. Two of the contributing authors to the series, Lucy Vickers and Diamond Ashiagbor, have received awards from the Society of Legal Scholars in respect of their books.

ALSO AVAILABLE IN THE SERIES

Underpaid and Unrecognized
State-Induced Unfree Labour
Katie Bates, Amir Paz-Fuchs

Workplace Investigations
Justice and the Legal Regulation of Employer Conduct
Adriana Orifici

Shaping Contracts for Work
The Normative Influence of Terms Implied by Law
Gabrielle Golding

Human Rights Due Diligence and Labour Governance
Ingrid Landau

Catholic Social Teaching and Labour Law
An Ethical Perspective on Work
Mark Bell

Freedom of Association

From Labour Law to the Constitution

Alan Bogg, *BCL, MA, DPhil*

OXFORD
UNIVERSITY PRESS

OXFORD
UNIVERSITY PRESS

Great Clarendon Street, Oxford, OX2 6DP,
United Kingdom

Oxford University Press is a department of the University of Oxford.
It furthers the University's objective of excellence in research, scholarship,
and education by publishing worldwide. Oxford is a registered trade mark of
Oxford University Press in the UK and in certain other countries.

Published in the United States of America by Oxford University Press
546 Fifth Avenue, New York, NY 10036, United States of America.

British Library Cataloguing in Publication Data
Data available

Library of Congress Control Number: 2026937055

ISBN 9780198790440

DOI: 10.1093/9780191831690.001.0001

Printed and bound by
CPI Group (UK) Ltd., Croydon, CR0 4YY

The manufacturer's authorized representative in the EU for product safety is
Oxford University Press España S.A. of Parque Empresarial San Fernando de Henares,
Avenida de Castilla, 2 – 28830 Madrid (www.oup.es/en or product.safety@oup.com).
OUP España S.A. also acts as importer into Spain of products made by the manufacturer.

FSC
www.fsc.org
MIX
Paper | Supporting
responsible forestry
FSC® C013604

Series Editors' Preface

This fascinating book takes a bold and refreshing look at freedom of association.

Labour lawyers standing on the outside have been highly critical of the judicial role in this field, whether in the development of the common law, the construction of statutes, or the application of constitutional and human rights. Professor Bogg inverts that process by pursuing an internal interpretative approach, in which he sets out to understand the underlying values that have informed the judicial approach to freedom of association.

In doing so, he is concerned to develop his argument through the lens of an enigmatic sentence from the writings of Kahn-Freund, where freedom of association is described as both a human right and an essential feature of labour law. This gives rise to an intriguing question of whether human rights law would shape the understanding of freedom of association as it applies in labour law, or whether labour law would shape the understanding of freedom of association as it applies in human rights law.

The answer is perhaps counter-intuitive. Professor Bogg persuasively demonstrates the deep roots of freedom of association in the common law and argues convincingly that it emerged to permit workers to do collectively what they could do individually. That is to say to engage in '*association as activity*, a periodic process whereby wages were adjusted and settled through strikes and collective negotiations', in contrast to '*association as organisation*' which was 'an object of suspicion'.

But in recognising the freedom of workers to bargain collectively, it was also recognized that 'the worker should always be protected from coercive interference from others in seeking his own contractual bargain'. The latter was a powerful theme in the jurisprudence of the 19th century, as the courts sought by various means to address 'the perennial paradox of freedom of association identified by Dicey', namely that 'its collective exercise posed a standing threat to individual freedoms', the threat being the trade union as much as the employer.

What has been the effect on these underlying values and principles by the increasing influence of constitutional and human rights law on labour law? Has this influence intruded on the autonomy of labour law, as had been feared by authors such as Wedderburn in the past? Paradoxically, the answer is no: 'the direction of normative influence has been *from* labour law back into constitutional norms, not the other way round', courts tending to integrate labour law values and norms into their constitutional jurisprudence.

The argument is presented elegantly in four chapters dealing with the personal scope of freedom of association, the right to bargain collectively, the right to strike, and the closed shop. Professor Bogg demonstrates that the constitutional and human rights courts are much more comfortable when dealing with cases brought by individuals who have been the victims of discrimination, exclusion or other mistreatment, than with cases brought by trade unions seeking to challenge the collective parameters of freedom of association law.

Drawing on constitutional theory, Professor Bogg reveals not only a consistency of judicial approach (which might be said to be exemplified by the decision in *Wilson v United Kingdom* [2002] ECHR 552) but also that the underlying themes applied by the courts are grounded in constitutional principle. On the basis of equality, this justifies intervention on behalf of excluded or disadvantaged individuals, and on the basis of democratic legitimacy it requires deference to be shown to legislatures on matters of structural design.

Those familiar with Professor Bogg's work will recognise his deep personal concern with the 'equal moral standing of citizens', his unrivalled ability to synthesise legal philosophy, constitutional law, and labour law, as well as his mastery of the jurisprudence from multiple jurisdictions. No surprise then that the book enhances understanding—in quite profound ways—of the underlying values which continue to inform the legal process, enabling us better to predict and critically engage with judicial decisions.

It also emphasises the autonomy of labour law in a human rights era, even if—with some exceptions—that autonomy has triumphed at a time when labour law is in retreat.

ACLD, KDE, MRF
19 January 2026

Acknowledgements

In the preparation of this monograph, I have incurred many debts, both personal and institutional. The ideas for an extended study of Freedom of Association started to form a decade ago. I was immensely fortunate to be awarded a Philip Leverhulme Prize in 2014 while I was still based at Oxford. They were themes that we wrestled with each year in teaching the BCL with the incredible Oxford Labour Law group. Through the support of the Prize, I wrote a number of articles and book chapters on disparate themes from freedom of association. I was still struggling to see the connections between the parts and to gain a view of the totality. It is the great virtue of the Leverhulme Trust that it allows its recipients the freedom to wander down blind alleys without berating them or submerging them in bureaucracy. The Trust represents how academia ought to be. I could not have delivered on this book without that initial start from the Prize.

For many years, my dear mum would enquire periodically as to the whereabouts of this book (i.e., every time we spoke). Unfortunately, she died before I finished it. That is the standard risk of missing deadlines as a middle-aged author. Let that be a salutary lesson, dear reader. As I finished the book, she was very much in mind. As a young man, I ended up in a Rehab in my early 20s. Indeed, I celebrated my 21st birthday while there. Every week of that nine months she would get the train across from Darwen to Blackpool to see me, never missing. I graduated successfully from Pierpoint House Treatment Centre, clean and sober, and worked for a short while as a plasterer's labourer. They were very happy times in my little bedsit. When I gently enquired if I had any talent for this, it was gently suggested that I might try something else. I knew that I loved books and learning. As a boy, my mum would take me to Darwen Public Library where I consumed biographies of great scientists voraciously. When I was 9 years old or thereabouts, I harboured a fantasy that I might one day be Lucasian Professor of Mathematics in Cambridge. I never managed that. I did end up eventually in the other place teaching and writing about law and reading old books and law reports in very old libraries. I could not have fulfilled that dream from whence I came without someone believing in me when very few people did. That was Mum. Wherever she is now, I send her my love, and I hope she is reading this book.

There are five people in particular whose reflections on freedom of association have influenced my own thinking profoundly over many years: Cynthia Estlund, Keith Ewing, Michael Ford KC, Brian Langille, and Tonia Novitz. As well as being brilliant thinkers, they have been as kind and supportive in intellectual collaboration as in intellectual disagreement. While I have no doubt that they will disagree with much in these pages, whatever is of merit owes a great deal to their work and generosity.

Beyond this group, I have been blessed with the support of many other scholars and practitioners in the development of the arguments in this book. It is an embarrassingly long list. I would like to thank Jeremias Adams-Prassl, Gordon Anderson, Joe Atkinson, Catherine Barnard, Stuart Brittenden KC, Douglas Brodie, David Cabrelli, Hugh Collins, Philippa Collins, Nicola Countouris, Shantha David, A.C.L. Davies, Paul L. Davies, Paul S. Davies, Manoj Dias-Abey, Ruth Dukes, Anthony Forsyth, Sarah Fraser Butlin, Sandy Fredman, Mark Freedland, Lord Hendy KC, Ioannis Katsaroumpas, Virginia Mantouvalou, Dan Schaffer, and Eric Tucker.

I am very grateful to the University of Bristol. It has kept the lights on at home following a family move to South West England in 2017. It also generously provided me with a period of research leave which enabled me to finish this book. I would like to convey my thanks to Old Square Chambers which has provided a source of collegiality, warmth, and new intellectual challenge. It has been fantastic to don the wig from time to time in my other life as a barrister with such fine colleagues. Finally, sincere thanks are due to the team at OUP for its patience in waiting for this manuscript to appear, and for their support in the production process.

In my first monograph back in 2009, I wrote the following: 'Finally, and most of all, I would like to thank my wonderful wife, Sarah Green . . . As a legal critic, best friend and wife, she is second to none.' It is my extraordinary good fortune that I am still able to write this in 2025.

Since 2009, we have added Alfie and Ben (and two labradoodles, Noodle and Nellie). This book is dedicated to Alfie and Ben, with much love from their Dad.

Contents

Table of Cases

UNITED KINGDOM

EUROPEAN COMMISSION OF HUMAN RIGHTS

EUROPEAN COMMITTEE OF SOCIAL RIGHTS (ECSR)

EUROPEAN COURT OF HUMAN RIGHTS

NATIONAL COURT

Canada

Ireland

United States

Tables of Treaties and Conventions

TABLES OF NATIONAL LEGISLATION

Canada

Iceland

Ireland

Sweden

United Kingdom

United States

1
Freedom of Association and the Autonomy of Labour Law

I. Freedom of Association in Constitutional Law and Labour Law

According to Sir Otto Kahn-Freund, freedom of association had two legal lives:

> Freedom to organise has two social and therefore two legal functions. It is a civil liberty, a human right, an aspect of freedom of association . . . its existence and adequate guarantees for its exercise are, however, also indispensable conditions for the operation of collective labour relations.[1]

This book on freedom of association is an extended reflection on this Kahn-Freund quotation. Since I first read it as a young graduate student, cited in one of Lord Wedderburn's famously searing critiques of the European Convention on Human Rights (ECHR), it has puzzled, illuminated, and provoked my own reflections on freedom of association. Like a great Victorian novel, I see something different each time I return to it. The puzzle is enhanced at the intriguing prospect that Wedderburn and Kahn-Freund probably intended to convey different things in drawing the distinction. To be sure, Wedderburn did not reject the idea that individual freedom is an important value in labour law.[2] Or that we should care about civil liberties. Nevertheless, his main concern was that human rights were too heavily skewed in favour of the individual freedom because collective interests were enshrined in instruments (like the European Social Charter [ESC]) with weaker mechanisms of protection. For this reason, the civil liberty might even pose a destabilising threat to collective labour law.

[1] Kahn-Freund, cited in Lord Wedderburn, 'Freedom of Association or Right to Organise? The Common Law and International Sources', in Lord Wedderburn, *Employment Rights in Britain and Europe* (Lawrence & Wishart 1991) 142.

[2] Ibid. 142–143.

Freedom of Association. Alan Bogg, Oxford University Press. © Alan Bogg 2026. DOI: 10.1093/9780191831690.003.0001

For Kahn-Freund, by contrast, the civil liberty and its corresponding individual freedom were 'indispensable' to collective labour relations.

More remarkably still, the entire legal development of freedom of association in labour law may be understood as the complex interplay between the civil liberty and the labour law conceptions. The reader is invited to see the world in a grain of sand (or in a few short sentences). At least, that is what I shall argue in this book.

What is at stake in this bifurcation? A useful general starting point is the 'autonomy' of labour law.[3] This emphasises the separation of different legal compartments in a single legal system. For example, labour law is 'autonomous' of the private law of contract because labour law's purposes and rules are directed at the protection of workers rather than contract law's facilitation of freely negotiated individual bargains. A similar idea of autonomy might also be true of freedom of association as it has developed in constitutional law and labour law.

In its guise as a general 'civil liberty', freedom of association is enshrined in many liberal constitutions. The basic starting point for freedom of association as civil liberty is the general freedom to do collectively with others that which one is at liberty to do as an individual.[4] At this level of generality, it encompasses a wide range of collective activities and associations: political parties, religious and confessional groups, protests and assemblies, book clubs, social and recreational associations, and trade unions. In constitutional terms, freedom of association is often protected as a general freedom relevant to a wide range of associational activities in different domains of social and civic life. Its abstract legal formulation as a constitutional freedom is sensitive to its generality of application to many different associations with their own needs and logics of collective action. General freedom of association considers matters such as the right of associations to discriminate and exclude members, the freedom of individuals to disassociate, and the extent to which liberal democratic governments must tolerate illiberal associations.[5] While these matters are obviously relevant to trade unions, they also arise in a wide range of diverse associational contexts, from churches to social clubs to networking groups for entrepreneurs.

By contrast, labour law as a discipline was addressed to the empowerment of workers who otherwise experienced inequality of bargaining power in

[3] See, generally, Alan Bogg and others (eds), *The Autonomy of Labour Law* (Hart 2015).

[4] A modern elaboration of this intuitively powerful idea is Brian Langille, 'The Freedom of Association Mess: How We Got into It and How We Can Get out of It' (2009) 54 McGill Law Journal 177, 183.

[5] See Amy Gutmann, 'Freedom of Association: An Introductory Essay', in Amy Gutmann (ed), *Freedom of Association* (Princeton University Press 1998) chapter 1.

the labour market. Workers were subordinate and dependent on employers. This meant that they were vulnerable to exploitation and unfair treatment.[6] Collective institutions, such as trade unions and collective bargaining, gave workers a democratic voice in their working lives. Trade unions enabled workers to shape their terms and conditions, to demand dignity and respect from their managers, and to challenge exploitative practices. It also empowered workers to participate in the wider democratic process to secure basic minimum labour standards through legislation. The purpose of freedom of association was to support the empowerment of workers through trade union activities.[7] This included collective bargaining and the right to strike. We might describe this as the 'industrial' or 'labour law' conception of freedom of association.[8] This is because the protective purpose of freedom of association is continuous with the protective purpose of labour law itself.

Historically, at least in English law, this industrial conception of freedom of association came first.[9] That historical story is the focus of Chapter 2. The general constitutional idea of freedom of association in English law only started to develop in the second half of the 20th century under the influence of civil and political human rights treaties like the ECHR. By the early part of the 20th century, British freedom of association had developed almost exclusively through economic conflict and legal accommodation through labour legislation. Indeed, for that great English constitutional lawyer A.V. Dicey, 'freedom of association' in English law was essentially synonymous with labour law.[10] The legal settlement in the Trade Disputes Act 1906 has been remarkably enduring, and it is still visible today in terms of the basic legal structure of freedom of association in British labour law. During the 20th century, with the extensive growth of the administrative state, freedom of association for trade unions in many legal systems was integrated into the vast and intricate body of statutory law protecting and regulating collective labour law. This machinery

[6] David Cabrelli, 'Traditional Justifications of Labour Law', in Guy Davidov, Brian Langille, and Gillian Lester (eds), *The Oxford Handbook of the Law of Work* (OUP 2024) chapter 8.

[7] Kalina Arabadjieva, 'Worker Empowerment, Collective Labour Rights and Article 11 of the European Convention on Human Rights' (2022) 22 Human Rights Law Review.

[8] This empowerment justification is not unique to trade unions. It would apply to other associations that represent disadvantaged and disempowered groups, such as civil rights activism, renters, irregular migrants, and welfare recipients. On associational activities as a response to structural injustice and disadvantage, see Alan Bogg, 'Freedom of Association and Structural Injustice', in Virginia Mantouvalou and Jo Wolff (eds), *Structural Injustice and the Law* (UCL Press 2024) chapter 6.

[9] The early history from the 18th century onwards is examined in John V. Orth, *Combination and Conspiracy: A Legal History of Trade Unionism 1721-1906* (OUP 1991). The development of the law on churches and religious associations in the 18th and 19th centuries raised distinctive issues to trade unions. For discussion, see Julian Rivers, *The Law of Organized Religions: Between Establishment and Secularism* (OUP 2010) chapter 1.

[10] Albert Venn Dicey, 'The Combination Laws as Illustrating the Relation between Law and Opinion in England during the Nineteenth Century' (1904) 17 Harvard Law Review 511.

regulated the constitution and operation of trade unions, the scope for compulsory membership through 'closed shop' arrangements, collective bargaining (sometimes including legal enforcement of a duty to bargain in good faith), collective agreements, and strike action. The enforcement of this specialist body of law was often entrusted to specialist labour courts and labour arbitrators. When general courts occasionally strayed over this boundary, it was often with disruptive effects, such as the enforcement of rediscovered economic torts against trade unions[11] or striking down protective labour legislation as unconstitutional.[12]

The civil liberty lies in the province of the constitution and the judges. The industrial conception lies in the province of labour law itself and its detailed statutes, codes, and voluntary collective bargaining practices. Kahn-Freund was astute enough to realise that labour law could never be fully autonomous of constitutional law.[13] The point of a constitution is to provide a basic legal structure and to set generally applicable limits to different compartments of the law. However, later scholars like Wedderburn harnessed the opening statement as a call for the civil liberty (and the judges) to be more tightly confined. This assertion of strong disciplinary borders reflected a broader scepticism about the role of courts (and especially the *common law courts*) in collective labour relations. It was better that trade union rights should be developed internally within labour law rather than externally in constitutional law. And it was better that this should be done through legislation and specialist labour courts interpreting that legislation in accordance with its social purposes.

As we have seen, this bifurcation between the civil liberty and industrial conceptions formed the basis of one of Lord Wedderburn's most famous pieces on freedom of association, 'Freedom of Association or the Right to Organise? The Common Law and International Sources'.[14] For Wedderburn, freedom of association as civil liberty was not so much 'indispensable' to collective labour relations as potentially subversive of it. Wedderburn was particularly critical of freedom of association under the ECHR in the late 1980s. This critique was focused on the Court's vigorous protection of the individual's freedom to disassociate from the trade union, undermining closed shop arrangements;[15] and its reticence in giving strong protection to collective

[11] As in the landmark case of *Rookes v Barnard* [1954] AC 1129.

[12] This arose most dramatically in disputes over the constitutionality of US New Deal legislation. For an introductory account, see Matthew W. Finkin and Timothy P. Glynn, *Cox, Bok & Gorman's Labor Law* (18th edition, Foundation Press 2024) 40–48.

[13] O. Kahn-Freund, 'The Impact of Constitutions on Labour Law' (1976) 35 Cambridge Law Journal 240.

[14] Wedderburn (n 1).

[15] Wedderburn focused on the controversial closed shop case *Young, James and Webster v United Kingdom* [1981] ECHR 4.

bargaining and the right to strike. Wedderburn also recognised that the ESC and the International Labour Organisation (ILO) protected collective rights.[16] This could be explained by the fact that these other legal orders were 'internal' to labour law because they were focused specifically on labour and socio-economic rights. The norms were usually developed by specialist committees rather than generalist courts. By contrast, the ECHR was an 'external' set of norms, or external to labour law at least. As a comparatist, Wedderburn also acknowledged that the constitutional norms in many European political systems were based (in different ways) upon social democratic consensus, such as in Italy, Germany, and Sweden.[17] This influenced the approaches of their courts. This did not extend to the English courts imbued with common law ideas of private property, class hierarchies, and the maintenance of the established social and economic order.[18]

Over the last three decades, Wedderburn's critical stance has been outflanked by social and legal developments. In many countries, there has been a shift towards a more hostile politics of organised labour and the disintegration of political consensus on trade unions and collective bargaining as public goods. This has been reflected in the deregulation of protective labour statutes and more restrictive public policies. It has led trade unions to engage strategically with constitutional and human rights courts to advance their collective interests.[19] Whereas for much of the 20th century, courts were viewed as a threat by organised labour, there is now a much greater willingness for trade unions to litigate freedom of association in the courts. That is why the topic of this book is so interesting. Trade unions and workers have turned to the courts, using constitutional norms and the civil liberty conception to bolster the industrial conception in a deregulatory political environment.

In response to this greater willingness of trade unions to pursue strategic litigation in the courts, there have also been radical shifts in constitutional jurisprudence. The European Court of Human Rights (ECtHR) has now recognised the right to bargain collectively as an essential trade union freedom under Article 11.[20] It has also recognised that the right to strike is protected

[16] Wedderburn (n 1) 141.

[17] Wedderburn (n 1) 149–150.

[18] In this respect, Wedderburn was influenced by the political constitutionalist approach, exemplified in the famous book J.A.G. Griffith, *The Politics of the Judiciary* (1st ed, Fontana 1977) chapter 3. This broader intellectual milieu at the London School of Economics, and its influence on Wedderburn's own thinking, is explored in Alan Bogg, 'The Hero's Journey: Lord Wedderburn and the "Political Constitution" of Labour Law' (2015) 44 Industrial Law Journal 299.

[19] For an assessment of this shifting constitutional context, see Judy Fudge, 'Constitutionalizing Labour Rights in Canada and Europe: Freedom of Association, Collective Bargaining, and Strikes' (2015) 68 Current Legal Problems 267; Jack Meakin, 'Mobilising Transnational Labour Law in Search of Transformation in Europe' (2025) 54 Industrial Law Journal 458.

[20] See *Demir and Baykara v Turkey* [2009] 48 EHRR 54 on Article 11 and the right to collective bargaining.

as part of the general protection of trade union activities.[21] As a result of the Human Rights Act 1998 (HRA), British courts have also been engaged with collective human rights to an extent that would have been unthinkable fifty years ago. In Canada, the Supreme Court of Canada (SCC) has recognised rights to bargain collectively and to strike under the Charter's general protection of freedom of association.[22] In these various legal orders, many important trade union rights are now recognised as constitutionally protected.

There has also been a much closer alignment between 'civil and political' and 'socio-economic' rights in adjudication, supported by the broader academic challenge to this division between 'types' or 'generations' of rights.[23] This alignment or integration has certainly supported a more expansive approach to labour rights in constitutional courts. This has included the constitutional recognition of the right to organise, the right to collective bargaining, and the right to strike. Some constitutional courts have even recognised that private parties such as employers should be subject to legal duties, such as the duty not to discriminate against individual trade unionists or the duty to bargain in good faith. States and governments have positive duties to protect workers and trade unions from interference by stronger parties in the private sphere (usually employers) and sometimes even to promote collective bargaining as a public good.

So, the 'autonomy' thesis must be reconsidered. That is what this book aims to do. The two lives of freedom of association are no longer being lived in enforced separation and on parallel juridical tracks. They are interacting in complex ways. Given the increasing importance of constitutional adjudication in the sphere of trade union rights, does this mean that the autonomy of labour law is dead? And has it now been superseded by a civil liberty conception led by a new and enlightened judiciary?

That conclusion would certainly be premature. The dense statutory framework of trade union law was already deeply entrenched in most countries long before the 'constitutionalisation' of labour rights emerged as a serious discourse.[24] This has established a high degree of 'path dependence' for legislated

[21] See *Enerji Yapi-Yol Sen v Turkey* [2009] ECHR 2251 on Article 11 and the right to strike.

[22] For a compelling critical assessment, see Brian Langille and Benjamin Oliphant, 'The Legal Structure of Freedom of Association' (2014) 40 Queen's Law Journal 249. Throughout this book, I will be engaging with the arguments of these scholars.

[23] The literature is huge, but for two leading examples, see Sandra Fredman, *Human Rights Transformed: Positive Rights and Positive Duties* (OUP 2008); Jeff King, *Judging Social Rights* (Cambridge UP 2012).

[24] Although the historical pattern is complex considered from a comparative perspective, the shift from legal 'repression' to legal 'recognition' was not necessarily linked to formal constitutionalisation of trade union rights in the constitution. On the varieties of European historical development, see Antoine Jacobs, 'Collective Self-Regulation', in Bob Hepple (ed), *The Making of Labour Law in Europe* (Hart 2010) 193. Jacobs notes the early constitutional recognition of trade union rights in the Weimar Constitution of 1919

labour law categories such as 'worker', 'trade dispute', 'trade union', 'good faith bargaining', and 'collective agreement'.[25] These categories were based in statutes conventionally regarded as being at the epicentre of labour law. In a constitutional democracy, courts (even constitutional courts) are subsidiary constitutional actors, and they usually operate as secondary decision-makers.[26] Their constitutional role is to ensure that primary decision-makers, such as the legislature and the executive, operate within the law. The courts do this through the techniques of judicial review. These techniques are sensitive to the subsidiary nature of courts, and this is reflected in doctrines like 'deference' or 'margin of appreciation'.[27]

I shall argue that courts have displayed a high degree of deference where legislators have defined the 'collective' parameters of freedom of association in legislation. They have been sensitive to their own institutional limitations in terms of expertise and democratic legitimacy. This has been reflected in the fate of many failed constitutional challenges to be discussed in detail in the book: on the legality of bans on secondary strikes, restrictions on strikes by civil servants in the German public service, defining 'representativeness' criteria in collective bargaining systems, and the repeal of special institutions protecting agricultural workers. By contrast, the courts have been more vigorous in protecting individuals from abuse of power, whether by governments, employers, or trade unions.

From the perspective of the autonomy of labour law, this leads to a surprising finding. Often, the direction of normative influence has been *from* labour law back into constitutional norms, not the other way round. The abstract constitutional norm is a relatively blank canvass. Generalist courts have tended to integrate the values and norms already embedded in labour law into their constitutional jurisprudence. This perhaps reflects a healthy self-awareness that these statutory rules reflect long-standing political compromises and that constitutional judges do not have the expertise or legitimacy to engage in large-scale reforms of labour law. For good constitutional reasons, the autonomy of labour law has been enduring. I shall argue that this persistence of labour law's autonomy is fundamentally sound.

and the Irish Constitution of 1937: 227. In many legal systems, however, the framework of labour was developed through legislation or codes.

[25] On 'path dependence' and legal concepts, see John Bell, 'Path Dependence and Legal Development' (2012) 87 Tulane Law Review 787.

[26] Aileen Kavanagh, *Constitutional Review under the Human Rights Act* (Cambridge UP 2009) 169.

[27] On the concept of deference, see Kavanagh, ibid. Also, Julian Rivers, 'Proportionality and Variable Intensity of Review' (2006) 65 Cambridge Law Journal 174. On the concept of margin of appreciation, see Andrew Legg, *The Margin of Appreciation in International Human Rights Law* (OUP 2012).

The remainder of this chapter will explain the arguments that will run through the book. In the next section, I will consider an important corrective to Wedderburn's autonomy thesis. Wedderburn's thesis seems to envisage separate spheres of (judge-made) human rights law and (legislated) statutory labour law. Against that view, Webber and others have argued that there is no special compartment of human rights law.[28] 'Human rights' are a matter of ordinary legislation that specify the complex sets of legal rights and duties (and adjudicative institutions and remedies) which give concrete and determinate content to abstract freedoms like freedom of association.

In Section III, I will explain and defend an 'internal' methodological approach to the material in this book. This 'internal' approach engages with legal reasoning as a committed participant, like a judge, and it is sensitive to the legal values and constitutional constraints that shape legal reasoning about freedom of association. While 'external' perspectives on legal phenomena are important and valuable, the 'internal' approach enables us to understand judicial reasoning better. Legal distinctions that might otherwise seem puzzling can be seen as coherent in light of internal legal principles. If we understand how judges think, from the inside as it were, this might also enable us to better anticipate developments in the case law.

In Section IV, I address a core issue that is central to understanding constitutional reasoning on freedom of association: deference. The orthodox position in labour law scholarship proceeds from a distrust of courts and judges.[29] This supports a strong default in favour of judicial non-intervention in collective labour relations. Historically, at least, labour law was regarded (at least by many scholars) as a 'no go' zone for the courts. Drawing upon modern public law scholarship on deference and judicial self-restraint, I argue that this orthodox analysis is no longer apt. Deference should be considered contextually, based on relevant factors and a balanced appraisal of the pros and cons of courts and legislatures. This enquiry is always context specific. It supports strong deference in some kinds of trade union cases, and it supports weak deference in other kinds of trade union cases. It rejects the traditional view of labour law or trade union law as a 'zone' which the courts should stay out of (or even be wary of).

In Section V, I identify an important category of case where deference tends to be weak. They involve violations of the equal moral standing of citizens, for

[28] Gregoire Webber and others, *Legislated Human Rights: Securing Human Rights through Legislation* (Cambridge UP 2018).

[29] These debates are considered in Alan Bogg, 'Can We Trust the Courts in Labour Law? Stranded between Frivolity and Despair' (2022) 38 International Journal of Comparative Labour Law and Industrial Relations 103.

example, where individuals are penalised for engaging in lawful trade union activities. I then consider a range of other ways in which the foundational legal value of equality before the law has shaped the development of the law on freedom of association. A full appreciation of the reach and significance of this value is facilitated by the internal perspective outlined in Section III.

Finally, in Section VI, I explain the core argument of the book and how the chapters develop this argument. In freedom of association cases, the constitutional courts have tended to defer to labour legislation on 'collective' matters; but they have intervened where individuals are exposed to risks of abuse of power, discrimination, and victimisation, whether perpetrated by the state, employers, or trade unions. In one sense, Wedderburn was right. These constitutional norms are based upon individualism. However, it is an individualism that is morally compelling. This is freedom of association that respects the autonomy of labour law *and* the moral and civic equality of persons.

II. Legislated Rights: Freedoms, Rights, and *Determination*

For Webber and others, the entirety of private law and specific compartments like labour law are all 'human rights law'.[30] If this thesis of *Legislated Rights* is true, then the legal gap between the civil liberty and industrial conceptions may not be so stark or dramatic as Wedderburn's arguments might suggest. 'Human rights' have been under our noses all along in the detailed statutory provisions of the Trade Union and Labour Relations (Consolidation) Act (TULRCA) 1992.

Trade union rights represent a paradigm case of what Webber and co-authors have described as 'legislated rights'. The semantic form of *freedom* of association in many international human rights instruments is misleading because 'it might be thought that human rights such as the freedom of expression, assembly, and religion are Hohfeldian liberties. The problem with classifying them as such, however, is that their two-term structure does not describe any particular relationship between persons'.[31] Without legislation, complex rights—like trade union rights—cannot be made fully determinate. If these rights are not determinate, they cannot be effectively realised in a

[30] Webber and others (n 28) 20–21.

[31] Ibid. 127. In other words, 'the two-term structure of rights signifies the importance of the subject matters x (life, liberty, security, privacy, etc) that persons (P) have by right, but does not identify which measures will realise everyone's right by identifying duty-holders and the content of their duties that correlate to the right(s) in question': ibid. 21.

political community. This is a task that can only be undertaken by a legislature. Courts resolve bipolar disputes between two parties. Legislation ensures that juridical relationships can be specified and defined while holding the common good of every person in the community in consideration.

As these authors explain, abstract freedoms like freedom of association function as directive guides to legislators, indicating that a certain kind of activity (i.e., collective bargaining or trade union activity) is of such importance that it is something citizens have by right. These 'broad goal-oriented' two-term formulae in human rights instruments then require further specification and translation into three-term rights through legislation.[32] This 'three-term picture' is that of a right-holder, a valuable thing or activity that is the subject-matter of the right, and a duty-bearer. This denotes a specified relationship between persons rather than a free-floating political evaluation that a certain activity is a good thing. The legislative specification of, say, a right to participate in trade union activity, therefore requires that 'a series of acts and arrangements—a combination of Hohfeldian relationships—must be selected from among more or less reasonable alternatives and authoritatively established'.[33] It is not enough to say 'everyone has the right to form and join trade unions for the protection of his interests'. Does everyone really have this right (including employers and independent businesses)? Does it include trade union activities during working time or activities that damage the employer's property? Who bears the duty not to interfere in this trade union activity? Without this further legislative specification, the legal implementation of freedom of association is incomplete.

Take the basic formulation of the right to organise in Article 1(1) of ILO Convention 98 on the Right to Organise and Collective Bargaining (1949): 'Workers shall enjoy adequate protection against acts of anti-union discrimination in respect of their employment.' The first thing to note is that it defines a certain class of persons—'workers'—as the relevant right-holders. This delimitation is not incompatible with the universality of human rights. As Webber and others have argued, the law's directive functions are often based upon distinctions between 'classes of persons'.[34] The important point is that the distinction between classes of persons is reasonable, given the nature of the right. Article 1 is still incomplete because it does not identify a class of persons as duty-bearers. Article 1(2) further specifies that the relevant acts

[32] Ibid. 21.
[33] Ibid. 42.
[34] Ibid. 53. This analysis on the delimitation of rights is also developed in Gregoire Webber, *The Negotiable Constitution* (Cambridge UP 2009).

include those that 'cause the dismissal of or otherwise prejudice a worker by reason of union membership or because of participation in union activities'. These kinds of prejudicial acts, like dismissal or imposing disadvantageous employment conditions, seem to presuppose *an employer.* Since the employer has the power to prejudice or dismiss the worker, it ought to be subject to a *duty* not to do so. Only then do we have something in the shape of a complete legal right.

All of this will be familiar to any student of labour law after a few weeks' basic study of employment law. In employment law, the general structure of a statutory labour right is based upon the juridical relationship between a class of right-holders (let's call them 'workers') and a class of duty-bearers (let's call them 'employers'). This 'right to organise' is elaborated across fifty-one separate statutory sections in Part III of TULRCA 1992. While this does not make for a pithy slogan ('trade union rights are human rights for everyone!'), it does mean that those using employment law in their daily lives have a more precise idea of their respective rights and duties and the appropriate means of legal redress. There is also a broader point here about the foundational role of employment status in labour law. The definitions of 'worker' (or 'employee') and 'employer' are probably inescapable because they flow from the basic correlativity of rights and duties.[35] Rights and duties denote juridical relations between right-holders and duty-bearers. It is entirely natural that the rights and duties of employment law should be allocated to workers (however defined) and employers. How else would such rights and duties be distributed? That is why employment status will endure for as long as there is a subject called employment law constituted by legal rights and legal duties.

The centrality of legislation to the realisation of human rights is also supported by the idea of *determinatio*. Based in the natural law theory of Aquinas, it has been deployed by natural law theorists such as John Finnis and Robert P George.[36] It describes the irreducible role of human creativity and choice in determining public regulation, including in the realm of human rights. There are many ways in which legislators can go wrong and, in so doing, violate the rights of persons. There are also many ways in which legislators can make reasonable choices to instantiate human rights through positive law. These choices select from a range of incommensurable yet reasonable options.

[35] This view of rights and duties as correlatives is derived from the work of Wesley Newcomb Hohfeld. See Wesley Newcomb Hohfeld, 'Fundamental Legal Conceptions as Applied in Judicial Reasoning' (1917) 26 Yale Law Journal 710.

[36] See, e.g., Robert P. George, 'Natural Law and Positive Law', in Robert P. George (ed), *The Autonomy of Law: Essays on Legal Positivism* (OUP 1996) chapter 11. John Finnis, 'The Truth in Legal Positivism', in Robert P. George (ed), *The Autonomy of Law: Essays on Legal Positivism* (OUP 1996) chapter 7.

For the sake of coordination, it is necessary for an authoritative choice to be made.[37] Those choices could have been reasonably different, but once enacted, they become salient for us in our political community. It enables us to know what we may or may not do, and what others with duties must do or not do, and how to proceed if those legal duties are breached.

Although the language of *determinatio* may be unfamiliar to labour lawyers, the concept itself will be very familiar. Take the 'right to collective bargaining'. In Chapter 4, we will examine the dazzling variety of legal models of collective bargaining in different countries. The levels, forms, and even the basic question of a 'legal duty to bargain in good faith' defy reduction into simple categories.[38] This comparative variety in the general realm of human rights was well understood by framers of international instruments such as the Universal Declaration of Human Rights 'who preferred not to stipulate which' of the range of reasonable formulations 'was to be selected for each and every community'.[39] Even within a single national system, take British labour law, the social practice and legal regulation of collective bargaining has changed radically since the early post-war period. Sectoral and multi-employer bargaining has diminished, 'indirect' legal supports for collective bargaining have been dismantled, and there is now a statutory recognition procedure focused on single-employer bargaining.[40] This incommensurability, particularly across legal systems, demands humility from courts in adjudicating on the right to collective bargaining. Legislators can reasonably expect creative latitude to make (and to re-make) the laws regulating collective bargaining. Courts must respect that legislative freedom within broad parameters until those legislative choices are unreasonable and violative of rights.

While the 'legislated rights' thesis is highly persuasive, and indeed labour law seems to represent a paradigm case of it,[41] this book endorses a more 'collaborative' vision of courts and legislatures.[42] There are many examples in this book where legislators have been either overtly hostile or indifferent to a plausible account of trade union rights as human rights. I therefore reject the Goldilocks theory of legislated rights, that the human right is whatever the

[37] John Finnis, 'Law as Co-ordination' (1989) 2 Ratio Juris 97.

[38] For a flavour of this variety, see Lord Wedderburn, 'Collective Bargaining at European Level: The Inderogability Problem', in Lord Wedderburn, *Labour Law and Freedom* (Lawrence & Wishart 1995) chapter 6.

[39] Webber and others (n 28) 31.

[40] This rich historical pattern is considered in Lord Wedderburn, *The Worker and the Law* (3rd ed, Penguin 1986) chapter 4.

[41] The dominance of legislation in the historical development of labour law is a central theme in the classic work Paul L Davies and Mark R Freedland, *Labour Legislation and Public Policy* (OUP 1993).

[42] Aileen Kavanagh, *The Collaborative Constitution* (Cambridge UP 2023).

relevant legislation says that it is. The legislation does not exhaust the content of the corresponding human right. Legislators can fail in their responsibilities, and they can (and do) make unreasonable legislative choices. There is space between the abstract constitutional standard and its legislative implementation, with the former providing a critical yardstick for the latter. It is obviously important that judicial power is exercised responsibly and with due restraint in a constitutional democracy. These considerations are even stronger for courts like the ECtHR in the face of significant incommensurability across national labour law regimes. However, these concerns can be addressed through a theory of judicial deference or self-restraint. We will return to this in Section IV of this chapter. Before that, a brief reflection on the book's methodology is in order.

III. Internal and External Theory

In his work on public law and constitutional theory, T.R.S. Allan draws an important distinction between 'internal' and 'external' theories of public law.[43] An 'external' theory or perspective examines the relevant legal rules and principles from the perspective of the historian or social scientist. This might be something like the legal realist enterprise, for example, examining causal patterns in constitutional development or predicting the outcomes of cases. An 'internal' theory adopts the perspective of the normatively committed legal official, paradigmatically the judge, and engages in argumentation to identify and apply the law. The internal perspective treats values, like democracy or equality, as immanent in the law and constitution and so continuous with the process of legal reasoning and interpretation. To reason internally, as a scholar or judge, is to engage with those moral values in a committed way.

This monograph takes an 'internal' approach to its subject-matter. This is not to deny that there are important and valuable external perspectives. There have been brilliant examinations of labour law phenomena from an 'external' perspective, for example, analysing the role (and limitations) of strategic litigation,[44] or the relationship between legal form and capitalist ordering.[45]

[43] T.R.S. Allan, *The Sovereignty of Law: Freedom, Constitution, and Common Law* (OUP 2013) chapter 1 and Appendix.

[44] Ruth Dukes and Eleanor Kirk, 'Legal Change and Legal Mobilisation: What does Strategic Litigation Mean for Workers and Trade Unions?' (2023) 33 Social and Legal Studies 479; Zoe Adams, 'Legal Mobilisations, Trade Unions, and Radical Social Change: A Case Study of the IWGB' (2023) 52 Industrial Law Journal 560.

[45] Zoe Adams, 'Labour law, Capitalism and the Juridical Form: Taking a Critical Approach to Questions of Labour Law Reform' (2021) 50 Industrial Law Journal 434.

Other external approaches might involve developing a normative theory of freedom of association, such as non-domination or capabilities, as a precursor to analysing and critiquing the law.[46] That is not the approach taken in this book because the book is concerned with different questions. The substantive chapters try to understand and apply legal reasoning on freedom of association from the inside, as a judge would understand and apply it, sensitive to constitutional values and the proper limits of the judicial role. This interpretive approach rejects the separability of legal reasoning from moral reasoning.[47] Legal reasoning is always laden with values. Those moral principles are immanent in the fabric of the law, justifying the settled legal rules and institutional practices, and include values such as legality, integrity, and equality.[48] The duty of the judge or (internalist) scholar is to be candid about those values. Judges who shout loudly about their agnosticism on matters of value are, of course, instantiating a set of values. It is inescapable in the judicial enterprise.

There are advantages to this internal orientation. It may mean that certain judicial outcomes do not appear as a shocking bolt from the blue when they flow from an appropriate judicial sense of constitutional restraint. There are many examples of such controversial judicial decisions in this book where judges have trodden more cautiously than scholars would like. For example, the recent Article 11 judgment in *Humpert and others v Germany* upholding the ban on strikes in the German civil service is one such example, to be discussed in Chapter 5.[49] From an internal perspective, however, this outcome was not so surprising because it reflected a well-settled theory of judicial deference. It enables the scholar to understand legal reasoning better when she is fully engaged as an insider in the practice of legal argumentation. There are also some risks, of course. The external perspective provides a measure of critical distance so that the scholar can understand and evaluate legal phenomena and judicial decision-making in a suitably dispassionate and detached way.[50] This enables the scholar to be a fearless critic of the judge and the legislator.

[46] For a republican theory of freedom of association based in non-domination, see Alan Bogg and Cynthia Estlund, 'The Right to Strike and Contestatory Citizenship', in Hugh Collins and others (eds), *Philosophical Foundations of Labour Law* (OUP 2018) chapter 13.

[47] In this respect, the book applies the account of doctrinal method defended in Alan Bogg, 'Doctrinal Method in Labour Law in Common Law Systems: Potential, Problems, Prospects', in Alysia Blackham and Sean Cooney (eds), *Research Methods in Labour Law: A Handbook* (Elgar 2024) chapter 13.

[48] As well as T.R.S. Allan, this approach is obviously indebted to Ronald Dworkin. See Ronald Dworkin, *Taking Rights Seriously* (Duckworth 1977).

[49] [2023] ECHR 1008.

[50] This relatively detached methodology may be a particular virtue in elucidating political shifts justifying different legislative programmes. See Davies and Freedland (n 41) 3, and the need to write about politics in an 'acceptably detached way'.

The danger of the internal perspective is that it degrades into apologism for whatever judges happen to do. I think that it is possible to be both internally committed *and* critical of judicial reasoning that is legally defective.[51] I must leave it to the reader to decide if this book manages to achieve this feat.

The internal viewpoint also places certain constraints on achieving a manageable comparative scope. The book is focused predominantly on British labour law, with some consideration of the ECHR and Canada. Given the constitutionalisation of trade union rights in each of these legal orders, it has been possible to study the interaction between civil liberty and industrial conceptions of freedom of association mediated through judgments. The internal viewpoint requires an immersion in the history and constitutional values of a legal order, especially in tracing the genealogy of freedom of association in Chapter 2.[52] While a cleverer academic could no doubt have managed a more ambitious comparative sweep, like a good appellate judge, I have been attentive to my own limitations of expertise and intelligence.

IV. Disagreement, Deference, and Democracy

How should we make sense of judicial disagreements about freedom of association, particularly where that disagreement relates to a legislated standard? One kind of disagreement reflects a first-order disagreement about the theory of freedom of association. There are different normative accounts of freedom of association. For example, Brishen Rogers has set out three concepts of workplace freedom of association that he terms social democratic, civil libertarian, and neoliberal.[53] There are no doubt many others. These underlying theories sometimes lead to divergent prescriptions on specific regulatory issues such as the closed shop, the duty to bargain, and the right to strike. When judges disagree with the legislature (or with other judges) about the constitutional requirements of the right to strike, this might reflect normative differences about the theory of freedom of association. For example, the social democratic concept, which promotes equalisation of economic power, would be more supportive of a right to strike than a neoliberal concept,

[51] Bogg (n 47) 215–216.

[52] This has some affinities with Bernard Williams' account of 'thick' moral concepts. These are concepts that must be understood in light of their specific cultural histories. See Bernard Williams, *Ethics and the Limits of Philosophy* (Routledge 2011). On law and legal phenomena as 'thick' concepts, see D. Enoch and K. Toh, 'Legal as a Thick Concept', in Wil Waluchow and Stefan Sciaraffa (eds), *Philosophical Foundations of the Nature of Law* (OUP 2013) 257.

[53] Brishen Rogers, 'Three Concepts of Workplace Freedom of Association' (2016) 37 Berkeley Journal of Employment and Labor Law 177.

which favours free markets. Standoffs between 'neoliberal' legislatures and 'social democratic' courts, or 'neoliberal' dissents within a 'progressive' constitutional court, are the heady stuff of many law review articles. Sometimes, judges might even tell us that their first-order theory leads to a generous interpretation of constitutional rights or that 'the arc bends increasingly towards workplace justice'.[54] Does it not follow that dissenting judges who favour a more restricted interpretation of constitutional rights favour workplace *in*justice? *Ceteris paribus*, it is surely better to pursue a theory that is 'generous' about the content of rights rather than mean or stingy. That is the surest way to be on the right side of legal history.

This account of disagreement, which is typical of disagreements between political philosophers, obscures another kind of disagreement that is integral to the judicial role in constitutional adjudication. We are more likely to see it when we adopt an 'internal' perspective on the law. It is captured in the concept of 'deference'. In one of the leading accounts of deference, developed by Aileen Kavanagh, she defines it in the following way: '*judicial deference occurs when judges assign varying degrees of weight to the judgment of the elected branches, out of respect for their superior competence, expertise and/or democratic legitimacy*.'[55] Deference flows from the subsidiary role of judges in a constitutional democracy. Ordinarily, courts are not primary decision-makers. Legislatures and executives have the primary responsibility to govern. Courts have 'a secondary responsibility to ensure that the primary decision-maker has acted in accordance with the requirements of legality'.[56]

In many of the freedom of association cases to be considered in this book, the primary decision-maker is the legislature which has enacted legislation to define specific freedom of association rights. This legislation is then challenged by an affected party in a court because it is alleged to be incompatible with constitutional standards. As Kavanagh has emphasised, it is certainly not legitimate for a court to substitute its own view of how that legislation ought to have been formulated or how it could be improved.[57] Some degree of deference to the primary decision-maker is properly to be expected. When elected representatives have introduced legislation based upon a 'social democratic' concept of freedom of association, judges should not override the legislature simply because they favour a 'neoliberal' or 'civil libertarian' concept. The conclusion that legislation has violated constitutional rights should

[54] *Saskatchewan Federation of Labour v Saskatchewan* [2015] 1 SCR 245, [1] (Abella J).
[55] Kavanagh (n 26) 169.
[56] Ibid. 172.
[57] Ibid.

not be determined primarily by first-order disagreements about theories of freedom of association. 'Deference' is the concept that ensures that this does not happen.

The legal scholar who has done the most to clarify the crucial role of deference in understanding judicial disagreements about freedom of association is Brian Langille, both in his own work and in joint work with Benjamin Oliphant. The most developed account is set out in their piece, 'From Rand to Rothstein: Labour Law, Fundamental Values and the Judicial Role'.[58] It assesses the jurisprudential legacy of Justice Rothstein, a Judge who has so often been a dissenting figure in the SCC in its expansive modern case law on freedom of association under s. 2(d) of the Charter. Langille and Oliphant analyse Rothstein J's jurisprudence through consideration of the appropriate limits of the judicial role. On this deference approach, it is a mistake to evaluate Rothstein J's judicial performance by its fidelity to a first-order theory of freedom of association. That is the wrong metric. Instead, his judgments reflect a particular conception of the judicial role in a democracy shaped by the institutional limitations of courts relative to legislators in the sphere of labour law. In other words, the key to understanding these recent judicial disagreements in the SCC is *deference*. Moreover, Langille and Oliphant argue that Rothstein J's deference is based in a deeply rooted and respectable constitutional tradition that treats courts as suspect constitutional actors in the labour field. On this traditional approach, courts are usually institutionally ill-equipped to adjudicate labour disputes. Historically, labour law (and especially trade unions and workers) did best when judges and the ordinary courts had least to do with them.

To return to our two concepts of freedom of association at the opening of this chapter, we can understand this deference argument in the following way. The civil liberty conception was developed by generalist judges who lacked relevant labour law and industrial relations expertise. The industrial conception was developed through democratically enacted labour legislation and handled by specialist courts and arbitrators. It was important to insulate the industrial conception from disruptive intervention by the civil liberty conception because intervention by constitutional courts was likely to be counterproductive. It risked disrupting the delicate political and economic compromises crystallised in labour legislation. Underlying this deference argument was a commitment to the strong autonomy of labour law from constitutional law. This autonomy could never be absolute, of course, and this is recognised by

[58] This essay is published in Ivo Entchev and Lisa M. Kelly (eds), *Judicious Restraint: The Life and Law of Justice Marshall E. Rothstein* (LexisNexis 2016) 251.

Langille and Oliphant. The constitution provides a basic structural framework for the different compartments of the legal system. However, constitutional review ought to be limited to extreme cases. In Langille's famous formulation, judges should not be drafting labour codes.[59]

Sometimes, distrust of courts was taken to be a distinctive feature of British labour law and 'collective laissez-faire'.[60] However, this sceptical attitude towards courts in labour law is evidently a more general feature of historical labour law development in other common law countries. So, Langille and Oliphant describe the Canadian position 'that judicial intervention in the labour relations sphere has often been unwise in principle, unhelpful in result, and sometimes, unauthorized in law'.[61] This norm against judicial intervention was 'long-accepted wisdom among labour law scholars'.[62] For Canadians, this was based in the substitution of a comprehensive statutory system, administered through labour arbitration and reinforced by ouster clauses, for a common law system of labour relations. The restriction of judicial intervention was justified by a range of arguments. Judicial expertise was sensitive to common law values and modes of reasoning, whereas industrial law required a broader understanding of labour relations.[63] Indeed, the common law tended to treat workplace hierarchies as natural, and it often struggled to view collective action as legitimate.[64] Labour law was highly political, most especially when the courts were called upon to adjudicate in industrial disputes. 'Neutrality' and judicial non-intervention ensured that the legitimacy of the law was not undermined.[65] In British versions of the institutional critique of courts, courts were regarded as structurally aligned with the values of property and freedom of contract that favoured market ordering.[66] This meant that impartiality was elusive in the judicial resolution of collective labour conflicts, even without any conscious bias on the part of individual judges. These considerations supported a 'broad consensus' in favour of judicial abstention,

[59] Brian Langille, 'Why are Canadian Judges Drafting Labour Codes—And Constitutionalizing the Wagner Act Model?' (2009–10) 15 Canadian Labour and Employment Law Journal 101.

[60] This 'distrust of courts' was famously presented as the historical leitmotif of British labour law by Allan Flanders, 'The Tradition of Voluntarism' (1974) 12 British Journal of Industrial Relations 352, 354.

[61] Langille and Oliphant (n 58) 251.

[62] Ibid.

[63] Lord Wedderburn, 'Labour Law—From Here to Autonomy? A Franco-British Comparison', in Lord Wedderburn, *Employment Rights in Britain and Europe* (Lawrence & Wishart 1991) chapter 5.

[64] This critique was not restricted to British labour law. From a US perspective, see James B. Atleson, *Values and Assumptions in American Labor Law* (University of Massachusetts Press 1983).

[65] The importance of state neutrality in industrial disputes was emphasised in Otto Kahn-Freund, 'Labour Law', in Otto Kahn-Freund, *Selected Writings* (Stevens & Sons 1978) 1, 23 (first published in 1959).

[66] Lord Wedderburn, 'Laski's Law Behind the Law. 1906 to European Labour Law' in Richard Rawlings (ed.), *Law, Society and Economy: Centenary Essays for the London School of Economics and Political Science* (OUP 1997) 25, 36; citing Harold Laski, *The State in Theory and Practice* (Allen & Unwin 1935) 182.

because of 'the courts' relative lack of competency, want of democratic legitimacy and legal authority, and apparent antipathy towards legislative policy'.[67]

Of course, many of these objections to judicial intervention were crafted in the specific historical context supporting a system of labour arbitration in collective bargaining law. There is a further question whether these institutional arguments favouring judicial deference vis-à-vis arbitrators extend into the different context of constitutional review. Langille and Oliphant argue that these deference arguments do apply to the constitutional review of labour relations statutes. They identify a range of deference considerations relied upon by Rothstein J in his dissents: that maintaining equilibrium in collective labour relations is principally a matter for democratically elected representatives; that labour relations policy is intensely political because it involves economic conflict and so it is less suitable to be resolved through judicial intervention; that 'constitutionalising' specific features of statutory bargaining models inevitably leads to the wholesale constitutionalisation of the entire legal framework, which ossifies that model and prevents democratic experimentation.[68]

For these reasons, Langille and Oliphant support the view that, in constitutional terms, labour law is not quite a 'no go' zone for judges, but it is certainly a 'proceed very cautiously and with due deference' zone.[69] As they say, the key idea in their account of deference is the 'zone'.[70] There is something about freedom of association in the zone of labour law that should trigger heightened judicial deference.

To what extent is this zonal analysis compatible with the modern treatment of deference in constitutional review? Langille and Oliphant are justified in emphasising the importance of deference. Many scholarly arguments are too quick to dispense with deference where it impedes the achievement of trade union successes in the courts. Sometimes, these critiques reach quickly for the word 'neoliberal' in describing the sin. However, there are two difficulties with Langille and Oliphant's argument. The first is the tendency to critique courts without a balanced consideration of the institutional weaknesses of other constitutional actors, such as the legislature of the executive. This could lead to a concept of deference that is unfairly skewed against courts because it does not reflect a balanced appraisal of institutional strengths and weaknesses. The second is the very idea of a spatial 'zone' of deference. Although the authors reject the idea that this is a 'no go' zone, many leading accounts of deference in

[67] Langille and Oliphant (n 58) 261.
[68] Ibid. 291–294.
[69] Ibid. 299.
[70] Ibid.

public law are sceptical about spatial approaches to its application. Deference is a variable concept that should be sensitive to a range of factors that arise in different ways depending upon the specific facts of a case. It is not warranted to proceed on the basis that certain zones are inherently ill-suited to judicial review. Even if our zone is a 'proceed very cautiously' zone, that could still foreclose an open consideration of relevant deference factors on the facts of the case. Let us consider each of these problems.

A. Are courts suspect constitutional actors in labour law?

The first difficulty, the institutional bias against courts, reflects the long-standing view in labour law that courts cannot be trusted to adjudicate fairly and impartially in disputes between employers and trade unions. It is hard-wired into the discipline, and it was often reflected in calls for procedural autonomy and a specialist system of labour courts.[71] Scholars with expertise in public law and labour law have been particularly well placed to scrutinise these claims.[72] A.C.L. Davies has examined the case for specialist labour courts in the context of the European Court of Justice, a generalist court with a broad constitutional remit.[73] In developing her own arguments, she drew upon Lord McCarthy's classic defence of labour courts (and which are implicitly critical of 'generalist' courts): the autonomy of labour law, expertise, accessibility and informality, and flexibility.[74]

Some of these arguments are addressed to first-instance courts adjudicating on disputes between employers and workers. For example, the accessibility and informality of proceedings is likely to be a particular virtue in circumstances where workers do not have formal legal representation and are seeking to vindicate their legal rights against an employer. It is less obvious that constitutional adjudication should be marked by informality in proceedings. Often, constitutional cases involving freedom of association are pursued by trade unions with well-resourced legal teams. Constitutional adjudication involves matters of fundamental importance to the constitutional order, and this should be reflected in a degree of formality that respects the dignity of the occasion. It is also not clear how 'flexibility' fits with constitutional adjudication. Flexibility is well-suited to the pragmatic resolution of industrial

[71] A classic example is Wedderburn (n 63).

[72] See A.C.L. Davies, 'Judicial Self-Restraint in Labour Law' (2009) 38 Industrial Law Journal 278.

[73] A.C.L. Davies, 'The Court of Justice as a Labour Court' (2012) 14 Cambridge Yearbook of European Legal Studies 145.

[74] W.E.J. McCarthy, 'The Case for Labour Courts' (1990) 21 Industrial Relations Journal 98.

disputes, where there is a need to conciliate between conflicting economic interests and to nudge the parties towards an enduring compromise.[75] It is less obvious that this is a virtue in constitutional adjudication. Often, there is a countervailing need for legal certainty in support of the rule of law. If legislation is declared to be incompatible with constitutional freedom of association norms, it is also important that the legislator understands what needs to be done to rectify the incompatibility through remedial legislation. This should not be a constitutional bartering exercise, nor legislators looking for answers in a crystal ball.

The remaining two factors, expertise and autonomy, are more obviously relevant to apex courts engaged in general constitutional review. It is less clear that they support a structural preference in favour of substantial judicial deference in labour law. Starting with expertise, this factor could encompass a range of considerations. Labour law rules must be workable in a diverse range of workplaces. This requires a deep contextual appreciation of the interactions between social norms, custom and practice, collective bargaining, and managerial prerogatives. Generalist courts and senior appellate judges often lack this understanding because of their social background, legal training, and professional practice. By contrast, elected political representatives are a more diverse group. Legislators consult widely with affected groups such as employers and trade unions before enacting labour legislation. This consultation ensures that legislation is responsive to labour market needs. Consultation also provides opportunities for democratic voice for the social partners in shaping legislation. These considerations all point in favour of substantial deference.

Sometimes, however, expertise argument might point away from substantial judicial deference. For example, imagine a statute that excludes gig economy riders from the scope of the right to organise because they are not defined as 'workers' under the legislation.[76] This exclusion then exposes them to the risk of anti-union victimisation because they are not protected from victimisation for trade union reasons. This may have arisen because the statutory definition of worker has not been revised in light of significant changes in the structure of modern labour markets. In these circumstances, where workers are exposed to discriminatory treatment because of a legislative gap, the court is well placed to intervene. The principle of non-discrimination is squarely within the expertise of the court. The vulnerability of economically disadvantaged groups may not always be safely entrusted to democratic majorities.

[75] Davies (n 73) 152.

[76] This is in fact what happened in *Independent Workers Union of Great Britain v Central Arbitration Committee and another* [2023] UKSC 43. This controversial judgment will be considered in Chapters 3 and 4.

Expertise is certainly a relevant factor to deference, but it would be preferable to treat it as a factor with variable impact on judicial deference depending on the facts. Sometimes, where legal values of equality and non-discrimination are engaged, the courts have significant expertise.

The relevance of the autonomy argument to deference is less clear. There is a danger that this is simply a reassertion of the spatial idea that labour law is a special 'zone' warranting its own institutional treatment. However, that doesn't help to advance our understanding of *why* autonomy matters particularly here. Apex courts are generalist courts, and they handle disputes arising in many different areas of law that require specialist expertise. Although it pains me to admit this, it is not clear that the doctrinal specialism in labour law is any more difficult or more exotic than other contextual subjects like tax law, medical law, or family law. Also, there might be a value in general constitutional norms being developed and applied by generalist courts with specific constitutional expertise. This reflects the overarching and general importance of the constitution and fundamental rights.

Sometimes, the autonomy argument seems to be a proxy for broader democratic arguments. These invoke the bitter historical experience of judges subverting legislation, especially in the context of strike law, to protect the common law rights of employers.[77] There is no doubt that judicial respect for democratic institutions is of paramount importance in a constitutional democracy. What Kavanagh has termed 'the argument from democratic legitimacy' means that courts should treat legislation with due respect for its democratic provenance.[78] This provides a justification for a default of 'minimal deference'.[79] That is to say, courts should *always* treat the decisions and outcomes of democratic institutions with a presumptive degree of respect. However, it is not clear that this democratic argument is any stronger in labour law than in any other context. The fact that a statute deals with a labour issue does not give it any special weight as a statute. For this reason, I think it confusing to obscure this general democratic argument by treating it as an aspect of the special autonomy argument.

So far, then, the 'labour law' arguments addressed specifically to the institutional limitations of courts do not support strong judicial deference. They are either not relevant to constitutional deference (such as flexibility, informality, and autonomy) or they are not as antithetical to courts as is often presented (e.g., expertise can point in different directions).

[77] Lord Wedderburn, 'Industrial Relations and the Courts' (1980) 9 Industrial Law Journal 65.
[78] Kavanagh (n 26) 190–196.
[79] Ibid. 192–193.

There is a final argument that has often been treated as a trump card by critics of judicial intervention, and that is Wedderburn's oft-repeated quotation of Lord Scrutton:

> The habits you are trained in, the people with whom you mix, lead to your having a certain class of ideas of such nature that, when you have to deal with other ideas, you do not give as sound and accurate judgments as you would wish. This is one of the great difficulties at present with Labour . . . It is very difficult sometimes to be sure that you have put yourself into a thoroughly impartial position between two disputants, one of your own class and one not of your class.[80]

Wedderburn always rejected the imputation of conscious judicial bias. Judges favoured the interests of capital because they were imbued with respect for private property, commerce, freedom of contract, and the maintenance of the existing social order.[81] These insights are still interesting, and we should not dismiss them too lightly. The difficulty is in treating this as a deference argument *directed specifically at courts*. In liberal capitalist economies, there is no reason to think that courts are any more prone than legislators or executives to supporting the interests of Capital. Indeed, the significant increase in strategic litigation by trade unions can be explained in part by a sense of political disempowerment because their economic leverage in the democratic process has waned. Legislatures (and legislation) are now more hostile to trade union interests, and courts have provided an alternative forum where legal argumentation does not depend upon economic heft for its persuasive power. For this reason, courts can provide something of a level playing field where there are severe economic disparities between the parties,[82] whereas the success of political lobbying is more overtly linked to economic power. The 'class bias' argument should therefore be treated as neutral insofar as judicial deference is concerned, because it applies to legislatures and executives as much as courts.

B. Is labour law a special 'zone' for deference?

There is no reason to think that there is a distinctive justification for strong judicial deference in labour law because courts embody unique institutional

[80] T.E. Scrutton, 'The Work of the Commercial Courts' (1921) 1 Cambridge Law Journal 6, 8, cited in K.W. Wedderburn, *The Worker and the Law* (Penguin 1965) 20.

[81] In this respect, there were significant affinities with Wedderburn's colleague at LSE, J.A.G. Griffith. See J.A.G. Griffith, *The Politics of the Judiciary* (1st ed, Fontana 1977).

[82] Bogg (n 29) 410.

shortcomings compared with other constitutional actors. We would do better to consider pro- and contra-deference factors in an open way, rather than stacking the analysis against courts at the outset. Is there anything left in the idea that labour law still constitutes a special deference 'zone'? Some of the Article 11 case law on freedom of association supports this spatial idea. For example, in *RMT v United Kingdom*, in considering whether severe restrictions on secondary strike action were necessary in a democratic society, the ECtHR stated that

> In previous trade union cases, the Court has stated that regard must be had to the fair balance to be struck between the competing interests of the individual and of the community as a whole. Since achieving a proper balance between the interests of labour and management involves sensitive social and political issues, the Contracting States must be afforded a margin of appreciation as to how trade-union freedom and protection of the occupational interests of union members may be secured.[83]

While the court considered a range of specific factors relevant to margin of appreciation on the facts of the case, this mantra of 'sensitive social and political issues' in 'trade union cases' indicates a spatial approach. To use Kavanagh's terminology again, this seems to establish a default of 'strong judicial deference' in trade union cases. This spatial approach is not unique to trade union cases, of course. What Kavanagh has described as the 'crude subject-based approach',[84] setting up predefined zones of deference, has sometimes been applied in national security and resource allocation cases.[85] Yet it is difficult to see what the justification for a zonal approach in labour law would be. Deference depends upon the context of the constitutional challenge rather than its zonal quality. For example, where the legislature enacts certain procedural requirements such as a ballot procedure for a lawful strike, there could be a powerful argument in favour of strong judicial deference. In circumstances where legislation permits an employer to selectively impose penalties on individual strikers, violating the basic principle of non-discrimination, the arguments in favour of judicial deference are much weaker. These are both 'trade union cases'. They both involve 'sensitive social and political issues'. Yet I would argue that the latitude for democratic choice should be far more restricted in the individual victimisation case.

[83] *RMT v UK* [2014] IRLR 467, [86].
[84] Kavanagh (n 26) 176.
[85] For an early and powerful critique of this approach, see Murray Hunt, 'Sovereignty's Blight: Why Contemporary Public Law Needs a Doctrine of "Due Deference"', in Nick Bamforth and Peter Leyland (eds), *Public Law in a Multi-Layered Constitution* (Hart 2003) 337, 351.

Treating deference as variable and contextual gives courts the ability to respond to these distinctions. The traditional labour law approach to deference is that 'the courts should presume themselves to have inferior competence, expertise or legitimacy across the board'.[86] It would be better to start from a different place. This would be to consider the issue of deference sensitive to *all* relevant factors on the facts of the case. The idea of a 'zone' is not helpful to that contextual evaluation. It should be dispensed with.

V. The Variable and Contextual Approach to Deference: Shifting the Deference Default

Having rejected the spatial approach, a better approach can be found in the work of Aileen Kavanagh and A.C.L. Davies on the variable and contextual approach to deference. The effect of this variable approach is that it would not treat strong judicial deference as an automatic default in the 'zone'. This does not mean that courts are treated as primary decision-makers in governing communities. However, 'substantial deference' is warranted only where the court has 'particular institutional shortcomings' relative to other constitutional actors.[87]

Which factors are relevant to deference for Kavanagh? She identifies three factors, and these are supported by the English public law jurisprudence. The first is 'institutional competence'.[88] This is concerned with the extent of legislative repair needed to achieve compliance with human rights standards. Where a human rights violation can only be rectified by extensive legal reforms, rather than a discretely targeted intervention, this would support a legislative remedy. Law reform can assess the broader consequences of changes to the law, and it can consider if wider changes need to be introduced to ensure that it is coherent with related rules and principles. Judicial repair is inevitably more circumscribed, and this reflects the bipolar nature of litigation.

The second is expertise. This requires a 'difficult and multifaceted inquiry' which will consider 'the degree of intrusion into Convention rights, the nature of the right at issue and the extent (and type) of law reform necessary to rectify the alleged rights violation'.[89] Essentially, this is concerned with an assessment of uncertainty and probabilities of error. The more that the court is

[86] Kavanagh (n 26) 175.
[87] Ibid. 182.
[88] Ibid. 182–183.
[89] Ibid. 187.

epistemically certain that the situation discloses a violation of rights, the less likely that the court will accord deference to the primary decision-maker.[90]

Finally, 'democratic legitimacy' indicates that courts should always accord a threshold of respect to the decisions of primary decision-makers in a constitutional democracy. It is less clear when democratic arguments justify substantial deference. Kavanagh suggests that where a political decision is highly controversial, political institutions might be better placed than courts to build a societal consensus in favour of that position.[91] The politically contested nature of some labour law issues, particularly in the realm of regulating strikes, might favour democratic modes of social change. There are some examples of this kind of approach to deference in some of the trade union cases to be considered in the book.

A. Institutional competence

Starting with 'institutional competence', an important example of this can be seen in the right to strike case of *Secretary of State for Business and Trade v Mercer*.[92] This involved a legal challenge under the HRA to the non-protection of lawful and official strikers from 'detriments'. This was excluded from the statutory protection in s. 146 of TULRCA 1992 because it was not a trade union activity 'at an appropriate time'. *Mercer* involved a human rights challenge to a long-standing exclusionary feature of the legislative framework of industrial action. This was a highly controversial matter of social and economic policy. It also engaged the fundamental constitutional value of non-discrimination, given that an individual trade unionist had been singled out for participating in lawful trade union activity.

The Supreme Court agreed that the absence of *any* statutory protection for individual strikers from detriment was a violation of Article 11. Nevertheless, Lady Simler concluded that it would not be appropriate to 'read down' the statutory provision using the HRA s. 3 interpretative obligation. This was because there was not 'a single, obvious legislative solution that will ensure compliance with article 11 while at the same time maintaining an appropriate balance between the competing rights of employers and their workers in this politically and socially sensitive context'.[93] According to Lady Simler, it was unclear

[90] Ibid. 171.
[91] Ibid. 194. She gives the example of changes to child support for homosexual couples.
[92] [2024] UKSC 12.
[93] Ibid. [102].

whether rights-compliant statutory protection should include all detriments, the situation of very long-term strikes, and coherence with the (then) 12-week limit on dismissal protections for 'protected' industrial action. These controversial matters of policy could not be resolved through interpretation: they were properly matters for legislative choice. In these circumstances, the Supreme Court issued a s. 4 declaration of incompatibility. This meant that these controversial policy decisions could be addressed in an appropriate way, with the scope for broader statutory amendments to ensure systemic legal coherence.[94]

B. Expertise

Another important epistemic guide to courts is the extent to which a violation is displayed to a 'substantial degree' or is manifestly serious or egregious.[95] This is because 'the more certainty, the less deference' for the reviewing court.[96] This is certainly a feature of some of the domestic and European case law on Article 11. For example, in *R (Boots Management Services Ltd.) v Central Arbitration Committee*, there was a voluntary recognition agreement with a non-independent association, the Boots Pharmacists' Association (BPA), which blocked a competing statutory application by the independent union, the Pharmacists' Defence Association Union (PDAU).[97] The agreement with the BPA did not encompass core issues such as pay. The only statutory mechanism for displacing the existing voluntary agreement was by an application of an individual worker to trigger a statutory derecognition ballot. The PDAU argued that the convoluted statutory process for displacing the voluntary agreement violated its Article 11 rights, and this argument included the fact that an individual worker was required under the legislation to 'pull the trigger' for the statutory derecognition process. Underhill LJ observed that 'there will inevitably be some choices which not only could have been made differently but could have been made better. But I think it is clear from the case-law of the ECtHR referred to above that article 11 cannot be used as

[94] For example, the Employment Relations Act 2025 has removed the 12-week period for protected industrial action in the dismissal protections in TULRCA s. 238A. This ensures temporal symmetry in the parallel detriment and dismissal protections for those engaged in protected industrial action. The time limitation in respect of dismissal protection is very unlikely to be compatible with Article 11, but it did not arise for consideration in *Mercer* itself.

[95] Kavanagh (n 26) 171.

[96] Ibid.

[97] *R (Boots Management Services Ltd.) v Central Arbitration Committee* [2017] EWCA Civ 66, [2017] IRLR 355 (*Boots*). This decision is considered in Alan Bogg and Ruth Dukes, 'Article 11 ECHR and the Right to Collective Bargaining' (2017) 46 Industrial Law Journal 543.

a tool to challenge this or that arguably sub-optimal element in a scheme provided that a fair balance has been struck.'[98]

It was only in more extreme situations, for example, where this derecognition route was not reasonably practicable for an individual worker, that this would be something more than 'suboptimal' legislative design. This emphasis on extremity was also a feature of the landmark case of *Demir and Baykara v Turkey*, which recognised the right to collective bargaining as an essential element of Article 11.[99] Under Turkish law, the union had not acquired legal personality, which meant that its collective agreement was annulled because it was of no legal effect. This required the reimbursement of sums that had been secured through the annulled collective agreement. The extremity of these facts has been emphasised by later courts in the reception of *Demir*.[100] This can be understood as an epistemic factor relevant to judicial confidence in their own judgement that there is a violation.

Another kind of epistemic consideration can be seen in the use of external legal materials to guide constitutional interpretation. For example, the SCC has attracted controversy in its engagement with international law material in its interpretation of s. 2(d) of the Charter. In *Health Services & Support-Facilities Subsector Bargaining Association v British Columbia (B.C. Health Service)*, the SCC referred to the ILO's recognition of the fundamental right to collective bargaining.[101] According to the Chief Justice and LeBel J, 'Canada's adherence to international documents recognizing a right to collective bargaining supports recognition of the right in s. 2(d) of the *Charter*.'[102] This appeal to international labour standards has been controversial.[103] Langille and Oliphant set out some powerful objections to treating the conclusions and recommendations of ILO committees as *authoritative* legal reasons in a national legal order.

The deference analysis provides a different perspective on the use of this material. The SCC is a generalist court. It is not a labour court. The appeal to international bodies with relevant expertise is a way of addressing its expertise deficit in labour matters. This is not the same as treating ILO committees as authoritative or legally binding. It is an epistemic tool that is rational to use for a generalist court dealing with specialist subject-matter such as the right

[98] *Boots* (n 97) [68].
[99] *Demir* (n 20).
[100] See, e.g., *R (on the application of the Independent Workers Union of Great Britain) v Secretary of State for Business, Energy and Industrial Strategy* [2021] EWCA Civ 260 [59] (Bean LJ).
[101] [2007] 2 SCR 391.
[102] Ibid. [70].
[103] 'From the Frying Pan to the Fire: Fraser and the Shift from International Law to International "Thought" in Charter Cases' (2012) 16 Canadian Labour and Employment Law Journal 181.

to bargain collectively. It ensures that general constitutional standards are permeable to the influence of labour law norms in trade union cases. Where international bodies have converged in condemning a practice as violative of human rights, this is relevant to the reviewing court's confidence in its own expertise and judgement that there is indeed a violation.

C. Democracy

The final deference factor is democratic legitimacy. Despite its intuitive appeal as a relevant factor in constitutional review, identifying its precise impact in particular cases is not easy. After all, it is a constant background factor in *all* human rights cases that involve a challenge to legislation. Can the democratic argument ever make an *extra* difference by justifying substantial rather than standard deference? Sometimes, the ECtHR has drawn attention to inadequate democratic procedures in determining the margin of appreciation. In *Ognevenko v Russia*,[104] for example, a train driver was dismissed for participating in a strike that was treated as illegal under Russian law because it was deemed an essential service. The ECtHR concluded that there was a violation of Article 11. It was particularly critical of the lack of solid evidence to justify the ban on striking in the railways sector.[105] And in *R (ASLEF) v Secretary of State for Business and Trade*, a group of unions challenged the Conduct of Employment Agencies and Employment Businesses (Amendment) Regulations 2022 through judicial review.[106] These amendments removed the restrictions on agencies providing workers as replacement labour during an official strike. The unions had made submissions on Article 11 and the right to strike, but Linden J focused on the multiple failures of the Secretary of State to comply with the administrative law duty to consult.

Respect for democracy can also be achieved by allowing governments a range of (incommensurable) legislative options for complying with the relevant constitutional standards. In *M.P.A.O.*, for example, the SCC concluded that the imposition of a 'Staff Relations Representative Programme' in the Royal Canadian Mounted Police Service (RCMP) violated s. 2(d) of the Charter.[107] The SCC articulated general constitutional principles, such as

[104] [2019] IRLR 195.
[105] Ibid. [76]–[77].
[106] [2023] ICR 1405. See Joanna Bell, 'Strike Cover, Consultation and Quashing: An Analysis of *R. (Associated Society of Locomotive Engineers and Firemen) v Secretary of State*' (2023) 52 Industrial Law Journal 930.
[107] *Mounted Police Association of Ontario v Canada (Attorney General)* [2015] 1 SCR 3 (*M.P.A.O.*).

'choice' and 'independence'.[108] These were more determinate than the abstract 'right to collective bargaining' but less specific than the statutory rules in the general Wagner Act model. As such, it was not mandating the adoption of a specific statutory model. These constitutional principles could be satisfied by a range of compliant statutory models. This principles-based approach preserved the latitude for democratic choice in responding to the judgment.

D. Deference and margin of appreciation

One final matter to be addressed is the relationship between the legal concept of deference in national law and the 'margin of appreciation' concept under the ECHR. Are these concepts related or are they distinct? This is a matter of theoretical interest but also of great practical importance. This is because of the 'mirror principle', which holds that the domesticated rights under the HRA 1998 must be interpreted in the same way by national courts as the Convention rights are interpreted by the ECtHR.[109] If the ECtHR treats the state's conduct as within the margin of appreciation, there is no violation for the purpose of the ECHR. Under the mirror principle, it follows that there is no violation of a Convention right for the purpose of the domesticated right either.[110]

I follow Kavanagh in treating the margin of appreciation as a 'doctrine of judicial self-restraint adopted by the Strasbourg court. It governs the extent to which, or the intensity with which, the Strasbourg court will scrutinise a decision made by a signatory state to the Convention'.[111] It is certainly true that there are factors relevant to the Strasbourg context that would not be relevant to a national court. For example, there are wide variations in collective labour law systems across Europe, reflecting diverse trade union histories, constitutional norms, and economic models. These variations in trade union

[108] Ibid. [85]–[90].

[109] *R (on the application of Elan-Cane) v Secretary of State for the Home Department* [2021] UKSC 56, [87]. See further Lord Sales, 'The Developing Jurisprudence of the Supreme Court on Convention Rights', Scottish Public Law Group Conference, 5 June 2023. See A.C.L. Davies, 'Article 11 in the Mirror: The Importance of Section 2 Human Rights Act 1998 in Understanding the Court's Approach to Article 11 of the European Convention on Human Rights' (2025) Industrial Law Journal advanced access https://doi.org/10.1093/indlaw/dwaf014.

[110] For an interesting alternative view that is critical of the mirror principle, see Joe Atkinson, 'Taking Human Rights Seriously at Work: The Past, Present and Future of Employment Law' (2025) 54 Industrial Law Journal 816. Atkinson highlights the important differences between 'margin of appreciation' and domestic 'deference'. However, the point remains that if the Strasbourg Court concludes that the domestic situation is within the margin of appreciation, there is no violation of a Convention right. If there is no violation, the rationale for 'bringing rights home' under the HRA is simply not engaged.

[111] Kavanagh (n 26) 208.

rights reveal reasonable yet incommensurable legal models. The Council of Europe is also committed to the organisational norm of 'subsidiarity', so that its human rights standards can be tailored in ways that are sensitive to local conditions.[112] Also, national institutions (including national courts) are often better placed to scrutinise relevant evidence justifying restrictions on Convention rights. For all these reasons, we should expect the default in favour of judicial deference to be stronger in the Strasbourg context.

Many of the principles relevant to Strasbourg margin of appreciation can be explained by reference to judicial self-restraint. For example, some relevant factors can be explained in epistemic terms. When state conduct is particularly invasive of a right,[113] or strikes at a 'core' aspect of a trade union right,[114] or interferes with an 'essential' trade union freedom,[115] this supports a narrower margin of appreciation. In different ways, these are all infringements that can be identified as especially severe. This means that a court will have more confidence in its judgement that there is a violation. Where there is a strong consensus in European law and practice on a specific issue, this would tend to increase the court's confidence in finding a violation.[116] The position under other international labour standards, such as the ILO and the ESC, is also treated as a relevant factor. Sometimes, this has been described as the 'integrated' approach to human rights adjudication.[117] Some caution is needed in using the terminology of 'integration' today. The position under the ILO standards is certainly not determinative of the position under Article 11, even though it is sometimes treated as relevant. For example, in both *RMT* and *Humpert*, the prohibitions on strike action in those cases had been subject to criticism by ILO committees and under the ESC. However, these national measures were still treated as within the state's margin under Article 11. There were other factors in those cases that supported a wider margin of appreciation. They will be considered in more detail in Chapter 5. It would be better to view ILO and other international standards as epistemic tools. Widespread

[112] On subsidiarity in international human rights law, see Paulo Carozza, 'Subsidiarity as a Structural Principle of International Human Rights Law' (2003) 97 American Journal of International Law 38.

[113] For example, dismissal is treated as a particularly invasive interference: see *Young, James and Webster* (n 15) [55].

[114] See *RMT v UK* (n 83) which drew a distinction between 'core' (i.e., primary strike action against a direct employer in defence of occupational interests) and 'accessory' (i.e., secondary strike action) elements of the right to strike: [77] and [82].

[115] There is a non-exhaustive list of 'essential' trade union freedoms under Article 11 that includes the right to form and join trade unions, the right that the trade union should be heard, prohibition of the closed shop, and the right to collective bargaining. These are rights of particular importance in the structure of Article 11.

[116] *Demir* (n 20) [151]–[154].

[117] Virginia Mantouvalou, 'Labour Rights in the European Convention on Human Rights: An Intellectual Justification for an Integrated Approach to Interpretation' (2013)] 13 Human Rights Law Review 529.

condemnation of national laws by other relevant bodies would give the ECtHR extra confidence in finding a violation, but in no sense are these standards presumptively binding or authoritative for the Strasbourg court. To the extent that 'integrated' implies indivisibility or even a fusion of norms, this is misleading given the more modest epistemic role of international standards in the margin of appreciation.

VI. Freedom of Association and Constitutional Equality

Let us return to the reflections of Langille and Oliphant on deference and the judicial function. They reject the proposition that labour law is a constitutional 'no go' zone, and of course, they are right to do so. What do they identify as the appropriate basis for judicial intervention? They propose the constitutional value of equality. They suggest that in many of the constitutional cases in the SCC, 'the underlying claim was simple: everyone else gets these labour rights, everyone else has had their freedom protected by the legislature, why not us?'[118] This would require the court to scrutinise the justification for the exclusion of occupational groups from the general statutory scheme, and to consider if the legislature had struck a fair balance between competing values and interests. There is something attractive in this proposal. It circumscribes the judicial role while targeting the judicial focus on a matter that is usually regarded as central to judicial expertise: the principle of non-discrimination.

The ideal of equality before the law provides a richer and more expansive basis for judicial intervention than simply the scrutiny of occupational exclusions from existing legislative schemes, however. Take the following example. Agricultural workers are unprotected from acts of anti-union victimisation by employers. This exposure to employer coercion has a serious chilling effect on unionisation. One kind of equality argument, which is developed by Langille and Oliphant, focuses on the justification for the statutory exclusion. In the Canadian context, this makes sense because there is a general baseline of statutory protection, and agricultural workers are excluded from it. But what if there is no such general statutory baseline? The agricultural workers cannot point to a specific occupational exclusion, perhaps because employment laws have been deregulated more comprehensively. There is still an equality concern in play, but it is different from the exclusion scenario. These workers are being exposed to *discriminatory sanctions* for exercising a fundamental

[118] Langille and Oliphant (n 58) 300.

freedom and engaging in lawful trade union activity. This exposure to victimisation is intrinsically wrongful, and it engages the constitutional norm of non-discrimination. This constitutional equality claim is freestanding from any general statutory scheme.

Equality as a constitutional value is a complex ideal.[119] It is connected to other constitutional values such as the rule of law and principles of non-discrimination. Different strands of equality before the law have influenced the development of freedom of association. It has also shaped legislative reforms as well as judicial reasoning. Constitutional equality in its different guises will recur throughout this book, and freedom of association as it has developed within the law cannot be understood without understanding these connections to legal equality.

As an example, Chapter 2 will examine the early historical development of trade union rights in English law. Until 1875, the criminal law regulated and restricted trade union activities. The liberalisation of penal suppression was based principally on considerations of legal equality rather than a theory of freedom of association. This led the legal historian John Orth to suggest that 'respect for proper procedure was hypertrophied, while knowledge of political economy was only slowly developing'.[120] For example, early legislation restricting combinations was tempered by a concern that these laws should be administered impartially. This augmented procedural rights, including rights of appeal, for those accused of crimes linked to combinations. It also justified restrictions on the legal officials empowered to decide these cases. For example, the hatters' combination act of 1777 disqualified master hatters from acting in a judicial capacity in any dispute involving journeymen hatters under that legislation.[121] As Foran has argued, 'the idea that law be impartially applied without fear or favour by an independent judiciary clearly presupposes a minimum degree of independence and impartiality within the law'.[122] These ideas of procedural fairness and impartiality were highly influential even during periods when the law was relatively repressive towards trade unions.

The momentous shift from criminal penalties to civil liabilities for trade union activities occurred during the great legislative reforms of the 1870s. The political debates during this period were shaped by ideas of impartiality and generality of laws, and hostility to partial 'class laws' directed specifically at

[119] Michael Foran, *Equality before the Law* (Hart 2023) chapter 1.
[120] Orth (n 9) 23.
[121] Ibid. 19.
[122] Foran (n 119) 23.

trade unions and workmen. There was opprobrium for one-sided master and servant laws that imposed heavy penalties for breaches of contract by workmen but not employers, and criminal offences directed at industrial tactics during strikes. These 'class laws' undermined the promise of equal citizenship in the political community. The coalition of support for the labour law reforms of 1875 was based upon 'the assertion of the right of equal treatment under the law for both masters and men', which required 'the removal of unjust and discriminatory laws'.[123] This led to the progressive removal of criminal liabilities for breach of employment contract. The notion of impartiality extended beyond the procedures and enforcement of the laws to encompass their substantive content. The debates around the generality of laws during this period also highlighted the connections between equality before the law and equal respect for the moral standing of citizens. There was something demeaning about the lop-sided nature of criminal liabilities because this was expressive of a diminished civic status of workers in the public realm.

Legal categories usually depend upon distinctions and differentiations between persons and groups. To define a legal right is to define a category of right-holders and a category of duty-bearers. This is necessarily exclusionary, because not everyone has the right or is subject to the duty. In his discussion of the Equal Protection Clause in the US Constitution, TRS Allan has observed, 'Since laws necessarily differentiate between persons for legitimate purposes, in practice the Clause requires differences of treatment to be justified. Legislative classifications are reasonable and permissible, rather than arbitrary and unconstitutional, where they relate to a legitimate statutory objective.'[124] The objection to the legislative classifications in 19th-century criminal laws was that they reflected demeaning stereotypes about workmen, trade unions, and unjust hierarchies in economy and society. However, there are many other legislative classifications distinguishing between persons and groups in the labour field. The fundamental distinction between workers and the independent self-employed, for example, is not inherently demeaning. The constitutional enquiry is whether these classifications can be justified by reference to legitimate statutory objectives.

Many of these category-based distinctions are considered in Chapter 3 on the 'personal scope' of freedom of association. It has been a frequent piece of rhetoric—and powerful rhetoric—that 'trade union rights are for rights for

[123] Jonathan Spain, 'Trade Unionists, Gladstonian Liberals and the Labour Law Reforms of 1875', in E. Biagini and A. Reid (eds), *Currents of Radicalism: Popular Radicalism, Organised Labour and Party Politics in Britain 1850-1914* (Cambridge UP 1991) 109, 114–115.

[124] T.R.S. Allan, *Law, Liberty, and Justice: The Legal Foundations of British Constitutionalism* (OUP 1993) 163–164.

everyone'. Since trade union rights are human rights, they should be guaranteed to everyone universally. Like other labour rights, such as the right to a fair wage or a right not to be unfairly dismissed, most legal systems developed a legal category of right-holder based upon some kind of personal employment contract or employment relationship. They are usually described as 'employees' or 'workers'. This was correlative to a legal category of duty-bearer, usually described as 'employer'. This was not an arbitrary or demeaning legislative classification. It reflected the normative justification for labour rights based in the need to protect workers in a subordinate and dependent relationship from exploitation and arbitrary treatment by their employer. Like many other labour rights, trade union rights are certainly human rights. This does not preclude the need for some kind of differentiation to ensure that those in need of the special protections receive them. The important enquiry is whether an exclusion can be justified by relevant reasons.

The 'rights for everyone' mantra is unhelpful because it fails in a basic way to engage with the fact that the very idea of 'labour law' is predicated on a defined category that excludes some relations (like relations between commercial parties or businesses) from its scope. This does not mean that equality considerations are irrelevant to the personal scope of freedom of association. Sometimes, occupations are excluded from the scope of general labour law coverage, such as the police or agricultural workers. Equality norms have been used to scrutinise the justifications for those occupational exclusions and to assess if they can be justified by reference to legitimate aims. More broadly, increasing numbers of workers are being classified as independent self-employed, yet they experience significant contractual vulnerabilities to exploitation and abuse. This has been a particular problem in the platform economy, though there is a wider problem of misalignment between personal scope and labour rights in other contexts. Chapter 3 explores the potential for adjusting this core category of an employment relationship to ensure that those in need of legal protections for freedom of association receive them. While this envisages more modest and incremental changes than the 'rights for everyone' approach, it does treat the existing labour law baseline as presumptively legitimate. The relevant enquiry is whether the law's discriminating categories are amenable to principled justification.

In Chapters 4–6, the book identifies a fundamental distinction between 'individual' and 'collective' aspects of the right to collective bargaining, the right to strike, and the closed shop. Constitutional courts have given a wide margin to legislators in defining 'collective' legal concepts (should 'representative' unions enjoy greater collective bargaining privileges? How should 'representative' be defined? Should there be a ballot requirement for lawful strike action? Should 'secondary' strikes be permitted?). By contrast, the courts have protected individual workers from acts of trade union discrimination by employers, and the idea of deference has had little influence on judicial reasoning. I will argue that this bifurcation reflects an equality concern. In his rich reflections on constitutional equality, T.R.S. Allan discusses the case of *Wheeler v Leicester City Council*.[125] This was a judicial review case that involved a challenge to a local authority's decision to ban the sports club from using council property for training. This was to punish the club for failing to pressurise some of its players to deter them from participating in a rugby tour of apartheid South Africa. The House of Lords concluded that the council's policy was ultra vires. According to Allan, 'The council's action was "irrational" in the sense that it violated the club members' equality—their rights not to be punished, or be subjected to adverse discrimination, on the ground of a public authority's disapproval of their characters or conduct.'[126] Similar concerns underlie many of the 'individual' freedom of association cases considered in Chapters 4–6.

Take the example of a striker engaged in a lawful and official strike who is subjected to penalties by her employer.[127] She is suspended from work and denied a promotion to penalise her for participating in a strike that is lawful and authorised by her trade union. There is no statutory protection from victimisation in these circumstances. Has her equality been violated? It has not been violated by an unjustified statutory exclusion, because there is no statutory protection from detriment *for any worker*. However, the exposure to sanctions by a private party, to punish her for participating in a lawful activity, violates *her equal moral status as a citizen*.[128] It is an affront to a citizen's dignity to be exposed to punitive sanctions by other private parties for doing things that are recognised as lawful and protected, like trade union activities. Private punishment treats adults like children, and it compromises the worker's independence and equal standing in the community. This explains why constitutional courts protect individual workers from discriminatory treatment by employers in such cases with little regard to considerations of deference. This kind of treatment is intrinsically wrongful, and it violates fundamental constitutional values.

This ideal of equality can be radical in its implications. It could certainly permit unequal treatment in certain circumstances where this is necessary

[125] [1985] 2 All ER 151, discussed in Allan (n 124) 168–169.
[126] Ibid. 169.
[127] This is similar to the facts in *Secretary of State for Business and Trade v Mercer* [2024] ICR 814, considered below in Chapter 5.
[128] Foran (n 119) 32–38.

to give effective legal protection to especially disadvantaged groups. Brian Langille has pointed to the dangers of 'condescension' when courts and constitutions identify specific groups, such as those dedicated to redressing social and economic imbalances, as warranting stronger constitutional protection.[129] It is certainly true that some kinds of public distinction between groups can violate equality, and they represent a kind of 'condescension' that we should reject. For example, Martha Nussbaum observes that 'even a benign religious (or anti-religious) establishment threatens equality by creating an in-group and a variety of out-groups. It says that all citizens do not enter the public square on equal terms.'[130] The point here is that religious differentiation is not a justified reason for a constitutional distinction in allocating legal protections for freedom of association. By contrast, targeted legal support for trade unions and other associations representing the disadvantaged is warranted because *they are already an 'out-group'*. The provision of affirmative support to associations that empower the disadvantaged is aimed at achieving rather than undermining substantive equality in the public square. It means that the disadvantaged can achieve the respect and equal moral standing that they would otherwise lack. In this way, special protections for the freedom of association of very disadvantaged groups, like agricultural workers and non-standard workers, could be justified by reference to equality before the law.

A rich idea of equality also provides a complete answer to A.V. Dicey's famous 'rule of law' criticism of the Trade Disputes Act 1906, to be considered in Chapter 2. The 1906 legislation provided a statutory immunity from civil liability for trade unions and organisers of industrial action where there was a 'trade dispute'. For Dicey, this violated the rule of law principle of the supremacy of the ordinary law by excluding specific named groups from liability for civil wrongs in the law of torts.[131] Many later judges were particularly exercised by this concept of a statutory privilege exempting private actors from responsibility for wrongful damage. Was this not simply another kind of 'class law' like the master and servant laws of the 19th century? It should be no less objectionable in principle simply because it privileges the class we favour. As I have already explained, the constitutional issue to be addressed is whether statutory distinctions and classifications are amenable to principled justification. Unequal treatment is not necessarily wrongful. The statutory immunity

[129] Brian Langille, 'The Condescending Constitution (or, The Purpose of Freedom of Association is Freedom of Association) (2016) 19 Canadian Labour and Employment Law Journal 335.

[130] Martha C. Nussbaum, *Creating Capabilities: The Human Development Approach* (Harvard UP 2011) 90.

[131] Kahn-Freund (n 65) 5.

in the 1906 legislation was justified because it was aiming (in Nussbaum's terminology) to restore equality in the public square for trade unions and workmen. Without this immunity, they could not engage in lawful strike action. This was a denial of their basic dignity and autonomy as equal citizens, no less offensive and demeaning than the Master and Servant laws repealed in the 1870s.

Finally, it is important to recognise that equality before the law can justify limits on the protection of trade union activity. A controversial example of this is *Baris v Turkey*, where employees were dismissed because they had engaged in strike action outside of the official union structures.[132] The strike was illegal under Turkish law. According to the ECtHR, this could not be described as protected trade union activity since it was not organised by the trade union. If anything, the strike on these facts was organised *against* the trade union. Although this *Baris* restriction is controversial, I suggest that it reflects a legally coherent limit. The relevant protective principle is equality *before the law*. If strikers are conducting themselves outside the law, their Article 11 protections ought to be attenuated.[133] Otherwise, the law would be speaking in two voices rather than one, by defining and enforcing the limits of a lawful strike *but at the same time* protecting individuals from the consequences of participating in that unlawful strike. This engages similar concerns to the public policy doctrine of illegality, where a claimant seeks to rely upon her criminal conduct in bringing a legal claim against a defendant.[134] Sometimes, this public policy would provide a defence to the legal claim to preserve the integrity of the legal system. *Baris* raises similar 'integrity of the legal system' considerations. This also indicates why 'radical' conceptions of the right to strike, that might justify actions such as property damage or mass sit-ins to counter structural economic oppression, cannot be anchored in constitutional norms.[135] The *legal* protection of rights must be grounded in the sense that these rights are an ordered and coherent whole protected in the legal system. This includes the employer's property rights. This must temper expectations of what can be achieved through legal argumentation and strategic

[132] App No. 66828/16, 27 January 2020.

[133] For another case demonstrating this principle, see *Trofimchuk v Ukraine* App No. 4241/03, 28 October 2010. However, the Court will still consider the severity of the individual sanction as part of the overall proportionality assessment even in unlawful strikes: see *Humpert and others v Germany* Applications nos. 59433/18, 59477/18, 59481/18, and 59494/18, 14 December 2023. As such, strikers engaged in unlawful strike action are not outlaws in human rights terms, but their protections are certainly reduced.

[134] For an extensive consideration of the doctrine of illegality in its many guises, see Sarah Green and Alan Bogg (eds), *Illegality after Patel v Mirza* (Hart 2018).

[135] On the 'radical' right to strike, see Alex Gourevitch, 'The Right to Strike: A Radical View' (2019) 112 American Political Science Review 905.

litigation. It is difficult to envisage a 'radical' right to strike as a blueprint for a constitutional right to strike protected in the law.

Throughout this book, we will return to this ideal of equality. As an internal legal value, it runs like a golden thread through many of the twists and turns in the legal development of freedom of association. The 'internal' methodology of the book is perhaps more attuned to its influence than externalist perspectives.

VII. Individualism and Collectivism in Freedom of Association: Redux

Many scholars in the pluralist tradition of collective laissez-faire were critical of judges in the context of freedom of association. Lord Wedderburn was the exemplar. This focused on the 'individualistic' values of judges, which subverted the 'collectivist' goals of freedom of association.[136] This 'individualism' critique was central to Wedderburn's sceptical view of Article 11. Article 11 was focused on individual rather than collective rights. It supported the individual's negative freedom to disassociate from the trade union. This undermined solidarity and other collective goods. The scope for restrictions on trade union rights under Article 11(2) also provided a medium whereby judges could uphold restrictions on trade union freedoms. This was effectively transferring political powers to unelected judges and transmuting what were essentially political questions into legal questions.[137]

One of the central arguments of this book is that the judicial approach to freedom of association is 'individualistic' but in a distinctive and appropriate way. In Chapter 2, the historical development of freedom of association will reveal a judicial disposition which was to protect the individual workman from the oppressive use of economic power. For reasons examined in that chapter, this was focused predominantly on the organised power of trade unions rather than the managerial authority of employers. In Chapter 6, judicial attitudes to the closed shop in the common law were rooted in a concern to protect workers from abuse of power. This justified the use of common law techniques to regulate the exercise of powers to discipline or exclude trade

[136] The permutations of the 'individualist' critique are considered in Alan Bogg, '"Individualism" and "Collectivism" in Collective Labour Law' (2017) 46 Industrial Law Journal 72.

[137] The classic critique in this vein is set out in J.A.G. Griffith, 'The Political Constitution' (1979) 42 Modern Law Review 1. It formed part of a critical functionalist tradition developed at the LSE, of which Lord Wedderburn was an important figure.

union members if this interfered with their 'right to work'. This was not confined to the common law courts, however. The ECtHR has also been strongly protective of the individual's right to disassociate from the trade union, and the prohibition of the closed shop is now an 'essential' element of Article 11.

In Chapters 4 and 5, on the right to bargain collectively and the right to strike, there is a strong distinction in the case law between individual and collective norms. The courts have been strongly protective where individuals have been victimised or exposed to discrimination for trade union membership or activities. There is little or no deference in these individual discrimination cases. By contrast, challenges to 'collective' issues such as the definition of 'representative' trade unions or the permissible scope for lawful strike action have attracted a high degree of deference. The courts are generally reluctant to interfere with democratic decisions crystallised in legislation.

This reflects a coherent judicial vision of freedom of association based upon appropriate deference and informed by norms of constitutional equality. Judicial attitudes to the closed shop, the right to organise, the right to collective bargaining, and the right to strike are not discordant. They reflect a unified approach that places the equal moral standing of workers at the core of freedom of association.

In this respect, Kahn-Freund was right all along, but perhaps not in the way that Lord Wedderburn thought. The civil liberty, understood through the lens of constitutional equality and non-discrimination, is indeed an 'indispensable condition' for the operation of collective labour relations. Individual discrimination for trade union reasons is an intrinsic wrong. Without norms of individual non-discrimination, safeguarded as a matter of high constitutional concern by judges, collective labour relations would be seriously undermined. Kahn-Freund articulated this most clearly in his Hamlyn Lectures, published as *Labour and the Law*, when he said of the civil liberty that workers must 'be free to join them [trade unions], to work for them, and to remain in them'.[138] This was 'a *conditio sine qua non* of industrial relations in all except totalitarian societies'.[139] As regards the machinery of *collective* labour relations, such as bargaining units or strike procedures, that is a matter properly amenable to popular democratic control. This reflects an appropriate division of constitutional labour in implementing freedom of association. Courts and legislators each have their part to play. This ensures that the autonomy of labour law is respected within appropriate constitutional limits. The argument in the book is developed in the following chapters.

[138] Paul Davies and Mark Freedland (eds), *Kahn-Freund's Labour and the Law* (3rd ed, Stevens & Sons 1983) 200.

[139] Ibid. 201.

Chapter 2 traces the historical development of freedom of association in British labour law. Freedom of association emerged as a freedom *within* the labour market rather than *against* the labour market. The chapter identifies a strong role for the autonomy of labour law in the legal history of freedom of association. Many familiar features of modern human rights and labour law, such as the focus on protecting primary industrial strikes and the marginal position of secondary and political strikes, were already visible in this early historical development. The judicial concern to protect the individual from oppressive economic power was also a significant feature during this formative legal period. This is echoed in modern human rights law on the closed shop.

Chapter 3 examines the 'personal scope' of freedom of association. It rejects the proposition that trade union rights are rights for 'everyone'. The labour law boundary of 'worker' for trade union rights is deeply rooted in most legal systems. The distinctive role of human rights law has been in scrutinising occupational exclusions from the scope of labour legislation. Human rights also provide a tool for extending the personal scope of 'worker' where self-employed individuals in need of protection, such as platform workers, are unable to satisfy existing legal definitions of employment status. While this can recalibrate the boundary, sometimes even in radical ways, *some* kind of boundary is presupposed by the logic of rights and correlative duties. However it may be defined, this is unlikely to be too remote from the conventional relation of worker and employer.

Chapter 4 examines the right to collective bargaining as an element of freedom of association. It identifies a bifurcation in human rights law between 'individual' and 'collective' cases. Where an individual has been exposed to discriminatory treatment by an employer, the courts generally eschew deference and require that the legislature introduce real and effective protections for individual workers. By contrast, legislative choices about the 'collective' aspects of legal models of collective bargaining, such as scope or level of bargaining, attract a high degree of deference. In these 'collective' cases, the autonomy of labour law is still a significant feature.

Chapter 5 examines the right to strike as an element of freedom of association. It identifies a parallel bifurcation between 'individual' and 'collective' cases, similar to the pattern identified in Chapter 4. When individual strikers have been penalised for participating in lawful and official strike action, the courts have been strongly protective. By contrast, legislative choices about the 'collective' aspects of the right to strike, such as its lawful purposes or procedural requirements, have attracted a high degree of deference. Again, the courts have respected the autonomy of labour law in these collective aspects.

The focus has been on ensuring effective judicial protection from discriminatory treatment for the individual striker.

Chapter 6 concludes with the closed shop and freedom of association. This was the principal focus in Wedderburn's critique of Article 11, which in his view provided the strongest example of an individualistic civil liberty disrupting the settled institutions of collective labour law. I argue that the Article 11 jurisprudence supports the opposite argument and undermines Wedderburn's critique. It is a myth to treat the closed shop as a core and legitimate institution of labour law. In most European labour law systems, in fact, the closed shop is treated as normatively suspect. The Article 11 case law integrates that labour law approach into its own human rights interpretation, reflecting the consensus in national labour laws and practices. Furthermore, the judicial protection of individuals from abuse of power in closed shop situations, and the correspondingly reduced margin of appreciation, is aligned with the ECtHR's general approach set out in Chapters 4 and 5. The closed shop is an 'individual' rather than a 'collective' issue. In this way, norms on the right to organise, the right to collective bargaining, the right to strike, and the closed shop are elements in a coherent interpretive approach to freedom of association.

This is a conception of freedom of association that respects the autonomy of labour law and the moral and civic equality of persons. As is so often the case, Kahn-Freund was right. Freedom of association depends upon the civil liberty and the industrial conception as complementary aspects. It is the vision defended in this book.

2
The Historical Foundations of Freedom of Association

I. The Legal Foundations of Freedom of Association

This chapter examines the historical foundations of freedom of association focusing on the development of English law from the late 18th to early 20th century. This may be regarded by some students of labour law as an unusual point of departure. It is conventional to treat this historical period as one of repression of trade union activities, especially through the criminal law.[1] The prohibitive shadow of the criminal law hardly seems promising in understanding the legal development of a freedom. Another issue is that the 19th century was a period of industrialisation and the legal construction of the 'labour market'.[2] Is this process of market-creation not antithetical to trade unions, which operated in restraint of trade and as an oppositional force to the marketisation of labour?

It would be a serious mistake to overlook this historical period. While the criminal law certainly regulated collective labour relations in the 19th century, the criminal law has been a continuous regulatory presence in this sphere through to the present day.[3] As a technique of regulation, criminal law prohibitions are used to specify the outer limits of freedom of association. It is too simplistic to view criminal law as the total negation of the freedom. The freedom is the thing that remains on the other side of the criminal prohibition. There is also a long legal history of social rights that can be traced back to the 18th and 19th centuries.[4] This is certainly true of freedom of association. In the early decades of the 19th century, the

[1] Antoine Jacobs, 'Collective Self-Regulation', in Bob Hepple (ed), *The Making of Labour Law in Europe* (Hart 2010) 194–196.

[2] Simon Deakin and Frank Wilkinson, *The Law of the Labour Market* (OUP 2005).

[3] Alan Bogg, K.D. Ewing, and Andrew Moretta, 'The Persistence of Criminal Law and Police in Collective Labour Relations', in Alan Bogg and others (eds), *Criminality at Work* (OUP 2020) chapter 19.

[4] Steven L.B. Jensen and Charles Walton (eds), *Social Rights and the Politics of Obligation in History* (Cambridge UP 2022).

Freedom of Association. Alan Bogg, Oxford University Press. © Alan Bogg 2026. DOI: 10.1093/9780191831690.003.0002

liberalisation of restrictive trade union laws was aligned with legal reforms to promote the free trade in labour. At that time, the creation of a labour market was viewed by some influential thinkers as a radical egalitarian project. The relationship between trade unions and free labour markets was quite different to its configuration today. Then, the justifications were regarded as complementary. Today, both critics and supporters of trade unions tend to regard trade unions and free markets as antithetical. It was not always like this.

An influential account of the legal history of freedom of association was provided by the great English constitutional lawyer A.V. Dicey.[5] Dicey viewed 'freedom of association' in English law as an issue almost exclusively of labour relations rather than general constitutional law.[6] The emancipation of trade unions was rooted in the individual workman's freedom to dispose of his labour on the market.[7] Freedom of association ensured that workmen could sell their labour collectively or even withhold their labour from the market. This justified a strictly voluntary conception of freedom of association. Where individuals preferred to bargain on their own, the law should protect their liberty to do so. This meant that the courts were often focused on safeguarding the contractual liberty of individual workers from trade union coercion.

This foundation in the individual freedom to dispose of labour on the market was conceptualised narrowly by judges and legislators. From 1824–25 onwards, the core case of legitimate trade union activity was centred on the primary bargaining relationship between an employer and its workers, negotiating their own terms and conditions of employment. This was reinforced by two related positions. The first was the deep suspicion of organised political activities by trade unions, which was always overshadowed by fears of sedition and treason. Trade union activity needed to be focused on the market rather than on politics. The second was the hostility to secondary boycotts. This was suspect because it was viewed as especially coercive, and it could be used as a tool of compulsion against unwilling workmen and masters. While primary industrial bargaining as the core trade union activity was not a logical necessity of the individual freedom to dispose of labour—after all, should freedom not mean that workmen should be at liberty to pursue *any* lawful object or lawful means collectively?—lawmakers were keen to reconcile collective

[5] Albert Venn Dicey, 'The Combination Laws as Illustrating the Relation between Law and Opinion in England during the Nineteenth Century' (1904) 17 Harvard Law Review 511.

[6] Ibid. 514.

[7] Ibid. 511.

bargaining with a functioning labour market. It was this concern with reconciliation that supported the narrow formulation of a core of legitimate trade union activity.

In sum, Dicey's account is fundamentally correct. Throughout this historical period, legislators and courts grappled with the regulatory challenge of reconciling individual and collective freedoms specifically in the labour market. It also mattered that this was being done through the medium of law. Legal ordering was generative of its own internal constraints on the use of state coercion. Over time, notions of legality and equality provided a powerful language for challenging the partiality of laws that imposed special restrictions on trade unions and workmen. This led to a significant emancipation of trade unions and workmen in the 1870s. It also meant that the special immunities for trade unions in the Trade Disputes Act 1906 jarred against judicial sensibilities. In the final section, the chapter indicates the ways in which the legal structure of the modern law of freedom of association was already visible by the first decade of the 20th century. Indeed, it is still with us today. And it was conceptualised by lawmakers as a labour law freedom, not a general constitutional freedom.

II. Freedom of Association, Labour Law, and Varieties of Laissez-Faire

Most students of British labour law are familiar with Dicey because Dicey's 'Lectures on the Relation between Law and Public Opinion in England during the Nineteenth Century' was the basis for one of Otto Kahn-Freund's famous essays from the 1950s.[8] Kahn-Freund's 'Labour Law' was published as a book chapter in a collection on Dicey's 'Law and Public Opinion' lectures, edited by the LSE sociologist, Morris Ginsberg.[9] This was the essay where Kahn-Freund popularised his brilliant term, 'collective laissez-faire'.[10] It was both a description of British labour law and a statement of values.[11] What is sometimes overlooked is that 'collective laissez-faire' emerged out of Kahn-Freund's dialogue with Dicey in that essay.

[8] Otto Kahn-Freund, 'Labour Law', in Otto Kahn-Freund, *Selected Writings* (Stevens & Sons 1978) 1.

[9] Morris Ginsberg (ed), *Law and Opinion in England in the 20th Century* (Stevens & Sons 1959).

[10] Kahn-Freund (n 8) 8, offered almost diffidently with the phrasing 'if you like'.

[11] This dual feature of collective laissez-faire is considered in Lord Wedderburn, 'Change, Struggle and Ideology in British Labour Law', in Lord Wedderburn, *Labour Law and Freedom* (Lawrence & Wishart 1995) chapter 1.

Dicey was imbued with the radical liberal tradition represented by utilitarians like Bentham and John Stuart Mill.[12] Dicey's *Law and Public Opinion* was based in lectures he had delivered in Harvard in 1898. These lectures traced the legal history of the 19th century examining the general relationship between public opinion and legal change.[13] Dicey had counterposed 'individualism' and 'collectivism' and, as Kahn-Freund noted, Dicey lamented what he saw as the disappearance of laissez-faire in the early decades of the 20th century.[14] Dicey's argument was that 'individualism' was disappearing. As the economic and political power of the working classes grew, and they organised in trade unions, the democratic pressures for 'collectivist' state intervention increased. This would lead to the eclipse of individual freedom. In 'Labour Law', Kahn-Freund argued that Dicey's prediction of state 'collectivism' had not come to pass in 20th-century British labour law. This was because of the primacy of voluntary collective bargaining through trade unions. Trade unions had sought a combination of indirect auxiliary support for collective bargaining and statutory immunity from common law doctrines. This enabled the British trade union movement to bargain with employers, and the collective parties preferred to negotiate their own arrangements and norms without state interference in bargaining outcomes. This was 'collective laissez-faire', and it charted a liberal course between 'individualism' and 'collectivism': 'The British labour movement, and especially the trade union movement, has, to an extent certainly not contemplated by Dicey, been heir not only to a Socialist tradition, but decisively also to the Liberalism of the nineteenth century.'[15]

This teaches us something of great importance about the continuity of legal structures. For Kahn-Freund, the legal framework of freedom of association in 20th-century Britain, 'collective laissez-faire', needed to be understood in light of its legal roots in 19th-century liberalism. In fact, Dicey published a separate lecture on the development of the law on freedom of association in the 19th century in the *Harvard Law Review*.[16] It was presented as an examination of the 'combination laws', which described the statutory and common law rules regulating labour associations. These laws were 'part of a far wider subject . . . which exists in every country, but, while under English law it has scarcely acquired a definite name, is known on the Continent and notably in France as the right of association'.[17] Dicey also noted that this 'right

[12] Mark D. Walters, *A.V. Dicey and the Common Law Constitutional Tradition: A Legal Turn of Mind* (Cambridge UP 2020) 53–54.
[13] Ibid. 342.
[14] Kahn-Freund (n 8) 4.
[15] Ibid. 8.
[16] Dicey (n 5).
[17] Ibid. 512.

of association' had developed in different countries in specific associational contexts. So, France was focused on religious associations, in the US it was on trusts, and in Ireland it had been the legality of boycotts in landlord and tenant relations.[18] In Britain, the law on freedom of association had been considered 'mainly, and indeed too exclusively, in reference to trade combinations either among workmen or employers'.[19] There were other kinds of association, such as churches and other religious associations, and there were important legal developments during the 19th century.[20] However, the legal problems of church and state were quite different to the legal problems of masters and workmen. There were no *general* legal principles of association that applied to these different associational contexts. As Dicey's historical examination made clear, the 'combination laws' were formulated as labour law statutes addressed specifically to problems of conflict in labour–capital relations. Indeed, by the early part of the 20th century, these 'laws on combination' provided the basic legal structure to labour law itself.

Freedom of association represented a paradox for a liberal individualist like Dicey: 'a right which from one point of view seems to be a necessary extension of individual freedom is, from another point of view, fatal to that individual freedom of which it seems to be a mere extension.'[21] Workmen might agree to combine and negotiate with an employer, as an aggregative exercise of their individual freedom to dispose of their labour. However, they might also seek to prevent individual workmen from defecting and negotiating their own individual bargains directly with an employer. This was the fundamental challenge which judges and legislators grappled with. It arose in the sharp economic conflicts between masters and workmen over picketing, union security, the closed shop, and the enforcement of union rules against employers and non-unionised workmen.

Dicey identified four distinct periods when the law on combinations shifted, and he examined the important influence of liberal public opinion on these shifts: the repressive combination laws culminating in the general legislation of 1799 and 1800; the 'Benthamite' liberalising reforms of 1824–25; the legislative settlement of 1875; and judicial decisions between 1890 and 1904. He traced the line of 'public opinion' through Adam Smith to Jeremy Bentham to John Stuart Mill. The fundamental liberal idea throughout was the significance of free trade in labour. At the turn of the 19th century, the

[18] Ibid. 514.

[19] Ibid.

[20] Julian Rivers, *The Law of Organized Religions: Between Establishment and Secularism* (OUP 2010) 25–32.

[21] Dicey (n 5) 514.

individual's freedom to dispose of his labour was a radical and emancipatory claim. It also provided the justification for the freedom to combine, because if workmen were free to dispose of their labour as individuals, they should also be free to dispose of it with others through collective bargaining. Free labour also imposed limits on the freedom to combine. This was because no individual should be coerced by the group and prevented from selling his own labour as he saw fit. This meant that some solidaristic practices such as picketing, enforcing closed shops, seeking the discharge of non-unionists were all regarded as morally suspect. By the end of the 19th century, free labour in mines and factories bore no relation to the artisanal ideal of civic independence and freedom in the work of Adam Smith. Yet the courts never quite shook the belief 'in the sacredness of individual liberty and a sense of the peril to which personal liberty was exposed by an unrestricted right of combination'.[22]

This chapter will now examine the early development of the law on freedom of association in Britain from the 18th century through to the Trade Union Act 1913. I shall argue that in every significant respect, Dicey was correct. In Britain, freedom of association developed almost exclusively as a labour law freedom rather than as an aspect of general principles of freedom of association. Its limits were policed strictly by the courts, which were usually concerned to shield workmen from molestation or obstruction by permanent trade union associations. The fact that this was a *legal* discourse also meant that the rule of law and legal equality shaped freedom of association in important ways. For example, special 'class' legislation that was not formulated through general rules, but specifically targeted at workmen and trade unions, was anathema to legal equality. Whatever their political and economic reservations about labour combinations, these ideas mattered to judges and other officials in the legal system. Equality before the law led to significant liberalisation of freedom of association throughout the 19th century. By 1906, when special legislation was needed to exclude tort liabilities for trade unions in the Trade Disputes Act 1906, the supremacy of the ordinary law had been violated. For Dicey, the supremacy of the ordinary law was fundamental to the rule of law.[23] This also demonstrated the ambivalent quality of legal equality to trade unions and workmen. What had liberated them in the 1870s threatened to stifle them in the early 1900s.

[22] Ibid. 532.
[23] Walters (n 12) 228–229.

III. The Radical Promise of 'Free Labour'

A. Egalitarianism and free labour

The work of Adam Smith and the ideal of a free-market society may not seem the obvious place to begin in understanding the legal emancipation of trade unions in the early 19th century. Today, Adam Smith's name is usually associated with right-wing libertarians and free-market think tanks.[24] We are accustomed to viewing free markets and trade union freedoms as antithetical poles rather than counterparts. The liberty of association was first secured in 1824–25 in the Combination Acts. This collective liberty of association was regarded by its proponents as a corollary of free trade and freedom of contract.[25] This justificatory basis would have the most profound consequences for the subsequent development of freedom of association as a labour right throughout the formative period from the 18th to the early 20th century. Indeed, we can still detect the cadence of some of these early developments in the modern law of freedom of association.

The liberalisation of combinations was led by utilitarian radicals, and it was linked to a wider utilitarian project of law reform and the promotion of free trade. However, the process of institutional reconstruction leading to the 1825 settlement was already underway in the 18th century. As the Webbs observed, 'when Adam Smith's masterpiece came into the hands of the statesmen of the time, it must have seemed not so much a novel view of industrial economics as the explicit generalisation of practical conclusions to which experience had already repeatedly driven them.'[26] This intellectual milieu is of fundamental importance in elucidating the earliest justifications for freedom of association in labour markets. It is vital to understand that the freedom to sell labour in a commercial society was rooted in a radical vision of emancipated citizens. In the 18th and early 19th centuries, the 'labour market' was a rallying call for civic freedom. By the late decades of the 19th century, of course, 'free labour' had encountered the 'cataclysm' of the industrial revolution.[27] By then, the

[24] For an important critique of this reductive treatment of Adam Smith, see Donald Winch, *Adam Smith's Politics: An Essay in Historiographic Revision* (Cambridge UP 1978).

[25] Indeed, Deakin and Wilkinson argued that by the time of legislative settlement of the 1870s, 'The collective right to combine could thereby be built up out of the individual freedom to contract of the union members': Deakin and Wilkinson (n 2) 207.

[26] Sidney and Beatrice Webb, *The History of Trade Unionism, 1666-1920* (Printed by the authors, 1919) 55.

[27] Elizabeth Anderson, *Private Government: How Employers Rule Our Lives (and Why We Don't Talk about It)* (Princeton UP 2017) 33.

labour market and free labour had become synonymous with degradation, domination, and structural exploitation.

In Elizabeth Anderson's Tanner lectures, *Private Government*, she retrieves this early radical case for the labour market in her first lecture, 'When the Market "Was" Left'.[28] In it, she provides a rich historical argument tracing the egalitarian foundations of free trade and civil liberty from the Levellers through to Paine and Lincoln. Anderson argues that Adam Smith's case for the market 'depicts market relations as egalitarian: the parties to exchange interact on terms of equal authority, esteem, and standing'.[29] In Adam Smith's work, the fundamental basis to this dignity and civic independence was the linkage between property and labour: 'the property which every man has in his own labour' is 'the original foundation of all other property, so it is the most sacred and inviolable'.[30] This freedom to dispose of labour tended to undermine servility and personal dependence. It was the mark of liberty, self-respect, and the free citizen.

This proprietary freedom required a labour *market* in which free citizens could trade their personal labour as a guarantor of their civic independence. The fundamental evil that impeded the realisation of egalitarian market relations through free trade was monopoly. The achievement of a commercial society required the dismantling of monopolies,[31] not just guilds in the economic sphere but in politics, religion, and family life. This would mean that 'far more people would be able to attain personal independence and become masterless men and women. Even those who remained servants would gain esteem and standing through enhanced income and bargaining power with respect to their masters'.[32] The collective freedom to combine flowed from this individual freedom to dispose of labour: 'the freedom to combine . . . was understood, in terms derived from Adam Smith, as an extension of the right of every man to dispose of his labour to the best advantage'.[33] There was no lightning moment for these ideas. They percolated slowly in legal and political circles throughout the 18th century as legal restrictions were gradually loosened. The moment of greatest visibility came in the Benthamite reforms of 1824 and 1825.

[28] Ibid.
[29] Ibid. 4.
[30] Adam Smith, *The Wealth of Nations Books I-III* (Penguin 1999) 225, discussing apprenticeship restrictions on the disposal of labour.
[31] Winch (n 24) 97.
[32] Anderson (n 27) 17.
[33] Mark Curthoys, *Governments, Labour, and the Law in Mid-Victorian Britain* (OUP 2004) 18.

B. The 18th-century combination laws as a negation of free labour

For much of the 18th century, collective activities of workmen were severely restricted. 'Combinations' of journeymen to raise wages or restrict working hours were often the formal object of statutory prohibition. This was linked to wider restrictions on private freedom of contract, for example through public regulation of wage rates or strict rules on numbers of apprentices. Typically, the statute would treat workmen's agreements as void, and it would subject the parties to any new agreements to criminal penalties. The coverage of these 18th-century anti-combination statutes was 'restricted to particular trades and places' and focused mainly 'on London and the clothing trade'.[34] In 1721, following a labour dispute, Parliament introduced a statute prohibiting combinations in the tailoring trade.[35] Later statutes extended this basic model, voiding existing agreements and criminalising new agreements, to weavers in the woollen trade (1726), papermakers (1796), hatters (1777), and the Spitalfield silk-weavers (1773, 1792). In 1749, an omnibus statute extended the first weavers' combination act of 1726 to 'dyers and hot-pressers, felt-makers and hatters, and all persons employed in the manufacture of silk, mohair, fur, hemp, flax, linen, cotton, fustian, iron, and leather'.[36]

This statutory law relating to combinations operated alongside the more draconian common law of criminal conspiracy. In the famous *Journeyman-Taylors of Cambridge* case of 1721, the court treated an agreement to refuse work to raise wages as an indictable conspiracy.[37] Other conspiracy cases involving labour combinations followed.[38] These 18th-century combination acts were often linked to mercantilist restrictions such as public wage-fixing by justices of the peace.[39] Some of them also included regulation of apprenticeships and restrictions on the intake of apprentices, as in the first Spitalfields silk-weavers Act of 1773.[40] For most of the 18th century, the prohibition of combinations was a counterpart of public limits imposed on the

[34] John V. Orth, *Combination and Conspiracy: A Legal History of Trade Unionism 1721-1906* (OUP 1993) 22–23.

[35] Ibid. 6. This statute was updated in 1768.

[36] Ibid. 15.

[37] *R v Journeymen-Taylors of Cambridge*, 88 E.R. 9 (1721).

[38] See, e.g., *R v Eccles*, 99 E.R. 684 (1783) (Liverpool tailors) and *R v Hammond and Webb*, 1 Leach 276-7 (1799) (London shoemakers), discussed in Orth (n 34) 32–33.

[39] See the discussion in Jim Moher, 'From Suppression to Containment: Roots of Trade Union Law to 1825', in John Rule (ed), *British Trade Unionism, 1750-1850: The Formative Years* (Longman 1988) 78–80.

[40] Orth (n 34) 16.

individual freedom to dispose of labour. The delinking of public wage-fixing from the prohibition of combinations occurred in the Papermakers' Act of 1796, which reflected the lobbying of larger employers in the trade.[41] This led to a crucial question: if wages were to be set freely through private bargaining, did it not then follow that workmen should be able to bargain collectively in relations with their master? It is in these gradual shifts that we can begin to see egalitarian ideals breaking through.

C. The high watermark of repression: the Combination Act 1800

The generalisation from specific 'trades' to 'workmen' occurred in the Combination Act 1799.[42] It was a ratcheting up of coercion against organised groups. This can only be understood by reference to the political anxieties of the time and the fears of insurrection and revolution because of the situation in France. The 1799 Act was highly significant because it marked the point at which 'parliament ventured its first general proposition concerning labour law' in the law of associations.[43] This was reflected in its title as 'an act to prevent unlawful combinations of workmen'. According to the Act's Preamble, 'whereas great numbers of journeymen manufacturers and workmen in various parts of this kingdom, have, by unlawful meetings and combinations, endeavoured to obtain advance of their wages, and to effectuate other illegal purposes'. The legislation provided a comprehensive response to such combinations.[44] It declared that certain agreements (i.e., to obtain an advance on wages, reducing or altering working hours, decreasing the quantity of work, preventing or hindering the employment of any person, controlling or affecting any person carrying on any manufacture, trade, or business, in the conduct or management of it) were void. In common with the earlier trade-specific acts, it was also criminal to enter into any such agreements or to combine for these purposes. These core prohibitions were supported by other offences aimed at disrupting the organisation of strikes, such as endeavouring to solicit or prevail upon any workmen to refuse work or to quit work. Like the Papermakers' Act of 1796, the general 1799 Act did not continue with public

41 Moher (n 39) 81.
42 39 Geo. 3, c. 81.
43 Orth (n 34) 43.
44 The details of the 1799 Act are set out in Orth (n 34) 45–49 and 156–161.

wage-fixing machinery. It also relaxed the strict rules on apprenticeships, which would be repealed altogether in 1814.[45] Shortly after the 1799 Act, the Combination Act 1800 modified some of its detailed provisions, especially on matters of procedure.[46] It also criminalised combinations by masters.[47] The legislation of 1799 and 1800 'had finally formulated a general proposition concerning the groups soon to be known as trade unions: they were illegal'.[48]

Although the Combination Acts of 1799 and 1800 were undoubtedly repressive, there were three features of this legislative activity that revealed something important about the fundamental structure of freedom of association as it eventually took shape in the 1824–25 reforms. These structural features were: (1) the boundary between 'industrial' and 'political' objects of collective action; (2) dismantling restrictions on public wage-setting and labour mobility; and (3) the influence of internal legal values, such as the rule of law, on legal developments.

The first element was reflected in the concern to repress subversive political activities by organised groups, including workmen's combinations. This consideration above all dominated the legislative activity during this period. During the febrile 1790s, amid fears of Jacobin insurgency, the public authorities suspended habeas corpus, and Parliament enacted a battery of restrictive laws including the Seditious Meetings Act 1795, the Treason Act 1795, and the Unlawful Oaths Act 1797. Industrial and political agitation could not easily be separated during times when nervous public authorities feared revolution and insurrection. The Unlawful Societies Act 1799 suppressed the London Constitutional Society and the London Corresponding Society by name.[49] E.P. Thompson described the general combination acts of 1799 and 1800 as having been 'passed by a Parliament of anti-Jacobins and landowners, whose first concern was to add to the existing legislation intimidating political reformers'.[50] These general combination acts were as much 'political crimes', related to sedition and treason, as they were 'labour market crimes' directed at collective bargaining.[51] These lines were often blurred. 'Industrial' disputes could encompass food rioting, wage bargaining, and political campaigning for

[45] Ibid. 48–49.
[46] 39 & 40 Geo. 3 c. 106.
[47] 39 & 40 Geo. 3 c. 106. S 17.
[48] Orth (n 34) 67.
[49] E.P. Thompson, *The Making of the English Working Class* (Penguin 1980) 191.
[50] Ibid. 551; Dicey (n 5) 518–519.
[51] See, e.g., the assessment of Professor Aspinall: 'The Act of 1800, though it cannot be compared in severity with the "Gagging Acts" which followed the outbreak of war with Revolutionary France, and of which it really formed part, was, nevertheless, an odious piece of class legislation': Arthur Aspinall, *The Early English Trade Unions* (The Batchworth Press 1949) xvii.

parliamentary reform.[52] There was also legal space for 'constitutional' forms of political action, such as peaceful petitioning and enforcing public wage rates fixed by the Justices.[53] Even for radicals like Adam Smith, it was generally preferable to pursue gradualist improvements to the existing constitutional order than to overthrow it through violent insurrection.[54] While the boundaries between the 'political' and 'industrial' are not 'ontological',[55] but always contested and in flux, the division continues to be a basic conceptual element of freedom of association. It was fundamental to the legal settlement of 1799–1800.

The second element was the dismantling of corporative restrictions on wages and the enforcement of apprenticeship rules. The public setting of wages and enforcement of apprenticeship rules was integral to a more communitarian ideal of labour as a fixed station in the social order. It was also bound up with a more benign view of guilds and monopolies and hence was (in Smithian terms) anti-egalitarian. This conception of labour was already disintegrating in the later 18th-century combination acts. Significantly, the general combination acts did not include provision for public wage-fixing machinery. The final abolition of wage-fixing and apprenticeship clauses of the Statute of Artificers occurred in 1813 and 1814 respectively. These shifts could certainly be traced to the ascendancy of Smith's ideas in political economy and his radical objections to monopoly.[56] With the eclipse of public regulation of wage rates, the arguments in favour of restrictions on combinations were much weaker. Moher described this selective market liberalisation as 'lopsided and oppressive'.[57] If there was a contractual freedom for the *individual* parties to negotiate the price of labour, it was partial and unjust to use the criminal law to restrict the *collective* exercise of that fundamental liberty. This unfairness was particularly evident in the disparity of enforcement as between combinations of masters and combinations of workmen.

[52] John E. Archer, *Social Unrest and Popular Protest in England 1780-1840* (Cambridge UP 2000) 43. There are also examples of 'industrial' crimes in the combination laws being used to prosecute political radicals: see Katrina Navickas, *Protest and the Politics of Space and Place 1789-1848* (Manchester UP 2016) 57, where she describes the arrest of political radicals in Manchester using the combination act in 1812. See also Moher (n 39) 86.

[53] This is described by the Webbs as a 'society to enforce the law': Webbs (n 26) 65. As Ulrich Preuss points out, the right to petition for the redress of grievances can be regarded as an element of freedom of association: Ulrich Preuss, 'Associative Rights (The Rights to the Freedoms of Petition, Assembly, and Association)', in Michel Rosenfeld and Andras Sajo (eds), *The Oxford Handbook of Comparative Constitutional Law* (OUP 2012) 949–951.

[54] Winch (n 24) 54–55.

[55] This famous line is from Lord Wedderburn, where his reflections on the distinction between 'industrial' and 'political' strikes continue to be fundamental in the modern law. See Lord Wedderburn, 'The Right to Strike: Is There a European Standard?', in Lord Wedderburn, *Employment Rights in Britain and Europe* (Lawrence & Wishart 1991) 285.

[56] Moher (n 39) 83; Orth (n 34) 59.

[57] Moher (n 39) 83.

The legitimacy of collective wage bargaining was also aligned with its essentially 'private' nature. This was what Alan Fox described as collective bargaining with a 'regulatory market function'.[58] This kind of bargaining supported the efficient adjustment of wage rates and it facilitated rather than obstructed the market order. It could be contrasted with forms of bargaining that were viewed as less legitimate by public authorities, for example (to use Alan Fox's term) 'market-restrictionist' bargaining (such as enforcing apprenticeship rules and other restrictions on labour supply) or political agitation. These forms of bargaining involved the reassertion of monopoly which was anathema to the radical vision of civic freedom. The explicit coupling of market liberalisation and collective freedom of association, which encapsulated the radical vision of free labour, only emerged clearly in the 1824–25 reforms. Once this linkage was clarified, the 'primary' labour dispute between the master and his own workers over issues of wages and working time would be the core instance of legitimate trade union activity. While the strict logic of individual freedom might have justified a wider conception of freedom of association, the public authorities were always keen to ensure labour conflicts were managed and adjusted within the contractual relations between an employer and his own workmen. Such disputes were more amenable to adjustment through market mechanisms and private ordering.

The third element was the influence of internal legal values, such as the rule of law, on the development of the law on freedom of association. For Adam Smith, domination was reduced and liberty secured through the rule of law and the impartial administration of justice.[59] These institutions tended to support the security of property and contracts, and this security reduced the dependence of workmen on the arbitrary will of the powerful. During periods of legislative contestation and change in the law on combinations, there was often intense preoccupation with the rule of law and procedural safeguards for the accused. This led Orth to suggest that 'respect for proper procedure was hypertrophied, while knowledge of political economy was only slowly developing'.[60] Many of the 18th-century combination acts provided for appeals to quarter sessions from convictions by the local justices. The higher courts jealously guarded their review power of certiorari over local justices which

[58] Alan Fox, *History and Heritage: The Social Origins of the British Industrial Relations System* (George Allen & Unwin 1985) 89.

[59] Paul Sagar, *Adam Smith Reconsidered: History, Liberty, and the Foundations of Modern Politics* (Princeton UP 2022) chapter 2. The left case for the rule of law as an 'unqualified human good' was articulated most famously by E.P. Thompson in *Whigs and Hunters: The Origin of the Black Act* (Breviary Stuff Publications 2013).

[60] Orth (n 34) 23.

could only be removed by express words in the statute.[61] These safeguards operated as a vital check on economic bias in the local dispensation of justice against workmen. This was extended in the hatters' combination act of 1777 which disqualified master hatters from acting in a judicial capacity in any dispute involving journeymen hatters under that legislation.[62] Monopoly power needed to be confronted in all its guises, economic *and* legal.

The replacement of the 1799 Act in 1800 was also testament to the growing salience of impartial justice and the rule of law in public debates. The new provisions of the 1800 Act reflected ideas of procedural fairness that had been eroded by the 1799 Act. Under the 1800 Act, cases were to be heard by two or more justices rather than a single justice. It also followed the approach of the earlier hatters' combination act in that no justice could sit if he was an employer in the trade in which the workman was employed. The 1800 Act removed the explicit bar on certiorari in the 1799 Act which restored the Court of King's Bench power of review.[63] The rule of law was not simply a matter of procedural safeguards for accused workmen, however. It also had substantive consequences for the content and scope of criminal laws. The supremacy of the ordinary law, that everyone should be equal before the law, supported the extension of criminal liabilities to encompass combination by masters.[64] This removed overt discrimination in the application of criminal liabilities, and it addressed the conspiracies of merchants that had been fiercely castigated by Adam Smith in *The Wealth of Nations*.[65] In due course, this ideal of equality before the law would be a double-edged sword for trade unions, as they sought special statutory immunities from common law tort doctrines in the early 20th century.

D. The Combination Act 1825 and the promise of free labour

During the early part of the 19th century, the dismantling of public restrictions on wage negotiation and the challenge to one-sided legal restrictions on workmen placed cumulative pressures on the repressive legislation of 1800. This culminated in the Combination Act 1825 (which quickly replaced the Combination Act 1824). This was the moment when the market-based

[61] Ibid. 13–14.
[62] Ibid. 19.
[63] Ibid. 54.
[64] Ibid. 51.
[65] Smith (n 30) 169–170.

egalitarian justification for collective bargaining was most visible, under the influence of Benthamite reformers.

Today, we tend to regard the Trade Disputes Act 1906 as the pivotal legislative event in the modern English law on freedom of association. As we shall see, the 1825 Act provided a basic legal structure for freedom of association which was of at least equal importance. This was reflected in the assessment of labour historians. The 1825 Act was described by the Webbs as a 'real emancipation', establishing 'the right of collective bargaining, involving the power to withhold labour from the market by concerted action'.[66] For Aspinall, it was a 'recognition for the first time of the right of collective bargaining and of the right to strike'.[67]

This recognition was linked to a broader project of utilitarian law reform orchestrated by the remarkable figure, Francis Place. Place had been a journeyman breeches-maker and then a master who became one of the leading Benthamite utilitarian radicals of his day.[68] He was a close companion of James Mill and Jeremy Bentham. This utilitarian liberty to bargain collectively was 'intended to establish free trade in labour . . . the sale or purchase of labour should be as entirely a matter of free contract as the purchase of boots and shoes'.[69] The 1825 Act was integral to the broader political movement in support of free trade and freedom of contract.[70] Atiyah observed that the utilitarian justification for workmen's freedom of association was coupled with freedom of contract arguments: 'freedom of contract ought to be extended to permit workers to combine on any terms they thought fit.'[71] Collective bargaining was the exact analogue of individual bargaining over wages and hours, and it was a market activity. This was 'freedom of combination' as the collective extension of individual 'freedom of contract'.[72] According to Curthoys, 'the right of every man to dispose of his labour to the best advantage' became 'an official orthodoxy' during the early to middle decades of the 19th century.[73] This flowed directly from Adam Smith's radical ideas around property, labour, and civic independence, and it was the animating idea of the 1825 settlement. In the hands of legislators anxious to ensure the pacification and integration

[66] Webbs (n 26) 108.
[67] Aspinall (n 51) xxx.
[68] Graham Wallas, *The Life of Francis Place 1771-1854* (4th ed, Allen & Unwin 1925).
[69] Dicey (n 5) 520.
[70] William Cornish, 'Labour Relations', in William Cornish and others, *Law and Society in England 1750-1950* (2nd ed, Hart 2019) 288; William Cornish and others, *Oxford History of the Laws of England Volume XIII 1820-1914: Fields of Development* (OUP 2010) 655.
[71] Patrick S. Atiyah, *The Rise and Fall of Freedom of Contract* (OUP 1979) 529.
[72] Curthoys (n 33) 18.
[73] Ibid.

of trade unions into liberal political economy, reconciling workmen to market ordering, collective bargaining between the primary employer and his own workmen was identified as the appropriate conduit.

While the parliamentary campaign for repeal of the 1800 settlement began in earnest in 1822, the extra-parliamentary movement for legal reform started years earlier in 1814.[74] Place had taken a leading role in the repeal of the paternalist regulation of the Statute of Artificers, with the wage-fixing provisions going in 1813 and the apprenticeship clauses in 1814.[75] In E.P. Thompson's view, Place and other radicals 'were devotees of orthodox "political economy", and had given active assistance in the dismantling of *all* legislation restraining the "freedom" of capital or of labour'.[76] In a letter to the President of the Board of Trade, Mr William Huskisson, in 1824, Place formulated his critique of the legal restrictions on combination in exactly these terms: 'The business is really very simple, and it lies in a small space. Repeal every troublesome and vexatious enactment, and enact very little in their place. Leave workmen and their employers as much as possible at liberty to make their own bargains in their own way'.[77] From 1814, Place had set his sights on freedom of combination, collecting data on trade disputes meticulously and corresponding with trade unions. Along with Jeremy Bentham, he also loaned money to support a political publication, the *Gorgon*, which published articles on the existing state of the laws and the case for reform.[78]

The Combination Acts were not simply the working through of deductions from classical economics.[79] Nor did the 1825 Act invent or create collective bargaining. There were already extensive social practices of collective bargaining in many crafts.[80] The task of wise utilitarian law reform was to adjust legislation to the existing habits and practices in economy and society.[81] The 1825 settlement continued the radical emancipatory politics identified by Elizabeth Anderson, but now in the form of Benthamite utilitarianism.

[74] Webbs (n 26) 98.
[75] Cornish (n 70) 282–283.
[76] Thompson (n 49) 565.
[77] Wallas (n 68) 210.
[78] Ibid. 204–205.
[79] William D. Grampp, 'The Economists and the Combination Laws' (1979) 93 The Quarterly Journal of Economics 501. On Adam Smith and the 'classical economists' in the legal history of freedom of contract, see Atiyah (n 71) 292–323. The Ricardian economist, J.R. McCulloch, published an important intervention in the *Edinburgh Review* of January 1824, which provided a market-based argument for repeal of the restrictive 1800 Act. According to McCulloch, such restrictions were 'unjust' and 'injurious' in impeding wage-setting through a self-regulating labour market: see Orth (n 34) 69–70.
[80] James A. Jaffe, *Striking a Bargain: Work and Industrial Relations in England 1815-1865* (Manchester UP 2000).
[81] Michael Lobban, *The Common Law and English Jurisprudence 1760-1850* (OUP 1991) 133–135.

There were two important strands to this wider radical project beyond economic liberalism. The first strand was the importance of law reform and legislative codification to the Benthamite reformers.[82] Law reform would promote rule of law values of generality and predictability for citizens, and this would protect their security of expectations.[83] The concern with defining the limits of the law through legislation in 1824–25 (and limiting the role of common law conspiracy) would have been important to Benthamites like Place. The second strand was the priority accorded to 'security' and the protection of reasonable expectations through civil order and stable legal rules. According to Kelly, Bentham's work on civil law was the reconstruction of Smith's economic liberalism 'in terms of his utilitarian science of legislation'.[84] The fundamental categories of private law established 'a system of personal entitlements or securities around the basic conditions of personal continuity and coherence; namely person, possessions, condition in life and reputation'.[85] This 'security-providing principle' placed strong emphasis on the inviolability of private property rights.[86] This benefited workmen as much as capitalists because labour was regarded in this radical vision as the most fundamental of all the property rights.

For Orth, the 1824 Combination Act achieved 'a revolution in the legal status of workmen's organisations'.[87] It repealed previous restrictive legislation on combinations. In terms of its positive enactments, it blended immunities with new crimes targeting coercive interference with the individual freedom to dispose of labour. Section 2 of the 1824 Act conferred a statutory immunity from common law conspiracy or statutory liability where there was an agreement concerning the rate of wages, the duration of working hours, or regulating the mode of carrying on any manufacture, trade, or business. It also exempted combinations of masters from criminal punishment 'in pursuit of the new ideal of legal equality'.[88] This immunity established a wide liberty for combinations. The legal limits of this liberty were drawn by criminal offences that punished interferences with the liberty of parties to dispose of labour and capital freely. One of the offences was focused on 'violence to the person or

[82] See ibid. 187–189, noting Bentham's focus on the reform of criminal law and procedure. See also James E. Crimmins, 'Bentham and Utilitarianism in the Early Nineteenth Century', in Ben Eggleston and Dale E. Miller (eds), *The Cambridge Companion to Utilitarianism* (Cambridge UP 2014) 38, 39.

[83] Gerald Postema, *Utility, Publicity and Law: Essays on Bentham's Moral and Legal Philosophy* (OUP 2019) chapter 12; Gerald Postema, *Bentham and the Common Law Tradition* (2nd ed, OUP 2019) 155–171.

[84] Paul J. Kelly, 'Utilitarianism and Distributive Justice: The Civil Law and the Foundations of Bentham's Economic Thought' (1989) 1 Utilitas 62, 64.

[85] Ibid. 66.

[86] Paul J. Kelly, 'Utilitarian Strategies in Bentham and John Stuart Mill' (1990) 2 Utilitas 245, 253.

[87] Orth (n 34) 76.

[88] Ibid. 79.

property, by threats or by intimidation' to force another to depart from his hiring or work before the end of the hiring term, or to return work, or to spoil or destroy machinery, tools, or work. Another offence penalised violence, threats, or intimidation used to enforce union discipline, for example where there was a failure to comply with or conform to any rules, orders, resolutions, or regulations to obtain an advance of wages or lessen hours of work.

Following a sharp upturn in strike action after the enactment of the 1824 Act, Parliament was anxious to protect the rights of capital from being overwhelmed by organised combinations.[89] In haste, it enacted the 1825 Combination Act. In structural terms, it was like the 1824 Act in deploying immunities circumscribed by substantive crimes. Overall, however, the 1825 immunities were narrower and the substantive crimes were broader. Section 4 of the 1825 Act provided for a more limited immunity for workmen 'who shall meet together for the sole purpose of consulting upon and determining the rate of wages or prices, which the persons present at such meeting or any of them, shall require or demand for his or their work . . . [2] who shall enter into any agreement, verbal or written, among themselves, for the purpose of fixing the rate of wages or prices.' The 1825 Act immunity also left the common law of conspiracy intact as a judicial tool for policing the boundary of legitimate combined activities. The substantive crimes now included the terms molestation or obstruction, which were of more uncertain ambit than violence, threats, or intimidation. Section 3 provided that it was a crime to use these coercive means 'for the purpose of forcing or inducing such person to belong to any club or association, or to contribute to any common fund, or to pay any fine or penalty'.

Like the 1824 Act, this 1825 settlement established freedom of association although it did so on more restrictive terms than the 1824 definition. The 1825 Act configured freedom of association as a freedom *within* the labour market rather than as a general associative liberty. Indeed, as we have seen, the Webbs regarded 1825 as a great emancipation establishing the liberty to bargain collectively. The 1825 settlement was also remarkably enduring: 'Between 1825 and 1871 labour law changed only in detail. Parliament acted once: in 1859 it passed a brief act concerning strikes to explain the meaning of the terms "molesting" and "obstructing" . . . Otherwise it left to the courts the task of construing the vague immunities and vaguer offences laid down in 1825.'[90] The next great legislative reset occurred in the 1870s, and it did so by reference

[89] Ibid. 85.
[90] Ibid. 92.

to the terms set by the 1825 framework. Across the intervening period, four aspects of this new freedom of association would be central to the persistent conflicts about its scope.

First, the justificatory foundation of collective freedom of association was rooted in the individual's freedom to dispose of his labour to his best advantage. This individualist justification imposed strict limits on the scope for the majority to restrict the freedom of the individual. The individual was free to combine with others and to seek an advantageous bargain through collective endeavour. Equally, the individual should be free to disassociate and negotiate his own contractual bargain. As Atiyah explained of the 1825 Act, 'workmen were now permitted to agree *among themselves* about the wages and hours of work which they would seek from their employers, but each worker was still left free to make his own bargain.'[91] After 1825, dissentient workmen and employers would turn to the courts for relief from collective boycotts to enforce union discipline and union security. The vigorous protection of individual property rights, even property in the disposal of labour, was well-suited to the judicial function and the common law judges. In the early 19th century, at least, this still had the aura of an emancipatory rather than a reactionary enterprise.

Second, Cornish noted that the terms of the 1825 'exemption from liability related only to workers and employers who fostered their own interests over wages and hours. Masters already feared the intervention of outside organizers with plans to coordinate action in ways which local associations of men were unlikely to achieve.'[92] The law was hostile to such 'permanent' combinations and federal associations seeking to regulate a trade or district. Indeed, 'legitimate combinations were conceived of in 1825 as occasional meetings of workmen to decide the level of wages for which they were willing to sell their labour.'[93] Periodic strike action by workers in a self-regulating labour market was accepted in a way that permanent organisations were not. Today, the 'right to form a trade union' is treated as the basic juridical starting point of freedom of association and collective bargaining is a more subsidiary aspect of this core right. In 1825, by contrast, the law was hostile to permanent trade union organisation while treating collective bargaining as presumptively legitimate. The foundation of the collective freedom to combine in individual freedom of contract was suspicious of any attempt by organised groups to restrict or

91 Atiyah (n 71) 531 (emphasis added).
92 *Oxford History* (n 70) 656–657.
93 Curthoys (n 33) 45.

coerce individual freedom of contract. The law was reluctant to facilitate that exercise of collective coercion. This was the perennial paradox of freedom of association identified by Dicey, that its collective exercise posed a standing threat to individual freedoms. The narrow focus of the 1825 exemption erred in favour of protecting individual contractual liberties from collective coercion by trade unions.

Third, the conceptual boundaries of molestation and obstruction would be the object of intense social and legal contestation in the courts until the 1870s. This contestation engaged the autonomy of labour law in a fundamental way. Should trade unions only be subject to the same general criminal laws restricting violence and threats like other legal subjects? This could be justified by considerations of legal equality in that it was subjecting workmen and their trade unions to the ordinary law of the land. Or did trade unions pose special threats to individual freedom on account of their strength in numbers wielded in working-class communities? This reflected an argument that trade unions posed special risks of coercion and it was therefore justified to regulate them using special definitions of criminal coercion. After 1825, the courts were wary of the coercive effects of trade unionism in situations where large numbers of pickets sought to prevent strike-breakers from undermining solidarity. Even 'black looks' from picketing trade unionists might be treated by the courts as sufficient to coerce the individual workman and thereby attack that inviolable proprietary freedom to dispose of his own labour.

Finally, statecraft after 1825 sought to depoliticise industrial relations and prevent industrial disputes from being treated as class conflicts in the political sphere. The centrepiece of the 1825 settlement was periodic adjustment of wages through collective negotiations between the work group and their master. This was a private market activity rooted in an early idea of the 'trade dispute'. The role of the state was limited to the police functions of ensuring public safety, suppressing violence and breaches of the peace, and maintaining civil order.[94] Beyond this, the state should maintain neutrality in industrial disputes, which itself reflected ideals of legal equality. Political crimes were a reserve power that could be used if industrial protests strayed into the political sphere. Following the Peterloo Massacre in 1819, for example, the infamous 'Six Acts' of 1819 tightened restrictions on mass platform meetings and the publication of 'seditious' and 'blasphemous' libels.[95] While the spectre of sedition never fully dissipated from trade unions, there was a broader tolerance

[94] Ibid. 28–29.
[95] Navickas (n 52) 97–105.

for criticism of governmental institutions as the 19th century progressed.[96] Ultimately, if the state could not prevent trade unions from operating as permanent organisations, there was a strong preference that these organisations should operate in the private realm of the market rather than the public realm of the polity.

The great and unresolved tension of 1825 was the clash between freedom of contract and the radical anti-monopolistic politics that animated the long political journey to the 1825 settlement. Freedom of contract could be used in a multiplicity of ways. Sometimes, the agreements resulting from freedom of contract could involve the reassertion of monopolistic tendencies: the enforcement of apprenticeship restrictions, limiting labour supply, enforcing closed shops on unwilling employers and individual journeymen. Freedom of contract thus exercised could extinguish free trade in labour. By the end of the 19th century, the material realities of industrialisation would leave 'free labour' unrecognisable to its early radical proponents such as Adam Smith and Bentham.[97]

IV. After 1825: Freedom of Association in the Courts

After 1825, there were two main areas where the boundaries between voluntary association and oppressive monopoly were contested. The first was in the legal status of trade unions, and the extent to which unions could enforce discipline and maintain solidarity through their contractual relations with members. The second was in defining the ambit of coercion in industrial disputes, especially where unions were seeking the dismissal of non-unionists or strikebreakers through boycotts of employers. These two areas raised similar issues, for as Lobban observed, 'molestation and restraint of trade clearly became close conceptual bedfellows'.[98] In both contexts, the courts (and legislators) were anxious to protect the individual's freedom to dispose of his labour. They were accordingly suspicious of collective coercion through majority rule in trade unions.

[96] Laurence Lustgarten and Ian Leigh, *In from the Cold: National Security and Parliamentary Democracy* (OUP 1994) 211. Michael Lobban, 'From Seditious Libel to Unlawful Assembly: Peterloo and the Changing Face of Political Crime c.1770-1820' (1990) 10 Oxford Journal of Legal Studies 307.

[97] Anderson (n 27) 33–36.

[98] Michael Lobban, 'Strikers and the Law, 1825-51', in Peter Birks (ed), *The Life of the Law* (Hambledon Press 1993) 232.

A. The legal status of trade unions

After 1825, the justification of freedom of association in free exchange of labour was a fertile source of instability for trade unions. In 1825, the law had accommodated itself to the idea of *association as activity*, a periodic process whereby wages were adjusted and settled through strikes and collective negotiations. By contrast, *association as organisation* was still an object of suspicion. It was not unusual for trade unions to be compared to restrictive guilds wielding monopolistic power or even to be characterised as tyrannical.[99] This was because strong and organised trade unions posed the standing threat of what many utilitarian radicals regarded as monopolistic domination of individual workmen.[100] The enforcement of union rules could restrict the individual's freedom to dispose of his labour. For the trade union, however, these restrictions were the basis for securing cohesion and collective advantage for the work group. Strong and permanent organisation meant that the majority will *should* override the contractual liberties of minorities and individuals. This would sometimes require collective coercion over dissenting workmen. Of course, these restraints were now imposed through voluntary agreements rather than involuntary means like royal grants or charters. Nevertheless, enforceable contracts between trade unions and members still had the potential to subvert the radical vision of free labour.

Throughout the 19th century, the line between legitimate combination and illegitimate monopoly was always a fine one for courts and legislators. The common law doctrine of restraint of trade treated restrictive rules as void and unenforceable where they tended to obstruct free trade unreasonably, and this included free trade in labour.[101] The rules of trade unions might include the provision of financial relief for strikers, fines for disobedience to union instructions, restrictions on members working for employers under boycott, or prohibitions on members working with non-members. This meant that the objects and rules of permanent trade unions were almost certainly in restraint of trade, and on that account were unenforceable in the courts. In Orth's assessment, 'trade unions were denounced as unlawful because in contemplation of law they were constituted by contracts, covenants, or agreements that

[99] The tyrannical description is that of Nassau Senior in the Royal Commission on Handloom Weavers, cited in Curthoys (n 33) 45–46. He was an economist whose work on trade unions was influential in the first half of the 19th century. See Atiyah (n 71) 317–319.

[100] This was the description of Baron Bramwell, cited in Curthoys (n 33) 83.

[101] John D. Heydon, *The Restraint of Trade Doctrine* (Butterworths 1971) chapter 1, setting out the historical context to the doctrine.

interfered with the "perfect freedom" of each individual workman to make his own agreement'.[102]

The policy around the judicial enforcement of rules between trade unions and members was a delicate one. On the one hand, courts were wary of becoming embroiled in enforcing contractual duties that required a workman to strike against his employer or pay a fine to the trade union.[103] This would have placed courts in the difficult position of enforcing contractual duties that contradicted the legal policy favouring the individual freedom of labour. On the other hand, the retreat of the courts from enforcement of union contracts left the property and funds of trade unions vulnerable to larceny, fraud, and misappropriation. Unlike friendly societies, which were given privileged protections from fraud in the Friendly Societies Act 1855, the exposure of trade union funds to criminal wrongdoing touched directly upon their basic civil and legal equality with other citizens and associations. It was an exclusion that conveyed overtones of class bias and hostility, and it demeaned the respectability of trade unionists and their standing in the community.[104] The civic demands of equality in law and politics were increasingly significant in public debates about trade unions. Proposals for granting corporate status to trade unions were often bound up with recognising the fuller integration of workmen into the polity as respected citizens.[105] These complex cross-currents of free labour and legal equality could sometimes be in tension with each other. The appropriate legal conceptualisation of the trade union was a prime example of this. As the law stood until 1871, trade unions were unincorporated associations whose purposes and rules were of dubious legality.

These issues came to the fore in the celebrated case of *Hilton v Eckersley*.[106] Interestingly, *Hilton v Eckersley* involved a combination of masters, not workmen, but trade unions were never far from the judges' minds in deciding restraint of trade cases. This also no doubt reflected the tangible influence of legal equality, and consistency of approach between masters and workmen's associations. The case concerned an agreement between mill owners in Wigan and Hindley to enforce a lockout during a strike for higher wages. The arrangement was based upon majority rule so that individual mill owners could not defect and break the collective resolve of the mill owners. This was enforced through a £500 penalty. James Eckersley agreed to reopen his mill in defiance of the majority's dictation and the association sought enforcement of

102 Orth (n 34) 101.
103 Curthoys (n 33) 49.
104 Ibid. 71.
105 Ibid.
106 (1855) 6 E&B 47, 119 Eng. Rep. 781.

the agreement against him. A majority of the Queen's Bench found that the arrangement was unenforceable because it was in restraint of trade, and this was upheld by the Exchequer Chamber.

The hostility of monopoly dictation pervaded the majority judgments. According to Crompton J, enforcement of such agreements would have a 'mischievous and dangerous tendency . . . with respect to strikes and combinations'.[107] It would lead to the parties giving 'up this right of judging for themselves, and place themselves and their trades under the dictation either of a majority or of a committee of delegates, which seems the same in principle'.[108] This extension to workmen could even lead to workmen being enjoined in equity to continue striking or to pay fines to the trade union.[109] From the perspective of the individual's fundamental proprietary right to dispose of his labour, this would transform voluntary association into monopoly subjugation. In a similar vein, Lord Campbell CJ raised the prospect of courts being called upon to enforce 'the fantastic and mischievous notion of a "Labour Parliament"' which could regulate wages and hours of labour 'in every branch of trade all over the empire'.[110] The adjustment of wages through periodic wage bargaining was permitted by the combination acts, but this did not envisage *permanent* organisational structures enforcing restraints on individual disposal of labour through majority rule. Erle J dissented, but it would be a mistake to view his as a pro-labour judgment. He noted the liberalisation effected by the combination acts, and that restraints of trade could be lawful at common law when they were adjudged to be reasonable and necessary. Erle J was particularly concerned about the consequences of excluding such bargains from the courts and judicial supervision. Without legal enforcement, 'the parties making them resort to social persecutions, fear and force for their enforcement'.[111] This pointed to something of much wider significance. By treating trade unions as fully fledged entities with legal personality, there was greater scope for legal control and public accountability for their activities. The courts could then adjudge the boundary between reasonable and unreasonable restraints. It was better for this to be done in the Queen's Bench than on a picket line in Wigan.

The facts in *Hornby v Close* were rather different from those in *Hilton*.[112] Charles Close had misappropriated funds from the Bradford Branch of the

[107] Ibid. 784–785.
[108] Ibid. 785.
[109] Ibid. 786.
[110] Ibid. 789.
[111] Ibid. 787.
[112] LR 2 QB 153 (QB).

United Order of Boilermakers and Iron Shipbuilders. The president of the Bradford Branch, John Hornby, had sought redress under the summary proceedings provided for by the Friendly Societies Act 1855. The Justices of the Peace ruled that there had been a misappropriation of funds, but the trade union was not entitled to summary proceedings. The trade union should not be treated as a friendly society because its purposes were illegal as in restraint of trade. Relying on *Hilton v Eckersley*, this was upheld by the Queen's Bench. The purposes of the Boilermakers and Iron Shipbuilders society were not analogous to the legitimate purposes of a friendly society. As Mellor J observed, 'some of the substantial objects of the society are those of a trades' union, and for the maintenance of its members when on strike, and these objects cannot be separated from the other objects, if any, of the society'.[113] It followed that its rules were unenforceable as between the trade union and its members. While common law proceedings were available to trade unions to protect their property, these were not as convenient as the summary proceedings provided under the 1855 Act.

In Joanna McCunn's sophisticated critique of *Hornby v Close*, she identified the recurrent tendency of judges at this time to regard contracts between union members and trade unions as akin to contracts of slavery.[114] Given this apparently extravagant equation between slavery and trade union contracts, she poses the following question: 'Why were these lawyers so opposed to workers binding themselves for the future, when, as Pollock pointed out, this is the effect of any contract?'[115] Her main answer is that it reflected judicial attachment to a kind of hyper-detached and atomised approach to individual contractual freedom. I think the judicial tendency was reflective of the special concern with *contracts affecting the individual disposal of labour.* As we have seen, the liberalisation of combinations was shaped by the radical promise of free labour and civic independence. On this view, contracts to restrict the disposal of labour *could* be viewed as akin to slavery contracts because they involved coerced submission to a private monopoly. This was a forfeiture of civic independence, quite unlike the ordinary restriction of future freedom that all contractual obligations entail. In a conflict between free trade and freedom of contract, free trade should always be the trump card in the labour sphere. And even by the time of *Hornby*, this could still be regarded as a radical rather than reactionary position.

[113] Ibid. 160.
[114] Joanna McCunn, 'Hornby v Close (1867): Freedom of Contract and Freedom of Trade', in Jeremias Adams-Prassl and others, *Landmark Cases in Labour Law* (Hart 2022) 45.
[115] Ibid. 46.

In the aftermath of *Hornby v Close*, a Royal Commission on Trade Unions was appointed in 1867 under the chairmanship of Sir William Erle.[116] It reported in 1869 and famously resulted in a majority and minority report. The fundamental philosophical difference between the two reports focused on the legal status of trade unions.[117] The majority favoured legal incorporation and much tighter public regulation of trade union rules and purposes. The minority rejected full incorporation because of the dangers of excessive state control of trade unions, proposing instead a minimalist approach of bare legal recognition and protection of trade union funds. This dichotomy was prefigured in Erle J's dissent in *Hilton v Eckersley*, which highlighted the ambivalent quality of corporate personality in its impact on group freedoms. Legal recognition was allied with public scrutiny and control.

Ultimately, the Trade Union Act 1871 reflected the minority report's philosophy. It conferred an immunity from restraint of trade by section 3. At the same time, section 4 prevented the judicial enforcement of any contracts between trade union members or between a trade union and a trade union member. This settlement provided a wide liberty for trade unions, but it also ensured that courts would not be called upon to enforce union instructions ordering members to strike or to pay fines. In this respect, it continued to reflect the anxieties of 18th-century radicals like Adam Smith about oppressive monopoly. By 1871, the material realities of 'free labour' in the industrial centres bore little relation to the context in which Adam Smith's arguments had taken shape. However, these justificatory arguments, rooted in the individual freedom to dispose of labour, were now too deeply embedded in the English law on combinations to be easily dismissed.

B. The ambit of trade union coercion

After 1825, the courts also grappled with the ambit of coercion in industrial disputes. Often, this arose in contexts where the union was seeking to enforce discipline against non-unionists or strike-breakers. It usually involved walking off the job or threatening to do so until the individuals had been discharged. These disputes were often supported by picketing to deter workers from breaking the boycott. This raised the spectre of majorities in combinations dictating terms to both masters and individual workmen. Many of

[116] *Eleventh and Final Report of the Trades Unions Commission* (1867-68), discussed in Curthoys (n 33) 97–107.

[117] Douglas Brodie, *A History of British Labour Law 1867-1945* (Hart 2003) 1–5.

these cases also involved 'market-restrictionist' bargaining,[118] with the union seeking to enforce apprenticeship rules or restrictions on labour-saving machinery. Judicial interpretations of the ambit of coercion expanded 'after 1850, the era when unions were becoming more established, permanent structures' which led to the deployment of the common law of conspiracy.[119] This reflected the concern that these larger federal organisations could enforce restrictive trade practices more effectively.

Political debates on legislative reform of criminal coercion from the 1850s onwards were focused increasingly on legal equality. Trade unionists were concerned that their activities were regulated by ideas of coercion that would not have been applied in non-labour contexts. This raised a suspicion that concepts like molestation were just 'class legislation' targeted at workers and trade unions. As the franchise widened and political reforms achieved greater traction, this supported the trade union case for regulating trade union activities using general criminal laws rather than special industrial crimes.[120] If boycotts did not involve violence, property damage, or threats thereof, there was no good justification for using the criminal law against them. The application of general crimes to workmen reflected their civic equality as full members of the political community.

By contrast, defenders of special criminal laws justified this by emphasising the distinctiveness of coercion in industrial disputes. In particular, the pervasive and insidious reach of coercive disapproval in working-class communities meant that hooting, name-calling, and even black looks could have a strong impact on the minds of individual workers. This was exacerbated when large numbers of workers engaged in picketing, hiding tools, and following and watching strike-breakers. Peaceful communication could easily shade into subtle coercion and intimidation in ways that were scarcely visible to outsiders. Given the fundamental importance of the individual right to dispose of labour freely, this context no doubt weighed heavily with judges. Across this period, until the great legislative settlement in the 1870s, judicial attempts to define the ambit of criminal coercion in industrial disputes were not exercises in conceptual analysis. Lawmakers' ideas of coercion and intimidation in working-class communities were shaped by politics of the time. The concepts of 'molestation' and 'obstruction' did not set precise boundaries to coercion. Even 'threats' were a flexible definitional category. As trade unions and

118 Fox (n 58).
119 Lobban (n 98) 228.
120 For a full account of the debates on 'class crimes' and legal equality, see Curthoys (n 33) chapter 6, discussing the Criminal Law Amendment Act 1871.

workers discovered, these criminal wrongs could be highly elastic, especially in the guise of common law conspiracy charges. The parameters of coercion were ultimately shaped by underlying views on whether there should be a general law of associations (regulated by the general criminal law) or a specific law of labour associations (regulated by special labour crimes).

In an early case, *R v Hewitt*, Charles Evans had worked with steam machinery which was against the rules of the Philanthropic Society of Coopers.[121] He was fined by the Society, and he then refused to pay the fine. Members of the Society refused to work with Evans and sought his dismissal by the employer. The coopers were indicted for offences under the combination act and for conspiracy. According to Campbell CJ, this behaviour fell within the parameters of the legislation in coercing the employer's management of his business and in enforcing the Society's fine. The coopers were convicted.[122] The ambiguities of free labour as a justification for freedom of combination meant that the courts could sometimes arrive at more liberal conclusions. In 1847, in *R v Selsby*, Baron Rolfe sought to demarcate 'threats' from persuasion. Where picketers were merely persuading others to associate with them and not take work at the foundry, this would not reach the threshold of bodily harm necessary for a criminal threat. Although the picketers were convicted because the jury found on the facts that the statements did imply criminal threats, the result of *R v Selsby* was that peaceful persuasion was not criminal. As Curthoys explained, 'since it was lawful for people to agree among themselves not to work except upon certain terms, he reasoned that it must [be] lawful for them to try to persuade the others to adopt the same view'.[123] The problem was persuading a jury that communications by large groups of picketing workmen and their families could ever be peaceful rather than intrinsically threatening or obstructive.

An expansive interpretation of molestation and obstruction was taken by Erle J in prosecutions arising out of a dispute between the National Association of United Trades (NAUT) and Edward Perry, a Wolverhampton tinplate manufacturer.[124] The criminal charges were focused on the freedom of Perry to carry on his mode of business. Even though the persuasion of workers to leave or refuse employment with Perry was peaceful, this was necessarily an obstruction to him in the conduct of his business.[125] Historians have identified the national scope of the NAUT as a factor that aroused special concern for

121 5 Cox CC 162 (QB 1851).
122 See Orth (n 34) 94.
123 Curthoys (n 33) 29.
124 *R v Rowlands* (1851) 5 Cox CC 436.
125 Orth (n 34) 98.

judges and legislators.[126] This was not the market-regulating 'collective bargaining' envisaged by the proponents of the 1825 settlement. The special and distinctive nature of coercive wrongs in labour disputes was given its fullest articulation by Baron Bramwell in *R v Druitt*: picketing would be criminal where it 'was calculated to have a deterring effect on the minds of ordinary persons, by exposing them to having their motions watched, and to encounter black looks'.[127] After *Rowlands* and *Druitt*, it was difficult to see how an effective picket could ever avoid criminal liabilities.

It is tempting to view these cases as the reactionary politics of a hostile judiciary, but progressive mid-19th century liberalism was itself struggling with the problems of reconciling individual free-will and organised social disapproval. John Stuart Mill had published *On Liberty* in 1859. His liberal defence of individuality and value pluralism was preoccupied with the insidious threats posed by societal pressures for conformity and the 'tyranny of opinion' rather than oppressive state coercion.[128] While Mill's later political economy was moderately supportive of trade unionism,[129] his famous example from *On Liberty* of the mob protesting corn prices at the corn dealer's house revealed his concerns about the delicate line between freedom of speech and incitement to violence.[130] In 1869, Mill's ambivalence about organised picketing was reflected in his concern that language and conduct should not threaten 'an infringement of an individual's personal security'.[131] This was not so very far from Baron Bramwell's references to 'black looks' and 'having their motions watched' in *R v Druitt*. This provided the liberal intellectual context to the legislative settlement of labour criminality in the 1870s. Although there had been a legislative attempt to define the limits of labour coercion in the Molestation of Workmen Act 1859, the choice between general crimes and specific labour crimes was addressed fully in the Criminal Law Amendment Act 1871 and the Conspiracy and Protection of Property Act 1875. The 1875 legislative settlement would finally limit the criminal law's encroachment on the regulation of trade union affairs and it would reconstitute freedom of association. The

126 Curthoys (n 33) 31.

127 *R v Druitt* (1867) 10 Cox CC 592 (Cent. Crim. Ct. 1867).

128 For perceptive discussion of this feature of Mill's liberalism, and Mill's particular concern with social oppression and conformity, see Alan Ryan, 'Mill's Essay on Liberty', in Alan Ryan, *The Making of Modern Liberalism* (Princeton UP 2012) 257, 260–261.

129 See Richard Reeves, *John Stuart Mill: Victorian Firebrand* (Atlantic Books 2007) 453–457, though as Reeves notes, Mill remained sceptical about 'many of their current goals and methods' such as the enforcement of restrictive trade practices. Significantly, Mill famously recanted on the popular 'wage fund theory', which had postulated a fixed and static national fund available for wage settlements. This meant that collective bargaining over wages was always at the expense of other more disadvantaged groups of workers. For discussion of the 'wage fund theory' in historical context, see Deakin and Wilkinson (n 2) 206.

130 John Stuart Mill, *On Liberty and The Subjection of Women* (Penguin 2006) 64.

131 Curthoys (n 33) 154, discussing Mill's contributions to debates on the labour question.

prime motivating factor for these legislative reforms was the eradication of unjust discrimination against workers and trade unions and the achievement of equality before the law.

V. After 1875: Legal Equality and Freedom of Association

The coalition of support for the Disraeli labour law reforms of 1875 was based upon 'the assertion of the right of equal treatment under the law for both masters and men' which required 'the removal of unjust and discriminatory laws'.[132] This was reflected in three major reforms: the removal of criminal penalties from breach of contract under Master and Servant legislation; the restriction of liabilities for criminal conspiracy; and the definition of criminal offences so that they were less overtly targeted at workers. Taken together, these reforms would promote the generality of laws by removing the vestiges of 'class legislation'.

The first change was the repeal of Master and Servant laws. The enforcement of labour discipline through criminal punishment had deep historical roots.[133] In the assessment of Daphne Simon, these types of law were so striking because they inscribed a status-based inequality into the form of the law: 'the very heart of this law of master and servant . . . contained statutory provisions which treated the employer and the workman as entirely unequal. Whereas the master who broke his contract was only liable in a civil action for damages or wages owing, the servant who broke his contract was punished as a criminal with imprisonment and hard labour up to three months'.[134] This status-based classification, allocating criminal liabilities unequally, was difficult to reconcile with the radical case for freedom of labour contracts. The Master and Servant Act 1823 'rendered virtually any breach of an employment contract by a servant a summary crime . . . with a maximum of three months' imprisonment'.[135] The injustice was compounded by the fact that the law was administered by Justices of the Peace who were usually sympathetic to

[132] Jonathan Spain, 'Trade Unionists, Gladstonian Liberals and the Labour Law Reforms of 1875', in Eugenio Biagini and Alastair Reid (eds), *Currents of Radicalism: Popular Radicalism, Organised Labour and Party Politics in Britain 1850-1914* (Cambridge UP 1991) 109, 114–115.

[133] Douglas Hay, 'England, 1562-1875: The Law and Its Uses', in Douglas Hay and Paul Craven (eds), *Masters, Servants, and Magistrates in Britain and the Empire, 1562-1955* (University of North Carolina Press 2004) 59.

[134] Daphne Simon, 'Master and Servant', in John Saville (ed), *Democracy and the Labour Movement: Essays in honour of Dona Torr* (Lawrence & Wishart 1954) 160.

[135] Cornish (n 70) 282.

the masters.[136] The legislation was often used as an effective countermeasure during strikes when ringleaders were arrested and imprisoned.[137] Although in practical terms the criminal laws on conspiracy were more dangerous to the strike weapon by the 1870s, at least in the hands of larger employers, repeal of master and servant legislation was symbolically important in terms of the wider arguments about legal equality.[138] The extirpation of the criminal law from breaches of the employment contract was achieved in the Employers and Workmen Act 1875. Employment contracts were treated like other contracts. Employers and workmen were now regulated equally through the civil law.

The second change was the exclusion of liability for criminal conspiracy in section 3, which provided that 'An agreement or combination by two or more persons to do or procure to be done any act in contemplation or furtherance of a trade dispute between employers and workmen shall not be indictable as a conspiracy if such act committed by one person would not be punishable as a crime'. This immunity was restricted to 'trade disputes' between employers and workmen. This core legal concept indicated that this legislation was in the sphere of labour law. Section 3 also reflected another idea of equal treatment, that between individual and collective liberties. Where an act would not be a crime if perpetrated by an individual, it was not transformed into a crime simply in virtue of the fact that there was coordinated action by a group. This would be to punish collective activities simply in virtue of their collective nature. Equality of treatment between individual and collective liberties would be central to later theoretical engagements with freedom of association.[139]

The third change was the definition of labour crimes. There was considerable debate about 'general' and 'special' criminal legislation, and the ideal of equality before the law.[140] The offences in the 1875 Act finally dispensed with the wrongs of 'molestation' and 'obstruction', but the specific offence definitions did not detach entirely from the labour sphere. These were unmistakeably industrial crimes, though the formal definitions removed the vestiges of overt class-based hostility. Under section 7, which imposed penalties for intimidation and annoyance by violence where the intention was to 'compel' a person to do or abstain from doing an act, these offences could be committed by a 'person' rather than a worker. However, the specific modes of wrongdoing were unmistakeably coloured by the industrial context. They included

136 Simon (n 134) 168.
137 Ibid. 172.
138 Ibid. 192.
139 See, e.g., Sheldon Leader, *Freedom of Association: A Study in Labor Law and Political Theory* (Yale UP 1992) 183.
140 Curthoys (n 33) 228.

persistent following, hiding tools, watching and besetting, and following in a disorderly manner. Other offences referred specifically to contracts of service, such as the offence in section 5 of wilful and malicious breach 'knowing or having reasonable cause to believe that the probable consequences of his so doing, either alone or in combination with others, will be to endanger human life, or cause serious bodily injury, or to expose valuable property whether real or personal to destruction or serious injury'.

There was also a crime in section 4 where a person 'wilfully and maliciously breaks a contract of service with that authority or company or contractor, knowing or having reasonable cause to believe that the probable consequences of his so doing, either alone or in combination with others, will be to deprive the inhabitants of that city, borough, town, place, or part, wholly or to a great extent of their supply of gas or water'. This would have ensured convictions in circumstances like *R v Bunn*, where conspiracy charges had been used in a strike of London gas stokers.[141] Threats to public amenities such as water, gas, rail transportation, and electricity could be disabling in the new industrial centres, and this provided a reason for retaining special criminal offences. These were not obviously 'class legislation' in the same way as master and servant laws. There was a public justification for differences in treatment, for these crimes responded to particular risks created by strikes for the general population. They were an early form of what would now be described as strikes in essential services.

The 1875 settlement secured the decriminalisation of trade unions, and this provided a statutory foundation for freedom of association based in legal equality. As Klarman put it, 'For British trade unions in 1875 everything seemed to be coming up roses'.[142] For fifteen years, 'no new statutes were enacted, and not a single controversial case was decided'.[143] Yet it did not provide a final legal settlement for the trade unions. After the London Dock Strike of 1889, the objectives and methods of trade unions were contested again by employers in the courts, but this time using civil rather than criminal liabilities. This contestation reflected important changes in the pattern of trade unionism and the contours of the labour market. The labour historian John Saville identified the strategic challenges faced by the new unions organising unskilled and semi-skilled workers where labour supply was high.[144] The

[141] 12 Cox CC 316 (Cent. Crim. Ct. 1872).

[142] Michael J. Klarman, 'The Judges versus the Unions: The Development of British Labour Law, 1867-1913' (1989) 75 Virginia Law Review 1487.

[143] Ibid. 1498.

[144] John Saville, 'Trade Unions and Free Labour: The Background to the Taff Vale Decision', in Asa Briggs and John Saville (eds), *Essays in Labour History* (Macmillan 1967) 317.

maintenance of solidarity depended upon militant tactics such as mass picketing, boycotts, and combating the use of strike-breakers by hostile employers. This was an era where 'free labour' was no longer integral to radical ideals of craft and civic independence. Organisations like the 'National Free Labour Association' were used to supply strike-breaking labour during industrial disputes.[145] 'Free labour' was now becoming synonymous with strike-breaking, often in bitter and protracted industrial disputes. The factory and the dockyard were not the guarantors of dignity and respect that the 18th-century proponents of free labour in the crafts would have recognised.

This period was memorably described by Professor Klarman as 'The Judges versus the Unions'.[146] The law of torts as it applied in the labour context reflected the judicially defined limits of freedom of association. The courts developed tort liabilities to restrict trade union activities to circumstances where the judges determined that collective power had not been misused.[147] This was particularly evident in the case law on conspiracy to injure, interference with trade, and inducing breach of contract. Indeed, the law of torts has always provided a tool for judges to define the limits of responsible trade unionism where legislation is viewed by the judges as too permissive.[148]

In his treatise on the economic torts, Murphy has observed that 'one of the most influential factors in relation to the genesis and early development of the economic torts was the rise of trade unionism . . . Indeed, it is no exaggeration to say that the emergence of civil liability for conspiracy represents, in significant measure, the civil law's attempt to "tame the beast".'[149] The common law was not univocally hostile to trade unions. In *Allen v Flood*, for example, a majority in the House of Lords held that the intentional infliction of economic harm was not a tort in itself, and a bad motive did not turn an otherwise lawful act into an unlawful one.[150] This case had arisen when the secretary of a trade union procured the discharge of shipwrights by indicating to the employer that the ironworkers did not wish to work alongside them. The 'taming' of trade unions was however reflected in a broad range of hostile judicial decisions. For example, in *Temperton v Russell*, the Court of Appeal applied the

[145] Ibid. 337.

[146] Klarman (n 142).

[147] This 'freedom of association' analysis of the economic torts is proposed in John Murphy, *The Province and Politics of the Economic Torts* (Hart 2022) 110–112. See also John Murphy, 'Malice as an Ingredient of Tort Liability' (2019) Cambridge Law Journal 355.

[148] For a particularly explicit statement of the civil law of wrongs as a mechanism of judicial control of labour activities, see Lord Hoffman, 'The Rise and Fall of the Economic Torts', in Simone Degeling and others (eds), *Torts in Commercial Law* (Thomson Reuters 2009) 109.

[149] Murphy (n 147) 225. See also Hazel Carty, 'The Modern Functions of the Economic Torts: Reviewing the English, Canadian, Australian and New Zealand Positions' [2015] Cambridge Law Journal 261.

[150] *Allen v Flood* [1898] AC 1.

tort of inducing breach of contract where a union boycott disrupting the supply of building materials had been organised to enforce certain union rules against a master builder.[151] And in *J Lyons & Sons v Wilkins*, the Court of Appeal confirmed that peaceful picketing could nevertheless still be criminal under section 7 of the 1875 Act.[152] It could be enjoined through injunction where it constituted a 'watching and besetting' of the plaintiff's premises (as in this case by relays of pickets). Although the strike itself was lawful, the picketing could be criminally wrongful even where it involved no violence or intimidation and consisted in peaceful persuasion. At the dawn of the 20th century, Klarman identified the following civil law propositions which may be understood as the common law perimeter of trade union association. While it was permissible for workers to associate and to agree between themselves on the conditions for sale of their labour,

> It was impermissible . . . to: (1) compel unwilling members of a union to abide by such an agreement; (2) coerce an employer into conceding the union's demands by threatening a (perfectly lawful) strike; (3) persuade, even peacefully, nonunion labor to stay away from a struck shop; or (4) pressure workers to join a union by threatening to strike against an employer who hired them.[153]

This was a conception of freedom of association that was now being overshadowed by the individual's freedom to dispose of his labour. The worker should be permitted to bargain collectively with others and to withhold that labour from the market. Equally, the worker should always be protected from coercive interference from others in seeking his own contractual bargain. Even on this justificatory argument, it was unclear why peaceful persuasion of reluctant workmen or even (lawful) economic pressure should be treated as wrongful. It was also not clear why strong economic pressure imposed on an employer in a bargaining dispute should be treated as wrongful. This revealed the legal fragility of freedom of association, particularly in the hands of judges, given its underlying basis in a labour market justification.

It is in the contrast between two leading judgments on conspiracy to injure and cartels that this judicial hostility to trade unions is usually demonstrated.[154] In the *Oxford History of the Laws of England*, for example, Lobban argues that 'judges were generally more hostile to trade unions than political

[151] [1893] 1 QB 715.
[152] [1896] 1 Ch. 811.
[153] Klarman (n 142) 1561.
[154] Murphy (n 147) 234–235; Brodie (n 117) 33–34.

opinion was . . . At the same time, the judiciary was much less hostile to businessmen or property owners using their economic power or assets in an aggressive way.'[155] This divergence is usually traced through the differences in outcome between *Mogul Steamship Company v McGregor, Gow & Co (Mogul)*[156] and *Quinn v Leathem (Quinn)*.[157] Clearly, any account of these cases that seeks to present Lord Halsbury or Baron Bramwell as progressive beacons forfeits any claim to intellectual seriousness. Nevertheless, this divergence between *Mogul* and *Quinn* could be explained by the fact that the individual freedom to dispose of labour *is* different in important respects to the freedom to dispose of capital. Recall that in Elizabeth Anderson's account, free labour was critical to self-respect, dignity, and civic independence. The ability to earn one's living by the sweat of one's brow enabled the worker to be liberated from the shackles of dependence. Labour was a species of property, and it provided the worker with the instrumental means to live as a free citizen and pursue his own purposes. Viewed in this way, the protection of the individual's proprietary freedom to dispose of his labour (as his own means) was within the moral realm of private law.[158] Its moral basis was quite different to the freedom to dispose of capital. On this view, it was natural to think that monopolies threatening free labour *were* more suspect and dangerous, especially in the eyes of judges, than monopolies in the shipping of tea and other commercial markets. Labour monopolies threatened the moral independence of workmen to use their own means (labour) as they saw fit. If there were salient moral differences between property in capital and property in labour, we should not necessarily expect the same judicial treatment of business cartels and trade unions.[159]

In *Mogul* a group of ship owners operated a cartel in the tea trade between China and Europe. This involved offering significant rebates on freights that used ships owned by the cartel. The arrangements made it impossible for other ship owners to secure trade at remunerative rates. These coordinated trade practices, which also involved aggressively undercutting competitors, were highly successful at driving competitors from the market. The non-cartel ship owners claimed damages for conspiracy and an injunction. A majority in

[155] William Cornish and others, *The Oxford History of the Laws of England Volume XII 1820-1914: Private Law* (OUP 2010) 1050.
[156] [1892] AC 25.
[157] [1901] AC 495.
[158] See, for example, Arthur Ripstein, *Private Wrongs* (Harvard UP 2016), defending an account of private law that protects the individual's person and property so that she is in charge of her own life (and no other person is in charge of her). These private rights protect her means to pursue her own goals independently of others.
[159] Cf. Klarman (n 142) 1508.

the Court of Appeal found in favour of the defendants in the cartel.[160] Bowen LJ emphasised that civil wrongs depended upon a violation of the defendant's rights. There was no right not to be harmed by competitors in the course of trade. Any judicial attempt to demarcate the boundaries of reasonable competitive behaviour, if unaccompanied by independently wrongful acts, was fraught with difficulty.[161] Fry LJ agreed that there was no basis for treating the defendants' collusive behaviour as wrongful. They were seeking a competitive advantage in a free market, and 'to draw a line between fair and unfair competition, between what is reasonable and unreasonable, passes the power of the Courts'.[162]

The Master of the Rolls, Lord Esher, dissented. Lord Esher considered that the behaviour of the cartel was a wrongful act akin to a molestation or obstruction of the plaintiffs' free right of trade. As such, it did not fall within the bounds of permissible competition. It is of particular interest that Lord Esher relied heavily on 'the most admirable essay' of Sir William Erle,[163] *The Law Relating to Trade Unions*. While the rights to dispose of labour and capital were treated as counterparts in Erle's treatise, I suggest that the greater judicial willingness to define the limits of competition flowed from Lord Esher's use of trade union analogies. There was something special about property in labour, and cartels that restricted the individual's freedom to dispose of labour raised special concerns. In retrospect, Lord Esher's reliance on Erle pointed to the different path taken by the House of Lords in *Quinn v Leathem*.

In the House of Lords in *Mogul*, the legal problem was analysed as commercial competition between rival traders. For Lord Halsbury LC, no right had been interfered with and no wrongful act had been done. While the cartel agreement was certainly unenforceable between its members because it was in restraint of trade, the plaintiffs had not been wronged by it. Lord Bramwell addressed Lord Esher's reliance on Erle's trade union treatise.[164] For Lord Bramwell, the critical distinction in *Mogul* (and unlike many of the trade union cases) was that no private right had been violated by the cartel. The judgments of Lord Morris and Lord Field were also strongly focused on the fact that this involved commercial competition between traders.

As Klarman recognised, *Mogul* 'was perceived by many observers to be one of great value to the trade unionist cause. A business cartel's attempt to drive

160 [1889] 23 QBD 598.
161 Ibid. 620.
162 Ibid. 626.
163 Ibid. 606.
164 *Mogul* (n 156) 48.

competitors out of the market by pressuring customers and third-party dealers appeared strikingly similar to a trade union's attempt to extend its control over the labor market by threatening to strike against an employer who refused to dismiss nonunion labor.'[165] Although the House of Lords judgment in *Quinn* frustrated those hopes, the separate path taken in that case may have been prefigured in Lord Esher's dissent in *Mogul.*

Quinn is still a controversial judgment, and one leading scholar has recently suggested that it should be quietly forgotten.[166] The plaintiff, Henry Leathem, was a flesher in Lisburn who employed non-union men. Following a meeting with the Belfast Journeymen Butchers and Assistant's Association, the plaintiff offered to pay the outstanding fines of the non-union men so that they might be admitted into the association. This offer was refused. To put pressure on the plaintiff, the union contacted a customer of the plaintiff, Munce, and threatened that it would instruct its members to strike against Munce if he continued to buy the plaintiff's meat. Munce acquiesced. The plaintiff sued for conspiracy and was awarded significant damages by the jury. This was upheld by the House of Lords. According to Lord Macnaghten, there was no 'trade dispute' with either the plaintiff or Munce.[167] The plaintiff had agreed to pay the men's fines to resolve the dispute. The union's actions were calculated to inflict 'a cruel punishment'.[168] Lord Shand agreed, and he referred with approval to Erle's treatise on Trade Unions.[169] The defendants' purpose was to injure the plaintiff rather than to advance their own trade interests, which set this apart from *Mogul* and *Allen v Flood*.

The judgment that articulates the labour aspects of *Quinn* most extensively is that of Lord Brampton. He emphasised the limits of freedom of association as established in the legislative settlement of the 1870s:

> The Legislature in conferring upon trades unions such privileges as are contained in the Trade Union Acts, 1871 and 1876, does not empower them to do more than make rules for the regulation of their own conduct and provide for their own mutual assistance, and leaves each member as free to cease to belong to it and to repudiate every obligation for future observance of its rules as though he had never joined it.[170]

[165] Klarman (n 142) 1504.
[166] Robert Stevens, 'Is There a Right to Work?', in Alan Bogg and Paul S Davies (eds), *Private Law and the Employment Contract* (Hart 2025) 219.
[167] *Quinn* (n 157) 511.
[168] Ibid.
[169] Ibid. 513.
[170] Ibid. 526.

In language redolent of the earlier radical concerns with monopolies and oppression, Lord Brampton also observed that 'such a conspiracy is a powerful and dangerous engine, which in this case has, I think, been employed by the defendants for the perpetration of organized and ruinous oppression'.[171] The power of numbers in conspiracies could 'become dangerous and alarming'.[172] Lord Lindley was also focused on the plaintiff's 'liberty to earn his own living in his own way'.[173] Echoing Lord Brampton, Lord Lindley drew the distinction between groups of workers resolving to withhold their own labour and groups of workers resolving to coerce other workers to prevent them from working.[174] Nor did he regard this as a genuine 'trade dispute': it was a malicious attempt to cause strife between employers and workers who had no dispute with each other.[175]

Quinn has few modern supporters. Labour historians have interrogated the historical record to examine if the facts were as unsympathetic to the defendants as presented in their Lordship's speeches.[176] From a theoretical perspective, it might be possible to rationalise *Quinn* as an instance where the economic torts are targeted at 'especially reprehensible defendants'.[177] The defendants in *Quinn* were certainly portrayed as reprehensible in the judgments. Or, that *Quinn* involved the wrongful use of coercion to punish an employer for having employed non-union labour.[178]

On the account presented in this chapter, the key to understanding *Quinn* is that it touched a judicial nerve because it involved a secondary boycott to obstruct the individual's free disposal of labour (and the plaintiff's freedom to employ such labour). Some of the speeches assumed that there was no 'trade dispute' at all because this concept was assumed to be limited to a *primary* dispute between a group of workers and their employer to negotiate about *wages and hours*. Given the basis of freedom of association in workmen's freedom to combine and to sell their own labour in combination, we can understand why the secondary boycott in *Quinn* was regarded by the judges as a wrongful misuse of collective power. This understanding could be traced all the way back to the scope of the immunity in the Combination Act of 1825. In this

171 Ibid. 531.
172 Ibid. 530.
173 Ibid. 534.
174 Ibid. 538.
175 Ibid. 541.
176 John McIlroy, 'The Belfast Butchers: Quinn v Leathem after a Hundred Years', in K.D. Ewing (ed), *The Right to Strike: From the Trade Disputes Act 1906 to a Trade Union Freedom Bill 2006* (Institute of Employment Rights 2006) chapter 3.
177 This general account of a distinctive rationale for economic torts is defended by Murphy (n 147) 246–253.
178 Allan Beever, *A Theory of Tort Liability* (Hart 2018) 128.

way, the wrong in *Quinn* was fashioned in the image of English law's theory of freedom of association at the turn of the 20th century. The economic torts were used by the courts to delimit freedom of association, which was still justified mainly by the individual's freedom to dispose of his labour in the market.

VI. To the Trade Disputes Act 1906 and the Modern Law of Freedom of Association

The foundations of the modern English law on freedom of association were shaped by two landmark judgments, both involving the Amalgamated Society of Railway Servants. Each judgment precipitated important statutory interventions providing a basic structural framework that is still familiar today. While these judgments have sometimes been regarded as surprising extensions of liability based upon the existing law at that time,[179] I will suggest that there were in fact strong continuities with the earlier English law on freedom of association. In *Taff Vale Railway Co v Amalgamated Society of Railway Servants*, the House of Lords considered the liability of the trade union itself for the wrongful actions of its officials during a strike.[180] In *Osborne v Amalgamated Society of Railway Servants (No 1)*, the House of Lords considered the lawfulness of the compulsory political levy sponsoring parliamentary candidates for the Labour Party.[181] As Brodie has argued, despite apparent differences in the factual issues, 'there is a clear thread running between *Osborne* and *Taff Vale* in terms of the judicial conceptualisation of a trade union'.[182] They treated the trade union as a quasi-corporate entity, with a personality distinct from that of its individual members. This was something more than a metaphysical theory of corporate personality. It was an attempt to use legal doctrines, such as the *ultra vires* rule, to curb what the judges viewed as the irresponsible use of power by an organised group.

A. *Taff Vale*

The *Taff Vale* case is perhaps the most famous case in the history of labour law. Unlike *Quinn v Leathem*, it arose out of a primary dispute between the

179 For example, Brodie (n 117) describes the contemporary reaction to *Taff Vale* as 'immense' surprise: 88.
180 [1901] AC 426.
181 [1910] AC 87.
182 Brodie (n 117) 110.

railway company and its employees about wages and the alleged victimisation of a union official.[183] The strike involved 1227 men, the majority of which had not given adequate contractual notice to the employer. The employer then attempted to use replacement labour to break the strike, which prompted a 'Blackleg circular' signed by the General Secretary of the union, Richard Bell.[184] In the High Court, Farwell J issued interim injunctions against named union officials and the Amalgamated Society of Railway Servants itself. The view that the union itself could be a defendant was based in an understanding of the legal effects of the Trade Union Acts 1871 and 1876. This legislation provided legal recognition to the lawful purposes of a trade union, and Farwell J regarded it as axiomatic that a powerful body recognised by statute should be liable for the wrongful conduct of the agents of a society. Farwell J's approach was upheld in the House of Lords. The key issue was whether trade unions should be regarded as 'above the law' or subject to the ordinary law of civil wrongs.[185] Lord Lindley expressed it in the following way: 'I entirely repudiate the notion that the effect of the Trade Union Act, 1871, is to legalise trade unions and confer on them the right to acquire and hold property, and at the same time to protect the union from legal proceedings if their managers or agents acting for the whole body violate the rights of other people.'[186] The effect of *Taff Vale* was to expose the funds of trade unions to damages claims arising out of strikes, and in this case the Society paid damages and legal costs of £42,000.[187]

Legal equality was integral to the legislative settlement of the 1870s. Trade unions and workers should not be singled out by special legal rules imposing disabilities and disadvantages upon them. They should be treated equally in accordance with the ordinary law. Since the supremacy of the ordinary law was central to the justification for the 1870s settlement, it was natural that it should also be central to defining its limits. It was therefore unsurprising that judges in *Taff Vale* would balk at the prospect of trade unions avoiding liabilities for civil wrongs. It was integral to the rule of law that trade unions should be liable for the wrongs of their agents, analogous to the legal situation of corporations.

If *Taff Vale* is the most famous case, the Trade Disputes Act 1906 that it prompted surely has a claim to be the most famous statute in the history of

[183] Graeme Lockwood, 'Taff Vale and the Trade Disputes Act 1906', in K.D. Ewing (ed), *The Right to Strike: From the Trade Disputes Act 1906 to a Trade Union Freedom Bill 2006* (IER 2006) 18–19.
[184] A copy of which is set out; Ibid. 22.
[185] Lord Macnaghten (n 180) 438.
[186] *Taff Vale* (n 180) 443–444.
[187] Lockwood (n 185) 26.

British labour law. The political debates around the issues raised by *Taff Vale* were not new. For example, the famous divergence between the majority and minority reports of the Royal Commission on Trade Unions 1869 had centred on the issue of incorporation of trade unions.[188] For the majority, it was a corollary of the legal concession of rights and duties to trade unions through incorporation that trade unions should submit to state control over their objects. Legal recognition betokened greater legal supervision and control. There were also dangers for the state with this process of legalisation. If trade unions could enforce contracts in the ordinary way, this would mean that they could exercise control over members through enforcing fines and union instructions during strike disputes.

The Trade Disputes Act 1906 adopted an immunity-based approach to the law of strikes. By section 3, an act done 'in contemplation or furtherance of a trade dispute' would not be actionable if certain torts were committed by the organisers. By section 4, any action in tort against a trade union 'shall not be entertained by any court'. 'Trade dispute' was defined as 'any dispute between employers and workmen, or between workmen and workmen, which is connected with the employment or non-employment, or the terms of the employment, or with the conditions of labour, of any person, and the expression "workmen" means all persons employed in trade or industry'. The statutory immunity raised concerns about 'privilege' from the ordinary law,[189] and the 1906 Act was certainly antithetical to Dicey's concern for the supremacy of ordinary common law.[190] In the immediate aftermath, judges sought to avoid the statutory immunity by interpreting 'trade dispute' narrowly. For example, in *Conway v Wade*, a dispute arising out of the employment of a worker who owed fines to the trade union was treated as outside the scope of a 'trade dispute'.[191] As *Quinn v Leathem* demonstrated, pursuing the dismissal of workmen who were not on terms with the trade union was often a step too far for the courts. Nevertheless, the 1906 Act has had a remarkably enduring influence on the modern law. Freedom of association for trade unions was addressed to the economic context of employers, workmen, and disputes about conditions of labour. This was captured in the 'trade dispute' formula. The terminology is still used today, though the current statutory definition is

[188] Brodie (n 117) 2–3.

[189] See the account of the parliamentary context in John Saville, 'The Trade Disputes Act of 1906', in Ewing (n 183).

[190] Walters (n 12) 229.

[191] [1909] AC 606. For a brilliant analysis of the case in its historical and legislative context, see K.D. Ewing, 'The South Shields Case - Subverting the Trade Disputes Act 1906?' in K.D. Ewing (ed), *The Right to Strike: From the Trade Disputes Act 1906 to a Trade Union Freedom Bill 2006* (IER 2006).

narrower than it was in 1906. For the judges, the central case of the 'trade dispute' was the primary strike between an employer and its own workers about core terms and conditions of employment. This continues to lie at the core of freedom of association today.

B. *Osborne*

Osborne involved a challenge to a compulsory political levy that had been imposed on Mr Walter Osborne, a levy which had been supported by a majority of the Society's members. The House of Lords concluded that the political levy was unlawful on two bases. The first basis involved the application of the doctrine of ultra vires to the union's objects. The statutory definition of trade union purposes in the Trade Union Act 1876 was defined in terms of trade purposes. This 'industrial' formulation was not surprising given the normative justification for collective bargaining in facilitating the free disposal of labour on the market. According to Lord Macnaghten, this meant that rules supporting political organisation were 'a thing very different' to trade purposes and were therefore ultra vires.[192] The ultra vires analysis was also adopted by Lord Atkinson and the Earl of Halsbury.

The second basis emphasised the constitutional distinction between representation and delegation. Lord Shaw was uncertain about the reach of the ultra vires argument because it might stultify the 'natural movements of the living organism', that is the 'living organism' of the association.[193] Instead, he objected to the payment on democratic and constitutional grounds. The political levy imperilled the independence and freedom of the elected representative to decide for himself on an issue, based upon a deliberative assessment of 'the real interests of the constituency which has elected him'.[194] For this reason, it was against public policy to enforce such a rule. Such arrangements strayed close to forms of political corruption. This constitutional analysis was supported by Lord James. Like *Taff Vale*, the effect of *Osborne* was reversed by Trade Union Act 1913 which provided for a separate political fund and an individual right to opt out of the political fund.

Osborne has been subjected to strong criticism by many of the leading labour law scholars of the modern era. In a recent consideration of *Osborne*, Cabrelli is unflinching in his criticism:

[192] *Osborne* (n 191) 97.
[193] Ibid. 108.
[194] Ibid. 111.

> What is particularly striking about the decision is how its effect was to ride roughshod over the freedoms of the workers who had voluntarily decided to apply a portion of their union dues towards the funding of political representation. To that extent, there is a strong case for the proposition that the freedom of association and expression of those workers was completely set aside.[195]

While this critique is very persuasive, we should not overlook the deeper alignments between *Osborne* and the legal theory of freedom of association at the turn of the 20th century. From the late 18th century, judges and legislators were suspicious of the political activities of associations of workmen. As we have seen, anxieties about political subversion through treason and sedition were central to the prohibition of combinations in 1799 and 1800.[196] The tight focus on 'trade' and its separation from 'politics' must be understood against this backdrop, and it still finds echoes today in the restrictive legal treatment of political strikes. *Osborne* also engaged concerns about the coercive use of organised collective power to compel individuals to provide political support or to vote in particular ways. This was certainly an extension beyond protecting the individual's freedom to dispose of his labour from what judges viewed as collective coercion. That said, *Osborne* can also be viewed as a counterpart of older cases like *Quinn v Leathem*. The individual's freedom to dispose of his vote or his political allegiance was no less important than his freedom to dispose of his labour. Both were aspects of civic independence.

VII. The Legal Structure of Freedom of Association in the Modern Era

The basic legal structure for freedom of association in English law was well established by the first decade of the 20th century. This structure had developed within the central domain of what we now describe as labour law. It was not conceived as a general constitutional freedom or civil liberty. Many of the normative elements of freedom of association in the early 20th century could be traced back to the early decades of the 19th century. Even more

[195] David Cabrelli, 'Financing the Parliamentary Representation of Labour: Amalgamated Society of Railway Servants v Osborne', in Jeremias Adams-Prassl and others (eds), *Landmark Cases in Labour Law* (Hart 2022) 97. K.D. Ewing, *Trade Unions, the Labour Party and the Law: A Study of the Trade Union Act 1913* (Edinburgh UP 1982).

[196] The legendary 'Tolpuddle Martyrs', agricultural labourers engaged in trade union activities, were prosecuted under the Unlawful Oaths Act 1797. This legislation had been introduced in response to naval mutinies during the anxious times of the late 1790s. The line between industrial and political criminality could be exceedingly thin: Orth (n 34) 112–115.

surprisingly, many of these elements are still integral to the law of freedom of association today.

By 1906, this basic legal structure was based in freedoms or liberties. There was an individual freedom to dispose of labour on the market (and this included the freedom to withhold labour), and workers should be free to do this collectively with others. There are strong similarities with Brian Langille's contemporary justification for freedom of association in the symmetry between collective and individual bargaining in the market.[197] Sometimes, there was looseness in the 'classics' in describing the relevant juridical relations. For example, the Webbs described the 1825 settlement as enacting 'the *right* of collective bargaining, involving the power to withhold labour from the market by concerted action'.[198] They did not have the advantage of familiarity with Hohfeld's work on jural relations.[199] Rights are correlative to duties, and during this period there were no legal duties on employers in the sphere of freedom of association. For example, there were no legal duties to bargain nor to refrain from dismissing or victimising trade unionists. There was a liberty to bargain, a liberty to associate, and so forth. This was exemplified in the settled legislative choice to use immunities rather than rights.

Wedderburn famously explained this in terms of union preference for industrial liberties, their experience of industrial power before full political emancipation, and reflected in pragmatism over political ideology.[200] It is perhaps equally pertinent that the elaboration of legal *duties* on private employers would have been unimaginable at this point in legal development. The English common law certainly stood as a bulwark against forced labour.[201] Yet key employer duties, such as the employer's legal 'duty to bargain', depended upon an extensive administrative machinery, usually enforced by specialist labour boards. This would not happen until the middle decades of the 20th century in the US and Canada.[202] In the UK, it would not happen until 1971. In relation to the fundamental legal duty not to dismiss for trade union reasons, the House of Lords affirmed the employer's wide dismissal prerogatives at common law in 1909.[203] It was not until 1971 that general statutory unfair dismissal protection was introduced in the UK. Without these general statutory

197 Brian Langille, 'The Freedom of Association Mess: How We Got into It and How We Can Get Out of It' (2009) 54 McGill Law Journal 177, 186–187.
198 Webbs (n 26) 108 (emphasis added).
199 Wesley Newcomb Hohfeld. See Wesley Newcomb Hohfeld, 'Fundamental Legal Conceptions as Applied in Judicial Reasoning' (1917) 26 Yale Law Journal 710.
200 Lord Wedderburn, 'Industrial Relations and the Courts' (1980) 9 Industrial Law Journal 65, 71.
201 The classic formulation of this is *Nokes v Doncaster Amalgamated Collieries* [1940] AC 1014.
202 See, e.g., Judy Fudge and Eric Tucker, *Labour Before the Law* (OUP 2001).
203 *Addis v Gramophone Co. Ltd.* [1909] AC 488.

protections, a rights-based framework for individual freedom of association could not be implemented. Freedom of association as a bundle of rights and correlative duties depended upon a more general statutory framework which would only start to develop in the UK from the 1960s.

Nevertheless, there was a normative core to 'industrial' freedom of association in the 19th and early 20th centuries that has proved to be remarkably resilient. In fact, we might even say that the law has come full circle. As we shall see in Chapters 4 and 5, the core element of freedom of association under Article 11 ECHR is the primary bargaining relationship between an employer and a trade union representing workers in respect of their own terms and conditions of employment. Political strikes by trade unions are likely to be treated as secondary or accessory freedoms with attenuated protection compared with primary occupational strikes. This is also true of secondary or sympathy industrial action. The proper realm of trade union action is the primary 'trade dispute', not the political or secondary dispute. It is remarkable how the contours of modern human rights law reflect the contours of 19th-century labour law.[204] These are not simply features of modern human rights law.

This judicial hostility to the secondary boycott was also reflected in the English courts and in other legal systems. For example, Forbath has observed of the US that boycotts 'provoked courts' anxiety and rage, in part because they mobilized whole working-class populations—broad networks of workers (and their families) not linked to individual workplaces or particular unions'.[205] These limits did not flow logically from the individual freedom to dispose of labour on the market (although they were compatible with it). They represented regulatory choices to define workmen's freedom of association so that it was less threatening to a functioning labour market and employers' property rights.

There is no doubt that 19th- and 20th-century judges were often hostile to organised labour and favoured the interests of capital.[206] Yet we must acknowledge that lawmakers were also attempting to formulate labour law limits to the boundary of lawful collective action. From 1824 onwards, it was too simplistic to view this as brute repression against trade unions. The courts were disposed to protect individual workmen from what they regarded as oppressive or unfair treatment by organised groups, especially trade unions. These notions of individual fairness and avoiding arbitrary treatment shaped

[204] The language of 'accessory' freedom is taken from the ECHR case law on 'secondary' industrial action: *RMT v UK* [2014] IRLR 467.

[205] William E. Forbath, *Law and the Shaping of the American Labor Movement* (Harvard UP 1991) 83.

[206] Mike Macnair, 'Free Association versus Juridification' (2011) 39 *Critique* 53.

judicial attitudes to picketing, the enforcement of union rules against members, the closed shop, and secondary boycotts. Then, as now, the closed shop was viewed as a fundamentally suspect institution from a judicial perspective. It is also regarded as fundamentally suspect in modern human rights law today. As Dicey recognised, if freedom of association is rooted in the individual's freedom to sell his own labour, association must be strictly voluntary. At times, this may have led the courts to detect wrongful coercion, particularly from trade unions, even where the industrial pressure on individual workers was rather light.

This chapter began with Elizabeth Anderson's powerful argument examining when 'the market was left' as an egalitarian project. The emancipation of trade unions in the early 19th century was strongly linked to the creation of a labour market. These new trade union freedoms, recognised in law, favoured modes of trade union action that facilitated a functioning labour market. For example, it was legitimate to bargain over wages but not to enforce apprenticeship restrictions. The latter activity smacked of oppressive monopoly. By the end of the 19th century, it was uncommon for small craft employers and workers to work together in the same workshop. Instead, there was 'a severe degradation of working conditions. Workers were subject to the relentless, grueling discipline of the clock and the machine . . . Conditions were harsh, hours long, wages low, and prospects for advancement, regardless of how hard one worked, minimal.'[207] Perhaps under the sway of older ideals of egalitarian relations between masters and journeymen, the courts continued to regard the main threat of oppression as emanating from trade unions rather than employers. This was discordant with the realities of industrial employment and large industrial employers. The robust protection of the *rights* of workmen depended upon the recognition and enforcement of legal *duties* on their employers. After the Trade Disputes Act 1906, that shift was still more than over half a century away in British labour law.

The legal model of freedom of association continues to be freedom *within* rather than *against* the market order. Today, that is more likely to be viewed as reactionary rather than radical in its import. Fundamentally, the historical period examined in this chapter marked the emergence of a distinctive 'labour law' concept of freedom of association. This was characterised by two fundamental features. On the one hand, the collective parameters of the freedom were *labour law* parameters specified principally through labour legislation. This identified a core set of familiar elements such as the trade

[207] Anderson (n 27) 34.

dispute, favouring primary occupational strikes over secondary or political strikes, and protection of the individual's freedom to disassociate. On the other hand, the courts policed the limits of those parameters strictly, guided by notions of equality, non-discrimination, and restraining abuse of power. In later decades, courts and legislators would begin to take the risks of abuse of power by employers far more seriously. This coincided with birth of modern labour law itself. In due course, these labour law elements would shape the emergence of trade union rights in modern human rights law. Over the next four chapters, we will see how the line between the civil liberty and the labour law conceptions of freedom of association can often be difficult to discern.

3
The ‘Personal Scope’ of Freedom of Association

I. Personal Scope and the Enduring Autonomy of Labour Law

Are trade union rights universal human rights for ‘everyone’? Or are they restricted to certain kinds of personal employment contracts and/or certain kinds of association such as a trade union? This will be familiar to all labour lawyers as the basic enquiry into the ‘personal scope’ of labour rights. It is usually treated as the most fundamental matter of all in labour law textbooks. The enquiry is relevant to full range of employment rights where those rights are allocated to employees or workers. It is not specific to freedom of association. The contract is the gateway into those statutory employment protections.

Litigation on this issue touches directly upon the autonomy of labour law. Usually, the legislated freedom of association right specifies a labour law boundary for freedom of association. This boundary will be defined in a labour law statute. In recent times, workers and trade unions have challenged that boundary using constitutional norms ‘external’ to labour law. These challenges have sought to expand the personal scope of labour law categories by invoking the universality of human rights.

As set out in Chapter 2, in the English legal system, freedom of association rights for workers developed *within* labour law across centuries. The boundaries of these rights were boundaries based upon labour law categories: the trade, occupations, workmen, employees, workers, and trade unions. This is now so deeply embedded that there is a high degree of path dependence favouring the labour law boundary.[1] It is a pattern that recurs across many different legal systems. Its persistence reflects the fact that the delimitation of the category of right-holders, let us call them workers, was aligned with the

[1] On the nature of path dependence and the persistent quality of established legal rules and categories, see John Bell, ‘Path Dependence and Legal Development’ (2012) 87 Tulane Law Review 787.

Freedom of Association. Alan Bogg, Oxford University Press. © Alan Bogg 2026. DOI: 10.1093/9780191831690.003.0003

traditional normative justification for labour rights.[2] Workers experienced subordination, dependence, and inequality of bargaining power. They were vulnerable to contractual exploitation by employers. Freedom of association through trade unions empowered workers so that they were able to meet with employers on a more equal footing. Similar anti-exploitation justifications applied to fair wages, dismissal protections, and working time rights.

Labour market changes have led to a misalignment between the conventional category of right-holders, workers, and the normative justification for labour rights.[3] Some of those who need freedom of association protections are excluded from it. Some occupational groups are specifically excluded from general labour relations legislation, such as agricultural workers, managers and supervisors, and the police. Yet these groups often have similar needs to other workers. Increasingly, many of the 'self-employed' in fissured labour markets are highly precarious and exposed to greater economic and social risk than 'standard' workers in secure employment.[4] The growth of the precarious self-employed has accelerated in the 'gig economy', but it is by no means restricted to that context.[5] This presents a more fundamental challenge to the worker category, and it has even led to calls for boundaryless freedom of association rights for all.

It is little surprise that trade unions and workers should have turned to strategic litigation using universal human rights 'for everyone' to respond to these challenges. If 'everyone' has these rights, and they are enjoyed universally, the legal system should not be creating exclusions through its legal categories. This chapter will consider examples from the European Convention on Human Rights (ECHR), the UK, Canada, and the European Social Charter (ESC). While there is some variation in techniques and outcomes across these systems, labour law categories of personal scope have remained sticky. Constitutional norms have led to adjustments of the labour law boundary, but by no means its overthrow. This no doubt reflects path dependence, given the long historical development of trade union rights as rights for workers within national labour law systems.

[2] David Cabrelli, 'Traditional Justifications of Labour Law', in Guy Davidov and others (eds), *The Oxford Handbook of the Law of Work* (OUP 2024) 103.

[3] For an early engagement with those changes, and their consequences for legal tests of employment status, see Hugh Collins, 'Independent Contractors and the Challenge of Vertical Disintegration in Employment Protection Laws' (1990) 10 Oxford Journal of Legal Studies 353.

[4] Bernd Wass and Christina HieBl (eds), *Collective Bargaining for Self-Employed Workers in Europe* (Kluwer Law International B.V. 2021).

[5] Ioannis Lianos and others, 'Rethinking the Competition Law/Labour Law Interaction: Promoting a Fairer Labour Market' (2019) 10 European Labour Law Journal 291.

I will argue that the fundamental legal idea underlying these constitutional challenges is equality before the law.[6] Equality before the law demands that distinctions in the law between persons and groups are amenable to principled justification. Discrimination between persons and groups need not violate equality before the law if it is a distinction that can be justified by reference to appropriate criteria.[7] Can the law's categories, exclusions, and distinctions in determining 'personal scope' be justified by reference to relevant reasons? We would do well to remember that the law *always* discriminates in defining legal rights: by identifying a class of right-holders, duty-bearers, and the content of relevant duties. To define a legal right is inevitably to include some and to exclude others. Discrimination through the law's categorisations is not necessarily wrongful. The constitutional question asks whether those categories are justified, given the purpose of the differentiation. This is the contribution of a human rights framework to the employment status enquiry.[8]

This is most obviously relevant in relation to a specific occupational exclusion from a general labour relations statute. Where the exclusion is unjustified, for example, because the excluded group is also in need of those protections, the simplest constitutional remedy would be the inclusion of the excluded group in general legislation. This could also be relevant to situations where individuals are vulnerable to contractual exploitation but do not satisfy the employment status tests, for example, because they are categorised as self-employed. There may also be more complex cases. For example, a group of workers experiences distinctive social and economic disadvantages compared with standard workers, such as agricultural workers. In these circumstances, the constitutional equality norm might even *require* positive targeted legislation to provide statutory protections beyond the general baseline. This is a way of achieving substantive equality for those disadvantaged groups: inclusion in the general statute is not sufficient to ameliorate those extra disadvantages.

As the case studies in this chapter demonstrate, the autonomy of labour law has been enduring in relation to personal scope. These studies confirm that

[6] See Michael Foran, 'Equality before the Law: A Substantive Constitutional Principle' (2020) *Public Law* 287. For an application of this idea in employment status contexts in labour law more generally, see Alan Bogg, 'Employment Status and Equality before the Law: Three Arguments from Equality' (2025) 29 Edinburgh Law Review 258. This equality argument has been developed most fully in the freedom of association context by Brian Langille, and my indebtedness to his thinking will be evident throughout this chapter.

[7] T.R.S. Allan, *Law, Liberty, and Justice: The Legal Foundations of British Constitutionalism* (OUP 1993) 163–164.

[8] For an excellent account of human rights and employment status, see Joe Atkinson, 'Employment Status and Human Rights: An Emerging Approach' (2023) 86 Modern Law Review 1166. I regard the potential impact of human rights on employment status as more modest than the approach defended by Atkinson.

the 'rights for everyone' idea remains elusive. This elusiveness is unsurprising. For rights to be made determinate and therefore enforceable through legal mechanisms, there must be *some* delimitation of the class of duty-bearers and the content of those duties.[9] Naturally enough, these tend to be formulated as legal duties on employers. There must be some kind of relationship between the right-holder and the duty-bearer. If the duty-bearer is an employer, it is natural to treat workers (however defined) as the relevant class of right-holders. The persistence of employment status flows from the correlativity of rights and duties, and the need for a juridical relation between the right-holder and the duty-bearer.

The chapter will consider a range of employment status problems that have arisen in different ways. In the ECHR, the European Court of Human Rights (ECtHR) has integrated an 'employment relationship' threshold into its formulation of trade union rights under Article 11. In the UK, the impact of human rights has led to some incremental adjustments to labour law categories. Some specific exclusions, such as foster carers and parks police, have been successfully challenged. The courts have also refined the general definition of worker through general purposive interpretation. In Canada, the Supreme Court of Canada (SCC) has scrutinised specific statutory exclusions from general labour legislation. Instead of pursuing an equality approach directly, the SCC has developed freedom of association protections for excluded groups such as agricultural workers. The effect of this has been a diluted constitutional standard of freedom of association for those excluded workers that falls short of the higher legislated standard. It has achieved less for those workers than a direct equality approach. The most radical approach has been under the ESC, where a substantive ideal of equality was used to challenge competition law constraints on the collective bargaining activities of the self-employed in Ireland. This ensured that the relational boundary of freedom of association tracked social and economic inequalities rather than formal contractual categories.

So far, I have been talking about 'trade union rights' as a general category. It might be useful at the outset to disaggregate the category because it could be relevant to the enquiry into personal scope:

(i) The *liberty* to form and join associations and to engage in collective activities.

[9] The central role of legislation in specifying determinate content for human rights (and their correlative duties) has been defended in Gregoire Webber and others, *Legislated Rights: Securing Human Rights through Legislation* (Cambridge UP 2018).

(ii) The *right* to be a trade union member and to engage in trade union activities and the correlative *duty* on employers not to dismiss or otherwise victimise individuals for trade union reasons.
(iii) The *right* to engage in collective bargaining correlative to the employer's *duty* to bargain.
(iv) The *right* to strike correlative to the employer's *duty* not to penalise those engaged in a lawful strike.

In relation to (i), the liberty to associate, this is a strong candidate for the broadest personal scope. All persons should be at liberty to form and join associations and to act collectively within the scope of the general law. Any justifications for state restrictions on these general associative freedoms should be scrutinised very carefully. Liberties do not need to be delimited by personal scope in the same way as rights because we do not need to define the right–duty relation with the same precision. This is reflected in our case studies. The broadest approach to personal scope occurred within the context of a challenge to state-imposed competition law restrictions on the bargaining activities of the self-employed in Ireland. This is a category (i) case.

Categories (ii)–(iv) are different. In each case, there is a defined duty-bearer, the employer. The employer is the duty-bearer either because (as under (ii) and (iv)) the employer presents a particular *threat* to the right-holder's interests[10] or because (as under (iii)) the *subject-matter* of the right (collective bargaining) is concerned with conditions of *employment* that require negotiation with an employer. The basic correlativity of rights and duties presupposes some kind of employment relationship. It does not tell us how broad or narrow this relationship should be. Generally speaking, the role of constitutional litigation has been to broaden the personal work category rather than to repudiate it entirely and to pursue a 'rights for all' approach.

Before considering these case studies, let us begin with the historical development of personal scope in English labour law. Over centuries, it coalesced around the personal employment contract. Legislated freedom of association rights were labour rights. For most of the 20th century, these labour rights were aligned with those relationships in the labour market that needed

[10] There is a strong argument that an employer should not victimise workers for participating in other types of association such as political parties or religious associations. I agree. Many of these situations would be caught either under unfair dismissal or discrimination law. This still presupposes an employment relationship because the relevant duty is addressed to the risks of abuse of economic power by an employer. I am grateful to Michael Ford KC for raising this point.

protection. From the 1970s onwards, the misalignment in personal coverage of rights started to become apparent.[11] This was a general feature of employment law, though it certainly applied to freedom of association rights.

II. The Legal History of Personal Scope

A. From wrongs to immunities

According to one leading scholar, 'Work law is born universal, yet it is filled with exclusions.'[12] This is certainly not true of freedom of association, as it developed in British labour law. There was no universality at its genesis. Instead, the early law of associations developed specifically within the domain of workmen's combinations. These associations were treated as specific problems of economic conflict rather than regulated through a general law of associations. In fact, the labour law of the 18th century was even more particularised in prohibiting concerted activities *in specific trades*. These early statutes typically prohibited agreements to advance wages or restrict hours in trades experiencing labour conflict and unrest. The statute would treat workmen's agreements to raise wages or restrict hours as void, and it would subject new agreements to criminal penalties. Different statutes covered weavers in the woollen trade, papermakers, hatters, and the Spitalfield silk-weavers.[13] The common law of criminal conspiracy was also used to punish combinations of workmen.[14] The generalisation from 'trades' to 'workmen' occurred in the Combination Act 1799.[15] For Orth, the 1799 Act was so significant because it marked the point at which 'parliament ventured its first general proposition concerning labour law'.[16] This generality was reflected in its title as 'an act to prevent unlawful combinations of *workmen*'. It was replaced shortly thereafter by the Combination Act 1800. This legislation used the criminal law to prohibit restrictive agreements of workmen and masters, and these included crimes related to the refusal or quitting of work.[17] These Acts 'had finally

[11] Collins (n 3).
[12] Gali Racabi, 'Excluded but Equal' (2024) 33 William & Mary Bill of Rights Journal 209, 210.
[13] John V. Orth, *Combination and Conspiracy: A Legal History of Trade Unionism 1721-1906* (OUP 1993) 22–23.
[14] For a discussion of its historical origins, and its extension to workers' collective action, see Christopher L. Tomlins, *Law, Labor, and Ideology in the Early American Republic* (Cambridge UP 1993) chapter 4. See further Francis B. Sayre, 'Criminal Conspiracy' (1922) 35 Harvard Law Review 393.
[15] 39 Geo. 3, c. 81.
[16] Orth (n 13) 43.
[17] The details of the 1799 Act are set out in Orth (n 13) 45–49 and 156–161.

formulated a general proposition concerning the groups soon to be known as trade unions: they were illegal'.[18]

The first significant statutory liberalisation of associative activities occurred in the Combination Act 1824. It is crucial to understand that this was responding to repressive measures directed specifically at workmen's associations. In no sense was the liberty for trade unions being derived from a general associative liberty. Instead, the freedom or liberty was being carved out of wrongs addressed specifically to problems of conflict over wages, hours, and job control. Section 2 of the 1824 Act conferred an immunity from prosecution for 'journeymen, workmen, or other persons who shall enter into any combination' to fix wages, to modify the duration of working time or the quantity of work, or to regulate the mode of carrying on any manufacture, trade, or business. Following an upsurge in strike action, the settlement was revised in the Combination Act 1825. While the 1825 Act was narrower in some respects than the 1824 Act, it continued to use this immunity technique. Since the immunity excluded labour wrongs, the corresponding liberties were for specific types of work relation or arrangement (i.e., 'journeymen' or 'workmen') and combinations (concerned with wages, or working time or quantity of work). The final extirpation of criminal conspiracy came through s. 3 of the Conspiracy and Protection of Property Act 1875, which held that 'an agreement or combination by two or more persons to do or procure to be done any act in contemplation or furtherance of a trade dispute between employers and workmen shall not be indictable as a conspiracy if such act committed by one person would not be punishable as a crime'. A 'trade dispute' was 'between employers and workmen'.

The effect of the 1875 settlement was to shift the battleground between capital and labour from criminality to civil wrongs, especially the common law of economic torts. In formal terms, these tort doctrines were neutral between capital and labour. In practice, the judges tended to be more hostile where the defendants were trade unionists, especially in civil conspiracy cases. In *Quinn v Leathem*, the House of Lords treated the boycotting activities of trade unionists differently and more restrictively to those of business cartels.[19] According to Klarman, 'the bulk of the cases finding liability during this era involved trade unions pressuring employers to dismiss unionists . . . the courts there were applying more restrictive antimonopolization rules to trade unions than business cartels.'[20] When the House of Lords decided that the trade union itself

[18] Ibid. 67.
[19] [1901] AC 495.
[20] Michael J. Klarman, 'The Judges versus the Unions: The Development of British Labour Law, 1867-1913' (1989) 75 Virginia Law Review 1487, 1508.

could be sued in tort in *Taff Vale Railway Co. v Amalgamated Society of Railway Servants*, the resulting crisis required fundamental legislative change.[21] This came in the guise of the Trade Disputes Act 1906. The legislation conferred an immunity on trade unions. In s. 5(3), it also defined 'trade dispute' as 'any dispute between employers and workmen, or between workmen and workmen, which is connected with employment or non-employment, or the terms of the employment, or with the conditions of labour, of any person, and the expression "workmen" means all persons employed in trade or industry'. There can be little doubt that the legal boundary of freedom of association was a correlate of the legal boundary of labour law itself. That is because the immunities were being crafted to exclude criminal and civil wrongs that were being developed in the specific context of *labour* conflicts, specifically 'trade disputes'. The scope of the immunity mirrored the scope of the civil wrong.

B. After the Trade Disputes Act: A patchwork of trades and occupations

It was not until the 1970s that the familiar general concept of the personal work contract specified the boundary of individual statutory rights not to be dismissed or victimised for trade union reasons. For most of the 20th century, British labour law was based upon a labyrinthine web of indirect legal and administrative 'props' to voluntary collective bargaining. This involved a complex set of administrative practices, fair wages resolutions, compulsory arbitration, and wages councils.[22] Many of these measures were focused on trades rather than general protective measures for workers. The law identified specific groups of workers or trades that were especially vulnerable to contractual exploitation, and it provided tailored support for their collective bargaining practices.

For example, the Trade Boards Act 1909 had its origins in political disquiet about the 'sweated' trades, where wages were so low that they could not meet the basic subsistence needs of workers. Many of these trades involved homeworking.[23] The 1909 Act created the basic legal model for what would later become wages councils. It adopted a procedural approach to the fixing of minimum wage rates, with trade boards composed of equal numbers of

[21] [1901] AC 426.

[22] For a comprehensive survey, see Lord Wedderburn, *The Worker and the Law* (3rd ed, Penguin 1986) chapter 4.

[23] K.D. Ewing, 'Homeworking: A Framework for Reform' (1982) 11 Industrial Law Journal 94, 96–99.

representatives from both sides of industry and including some independent members. The trigger for setting up a Trade Board reflected the concern with eradicating sweating in specific trades. It was provided in s. 1 (2) 'that the rate of wages prevailing in any branch of the trade is exceptionally low, as compared with that in other employments, and that the other circumstances of the trade are such as to render the application of this Act to the trade expedient'. The legislation included four trades: bespoke tailoring, paper and cardboard box-making, chain making, and machine-made lace.[24] The scope was extended to include five more trades in 1913.[25] As Bayliss observed, the purpose of this legislation was 'the need to protect the weakest workers against sweating'.[26]

The Trade Boards Act 1918 pursued an approach focused on the absence of 'adequate machinery' for collective bargaining in a trade.[27] Towards the end of the Second World War, the Wages Councils Act 1945 consolidated a trades-based approach where either adequate machinery for collective bargaining did not exist or the collective parties applied to the Minister because collective bargaining was 'likely to cease to exist or be adequate for that purpose'.[28] Specific legislation for vulnerable groups exposed to the risk of serious exploitation, identified by sector or trade, was also introduced in the Catering Wages Act 1943[29] and the Agricultural Wages Act 1924.[30] A similar pattern could be seen in the road haulage sector.[31] A sectoral approach was also evident in relation to machinery to support or extend collective agreements. There were examples in coalmining[32] and port transportation.[33] Another important example was the Cotton Manufacturing Industry (Temporary Provisions) Act 1934, referred to by Kahn-Freund in his famous 1959 essay, 'Labour Law'.[34]

[24] Frederic J. Bayliss, *British Wages Councils* (Blackwell 1962) 9.
[25] Ibid. 11.
[26] Ibid. 15.
[27] Trade Boards Act 1918 s. 1 (2).
[28] Wages Councils Act 1945 s. 2(1).
[29] For a sophisticated contextual analysis of catering sectoral regulation and its specific regulatory challenges, see Einat Albin, 'Labour Law in a Service World' (2010) 73 Modern Law Review 959, 967–970.
[30] Douglas Brodie, *A History of British Labour Law 1867-1945* (Hart 2003) 188. As Brodie notes, the Agricultural Wages Act 1924 was conceived as a regulatory measure to enforce a minimum wage, since there seemed to be little prospect of collective bargaining being established in the agricultural sector. It had originated in the Corn Production Act 1917. The Agricultural Wages Act 1948 adopted the standard wages council pattern of equal numbers of representatives of employers and workers, and independent persons appointed by the Minister.
[31] Ian G. Sharp, *Industrial Conciliation and Arbitration in Great Britain* (Allen and Unwin 1950) 384–385, discussing the Road Traffic Act 1930, Road and Rail Traffic Act 1933, and Road Haulage Wages Act 1938.
[32] Coal Mines (Minimum Wage) Act 1912. As Brodie (n 30) notes, it is difficult to view this as an intervention to protect a vulnerable group because there was strong collective organisation in the industry: 69.
[33] Dock Workers (Regulation of Employment) Act 1946.
[34] Otto Kahn-Freund, 'Labour Law', in Otto Kahn-Freund, *Selected Writings* (Stevens & Sons 1978) 1, 18.

Exceptionally, the law would sometimes restrict trade union membership or activities in certain occupations and sectors. For example, the Police Act 1919 prohibited trade union membership for police, following a strike in London in 1918.[35] An alternative mechanism for collective representation was established under the legislation, the Police Federation, but strike action was prohibited. In the aftermath of the General Strike of 1926, the Trade Disputes and Trade Unions Act 1927 s. 5 imposed severe restrictions on the unionisation of established civil servants. This was to ensure the undivided loyalty of civil servants to the state in the event of a conflict between the government and trade unions. It prohibited membership of organisations 'of which the primary object is to influence or affect the remuneration and conditions of employment of its members', unless the organisation was confined to those employed under the Crown, did not include political objects, and was not associated 'directly or indirectly' with any political party. In effect, this meant that civil service unions could not affiliate with the TUC.[36] There were also restrictions on industrial action in other occupational contexts such as the armed forces.[37] In comparative terms, however, these public sector restrictions were far less extensive than in other jurisdictions such as Germany.

By the 1960s, the legal boundaries of freedom of association for trade unions were indisputably 'labour law' boundaries. Indeed, it is difficult to see how it could be otherwise. As Kahn-Freund's seminal essays of the 1950s demonstrated, 'labour law' itself was *defined* in terms of the institutions of collective bargaining. Labour law in its focal sense was nothing other than the law (and social practice) of freedom of association. The little case law that existed on 'scope' in respect of Trade Boards was concerned with the scope of the 'specified trade' rather than the modern focus on contract types. For example, in *Skinner v Jack Breach Ltd.*, the King's Bench Division concluded that workers mending drift nets, engaged by fishing boat owners and drift fishermen, were within the scope of the 'trade' of driftnet mending and so protected under the legislation.[38] According to Shearman J, 'a "specified trade" must be a recognized species of industrial work'. By the time the Donovan Commission reported in 1968, during a discussion of the redefinition of 'trade union', it

[35] Sandra Fredman and Gillian S. Morris, *The State as Employer: Labour Law in the Public Services* (Mansell 1989) 95–96.

[36] For discussion, see Dave Lyddon and Paul Smith, 'The 1906 Act: The First Fifty Years—Industrial Relations, Picketing, and the Employers' Challenge', in K.D. Ewing, *The Right to Strike: From the Trade Disputes Act 1906 to a Trade Union Freedom Bill 2006* (IER 2006) 149, 161–165. The 1927 Act was repealed by the Trade Disputes and Trade Union Act 1946, s. 1.

[37] For a comprehensive review of legal restrictions on strikes in essential services, see Gillian S. Morris, *Strikes in Essential Services* (Mansell 1986) chapter 2.

[38] *Skinner v Jack Breach Ltd.* [1927] 2 KB 220.

observed that 'The term "workmen" in the definition is not defined. In practice it is today treated as equivalent to "employee" and in any amendment of the definition it would be preferable to use this term'.[39] While presented as an aside on technical drafting, this pointed to a fundamental reorientation of scope around a general personal work category, the contract of employment.

The English law of freedom of association for workers was not univocal: it was differentiated. It was often differentiated by reference to considerations of power and economic inequality. Some categories of work, usually defined through trades, needed tailored support because the work conditions were unusually harsh and/or collective bargaining was weak, defective, or non-existent. This was reflected, for example, in the system of trade boards and wages councils. Some categories of work, usually defined through occupational exclusions, restricted aspects of freedom of association. This included restrictions on union membership for the police or industrial action for the armed forces. Some of these exclusions and restrictions could be rationalised through specific risks of *abuse* of power presented to others, such as vulnerable service users or the public.

C. From 'trades' and 'workmen' to the personal employment contract

The Industrial Relations Act 1971 (IRA) marked a decisive shift in the statutory law on freedom of association. The basic right was set out in Part II, 'Rights of Workers'. S. 5 provided that 'every worker shall, as between himself and his employer, have the following rights', which included the right to be (or not be) a member of a trade union; and the right to take part in the activities of a trade union at an appropriate time. The duties of employers were set out in s. 5(2) through 'unfair industrial practices', which prohibited employers (or any person acting on behalf of an employer) from 'preventing' or 'deterring' or to 'dismiss, penalise or otherwise discriminate' against a worker in the exercise of s. 5 rights. The recognition procedure for collective bargaining was based upon the 'bargaining unit', defined in s. 44 as 'those employees or descriptions of employees of an employer, or of two or more associated employers, in relation to whom collective bargaining . . . is, or could appropriately be, carried on by an organisation of workers'.

[39] Report of the Royal Commission on Trade Unions and Employers' Associations (1965–1968) (Cmnd. 3623) [763], known as the 'Donovan Commission' because the Chair was Lord Donovan.

During the debates on the IRA, the question arose as to why s. 5 did not extend universally to persons. On Tuesday, 4 May 1971, Lord Delacourt-Smith moved an amendment to substitute 'person' for 'worker'.[40] Otherwise, there was a danger that those in need of protection would be excluded. The rationale for 'worker' was brilliantly articulated by Lord Windlesham, then Minister of State in the Home Office:

> What I think lay under the noble Lord's probing Amendment—I regard it as a probing Amendment because he has not actually proposed that the word 'person' should be inserted in the Bill and that it would be appropriate wherever the word 'worker' occurs—is, why should the right to join a union be contained at all? Why should not everyone have the right to join a trade union? The noble Lord nods his head, so we are in agreement on that point. Everyone has a right to join a trade union . . . What we are doing in the Bill, and we now come to the crux of this clause, is to provide a statutory right to which specific remedies are attached in Clause 5(2), the next subsection, for the exercise of that right in certain specific situations. Nobody is going to interfere with the right of a private individual to join a union if he wishes to do so whether he is a professional man or a man in these special categories or otherwise; but it is in the employment relationship that this right needs to be protected, and in Clause 5(2) there are specific remedies which we shall be discussing later this evening . . . Those are specific protected rights, because it is in the employment situation where there is an employer and a worker that there is a need for safeguards, and those safeguards are contained in subsection (2) of this clause.[41]

Lord Windlesham's response is of fundamental importance. While every *person* has the liberty to join a trade union (subject to the union's rules and its liberty to associate), only a narrower class needed the *rights* in s. 5. This is because the relevant *rights* in s. 5 must be correlative to *duties*.[42] In this context, the employer is the duty-bearer because it wields economic power.[43] So, the employer can dismiss, victimise, penalise, refuse to employ, and so forth, and

[40] Column 161.

[41] Column 170.

[42] While there is no reference to the work of Wesley Hohfeld on fundamental legal concepts, and no suggestion that Lord Windlesham was familiar with Hohfeld (although Lord Windelsham did read Jurisprudence at Trinity College, Oxford), Lord Windlesham's account of rights and duties reflects Hohfeld's approach. The scholar who has (rightly) emphasised the importance of these juridical distinctions in freedom of association is Brian Langille. For further reflections on Hohfeld, see Alan Bogg and K.D. Ewing, 'A Muted Voice at Work? Collective Bargaining in the Supreme Court of Canada' (2012) Comparative Labor Law and Policy Journal 379.

[43] There may also be situations where non-employed individuals need *rights* against the union. For example, retired employees no longer need rights against employers, but they may need rights against the trade union itself in respect of certain benefits and entitlements.

this must be restricted by duties. This echoes the Hohfeldian dimension of the 'legislated rights' thesis that we examined in Chapter 1.

In this way, the relevant distinction is between those self-employed who have an employer (and so need legal protection) and those self-employed who do not (and so with a reduced need for protection). Lord Delacourt-Smith's amendment in favour of 'persons' was incomplete because it failed to identify the party owing the relevant legal duties. Even if the right-holder in s. 5 was a 'person', the legislator would still need to identify the relevant duty-bearer who would 'dismiss, penalise, or otherwise discriminate'. The IRA was short-lived, but its shift to personal scope based on contract was enduring. The IRA was repealed by the Trade Union and Labour Relations Act 1974, but the IRA statutory definition of worker was retained for the 'social contract' legislation.[44] The Employment Protection Act 1975 introduced statutory protections from 'action short of dismissal' for trade union membership and activities for employees.[45] By contrast, the 'collective' provisions on union recognition were concerned with collective bargaining on behalf of workers.[46]

In UK law, the 'worker' category has now been adopted for most statutory freedom of association rights.[47] A similar pattern can be seen in other jurisdictions such as the US, Canada, and Australia.[48] For example, federal labour protections for collective bargaining in the US are allocated to 'employees'. This was to address the inequality of bargaining power between employers and employees.[49] There are also statutory exclusions, such as for agricultural labourers and supervisors. In Canada, provincial labour codes often protect the organisational and collective bargaining rights of employees or dependent contractors. This is supplemented by a patchwork of exclusions for supervisors and managers, agricultural workers, domestic workers, and the police.[50]

[44] Trade Union and Labour Relations Act 1974 s. 30(1).

[45] Employment Protection Act 1975 (EPA) s. 53

[46] See, e.g., EPA ss. 12(5)(b) and 14(1).

[47] There is a curious exception for refusal of employment for trade union membership, Trade Union and Labour Relations (Consolidation) Act 1992 (TULRCA) s. 137, which is still an 'employee' right.

[48] The distinction between employees and independent contractors in respect of collective bargaining is also a feature of Australian labour law: see Shae McCrystal, 'Collective Bargaining by Self-Employed Workers in Australia and the Concept of "Public Benefit"' (2021) 42 Comparative Labor Law and Policy Journal 253.

[49] For the historical context to the US legislation, see Karl E. Klare, 'Judicial Deradicalization of the Wagner Act and the Origins of Modern Legal Consciousness 1937-1941' (1978) 62 Minnesota Law Review 265, 281–284.

[50] See David J. Doorey, *The Law of Work* (3rd ed, Emond 2024) 59–62. The Canadian legal terrain is also set out in Cynthia J. Cranford and others, *Self-Employed Workers Organize: Law, Policy, and Unions* (McGill UP 2005) 14–21. This latter work is concerned specifically with the legal obstacles experienced by the self-employed in exercising freedom of association.

In the UK and Canada, constitutional litigation has been used to expand the existing coverage of statutory protections. This has sometimes been viewed as a clash between constitutional rights (for everyone) and labour law rights (presumptively for workers or employees). Let us call this the problem of the autonomy of labour law. It goes to the very root of the most fundamental matter of all: how to identify the right-holder. As Lord Windlesham perceived, this is not severable from the identity of the duty-bearer. We are interested in identifying juridical relations, not persons. It is very misleading to ask the question 'who is an employee/worker?' because that is only ever the half of it. While the constitutional techniques are different in each legal system, they are addressed to the same underlying basic issue: equality before the law. Is the law's differentiation between groups and persons in access to the right amenable to principled justification?

III. Freedom of Association and 'Personal Scope' under the ECHR

A. 'Everyone' or 'employment relationship'?

Let us begin with the ECHR. Under Article 11(1), 'everyone' has the right to freedom of association, including 'the right to form and join trade unions for the protection of his interests'. Article 11(2) provides that the Article 'shall not prevent the imposition of lawful restrictions on the exercise of these rights by members of the armed forces, of the police or of the administration of the State'. The ECtHR has adopted a strict approach to these occupational exclusions. It has construed the scope of 'administration of the state' narrowly, so that it does not include municipal civil servants.[51] Any restrictions must *regulate* the exercise of the right rather than impairing its very essence. This means that an absolute ban on associations is unlikely to be compatible with Article 11.[52] For example, a blanket ban on trade unions for military personnel impaired the essence of the right.[53] This text implies that there are very broad entitlements to trade union rights ('everyone'), and the occupational restrictions under Article 11(2) do not go to the issue of entitlement. The right is yours, but its exercise may be subject to regulation and restriction in

[51] *Demir and Baykara v Turkey* [2009] 48 EHRR 54 [97].

[52] *Tumer Haber Sen and Cinar v Turkey* [2006] ECHR 157 [36] and [40].

[53] *Matelly v France* App No. 10609/10, 10 February 2014 [75]. For discussion of trade union rights and the armed forces, see Maurizio Falsone, 'Union Freedoms in the Armed Forces: Still a Taboo?' (2022) 51 Industrial Law Journal 375.

accordance with proportionality. In fact, the question of personal scope does not seem to arise at all. Personal scope implies a division *within* the universal category of persons. Yet if these are human rights for 'everyone', the personal scope enquiry is otiose.

There are some Article 11 cases that could support this wide reading of personal scope.[54] However, the ECtHR has adopted a narrower 'labour law' framing of trade union rights in two of its leading Grand Chamber decisions. Let us begin with *Demir and Baykara v Turkey*. In *Demir*, the Grand Chamber was not concerned with the personal scope of trade union rights. However, it did examine the specific occupational position of civil servants, given that the impugned collective agreement in this case concerned Turkish civil servants. The Court used what has been memorably described as the 'integrated' approach to legal reasoning.[55] This 'integrated' approach supported a 'dynamic and evolutive approach' to interpretation,[56] with the Court using the instruments and decisions of the ILO to justify the recognition of the right to collective bargaining.

In a crucial paragraph, the Grand Chamber also stated that '*having regard to the developments in labour law*, both international and national, and to the practice of Contracting States in such matters, the right to bargain collectively with the employer has, in principle, become one of the essential elements . . . set forth in Article 11 of the Convention'.[57] While the 'integrated' approach has often been praised for its expansive effects on trade union protections, it is important here to notice its restrictive effects in *Demir*. The fact that the content of the Article 11 right was being shaped by 'developments in labour law' entailed the integration of the labour law approach into the content of the human right. For example, workers 'should be able to engage in collective bargaining in respect of their *conditions of employment, including wages*'.[58] Under Article 11, the union must have the freedom 'to protect the *occupational interests* of trade-union members' and it must be free 'to seek to persuade *the employer* to listen to what it had to say on behalf of its members'.[59] In *Demir*, the general issue of personal scope did not arise directly because the civil servants were clearly in some kind of employment relationship. Yet the nature of the

[54] For a discussion of the divergences in the case law, see Alan Bogg, 'Economic Coordination as Freedom of Association', in Sanjukta Paul and others (eds), *The Cambridge Handbook of Labor in Competition Law* (Cambridge UP 2022) 35–43.
[55] Virginia Mantouvalou, 'Labour Rights in the European Convention on Human Rights: An Intellectual Justification for an Integrated Approach to Interpretation' (2013) 13 Human Rights Law Review 529.
[56] *Demir* (n 51) [153].
[57] Ibid. [154] (emphasis added).
[58] Ibid. [147] (emphasis added).
[59] Ibid. [140] and [143] (emphasis added).

right to collective bargaining, its bilateral dependence on an employer, and its concern with wages and other terms and conditions of employment pointed towards some kind of employment relationship as a threshold. Otherwise, without an 'employer' and without 'wages' to negotiate collectively, it is difficult to see how such a right would satisfy the basic requirements of juridical intelligibility. This echoed the perceptive observations of Lord Windlesham in the parliamentary debates on IRA. In this way, *Demir* affirmed the 'autonomy' of labour law under the influence of 'integrated' interpretation.

The issue of personal scope was considered directly by the Grand Chamber in *Sindicatul 'Pastoral Cel Bun' v Romania*.[60] It concerned Romanian orthodox clergy and their right to form a trade union under domestic law. There is no doubt that the spiritual purpose of the clergy rendered their employment distinctive compared with other employees. However, the Court observed that 'the only question arising here is whether such duties, notwithstanding any special features they may entail, amounted to an employment relationship rendering applicable the right to form a trade union within the meaning of Article 11'.[61] In identifying and applying the relevant criteria of 'employment relationship', the Grand Chamber applied the indicative factors in ILO Recommendation No. 198 (2006) concerning the employment relationship. In line with this ILO Recommendation, the Court examined the facts of the relationship between the clergy and the Church, focusing on the performance of work and remuneration. The Grand Chamber concluded that the special features of religious employment were not sufficient to take it outside the scope of an employment relationship, effectively treating the presence of pro-indicators as giving rise to a presumption of employment relationship.[62] Since the clergy performed the work 'in the context of an employment relationship',[63] they were within the scope of Article 11 trade union rights.

Under Article 11, trade union freedoms are a special aspect of general freedom of association. The existence of this general freedom provides a safety net for those not in an employment relationship. In *Manole and 'Romanian Farmers Direct' v Romania*, self-employed farmers were unable to register their association as a trade union under Romanian law because they were not employees.[64] According to the Court, this refusal to register a

[60] (2014) 58 EHRR 10.
[61] Ibid. [141].
[62] This is envisaged by the Recommendation Part II 11(b).
[63] *Pastoral Cel Bun* (n 60) [148]. The Court's use of the phrase 'in the context of' an employment relationship is unlikely to suggest that the personal scope of trade union rights under Article 11 is *wider* than 'employment relationship', not least because that same phrase is in the ILO instrument itself: see Part I (1).
[64] Application no. 46551/06, 16 June 2015.

'trade union-type association' was an interference.[65] However, since the self-employed farmers were not treated more disadvantageously than other self-employed, and since they were able to set up a trade association to pursue their objectives, this refusal did not exceed the state's margin of appreciation. Since the general liberty to associate (for 'everyone') was not restricted for the self-employed farmers, their exclusion from the specific nexus of trade union rights was not a violation. *Manole* demonstrates that the general associative *liberty* provides some protection for the self-employed. *Everyone* should be free to form and join associations where those associations do not infringe the general law. In this sense, liberties are boundaryless, and personal scope should not matter. On the specific facts in *Manole*, the purpose of the association was to encourage a transition to the market-based organisation of agriculture, facilitated through legal information, political lobbying, accountancy advice, and legal assistance.[66] This was not collective bargaining in the sense envisaged in *Demir*. In other circumstances, however, the self-employed may have a stronger need for collective bargaining over employment conditions. The exclusion from trade union rights (and the correlative duties) would then be a more significant disadvantage, requiring a different analysis to *Manole*. The general liberty to associate would not be sufficient. Overall, Article 11's protection of trade union rights has been strongly influenced by labour law categories of personal scope.[67]

B. Article 11 and sectoral freedom of association

Agricultural workers experience high levels of precariousness and social and economic disadvantages, and this is often compounded by difficulties in accessing trade union representation.[68] The Agricultural Wages Board (AWB) provided a special protective system for nearly a century. Originating in the Corn Protection Act 1917, the AWB provided a substitute for voluntary collective bargaining through a wage-setting institution of employer and worker representatives and independent members. The Board set minimum wages and conditions in the agricultural industry. Following a short consultation, the

[65] Ibid. [62].
[66] Ibid. [8].
[67] Alan Bogg and Michael Ford, 'Employment Status and Trade Union Rights: Applying Occam's Razor' (2022) 50 Industrial Law Journal 717.
[68] See, e.g., Eric Tucker, 'Farm Worker Exceptionalism: Past, Present, and the Post-*Fraser* Future', in Faraday and others (eds), *Constitutional Labour Rights in Canada: Farm Workers and the Fraser Case* (Irwin UTP 2012) 30.

AWB was abolished under s. 72(1) of the Enterprise and Regulatory Reform Act 2013. After 2013, agricultural workers were able to access the general statutory mechanism regulating recognition and collective bargaining. However, this is subject to a 21-worker threshold, and the number of UK agricultural employers above this threshold 'was almost zero'.[69] This meant that collective bargaining in practice depended entirely on voluntary practices. The repeal of the AWB removed the only significant legal prop to voluntary collective bargaining practices, and it probably entailed the practical disappearance of collective bargaining in the agricultural sector.

This repeal was challenged by Unite the Union in the ECtHR. According to the applicants, the state breached a positive obligation to promote the effective realisation of the right to collective bargaining. The AWB's abolition would lead to the disappearance of collective bargaining 'since it was impractical for unions to gain recognition from so many small employers'.[70] The ECtHR rejected the union's claim as inadmissible.[71] It was relevant to the Court's assessment that 'the applicant *has not been prevented* from acting as a trade union to protect the general occupational interests of its members'.[72] The state had a wide margin of appreciation in positive obligation cases such as this. According to the Court, the Government had 'relevant and sufficient reasons' for abolishing the AWB,[73] and there could not be said to be a positive obligation to maintain special measures for collective bargaining in the agricultural sector. In the case of *Manole*, already considered, the ECtHR concluded that it was sufficient under Article 11 if self-employed agricultural workers were not *prevented* from forming and acting through a trade association. Accordingly, there was no positive Article 11 obligation to even register their association as a trade union.

After *Unite* and *Manole*, it is difficult to see what scope there is for an Article 11 positive obligation to promote collective bargaining through special sectoral regimes. *Unite* was an extreme case, given the data on employer size in the UK agricultural industry. The history of English freedom of association reveals a long tradition of sectorally segmented freedom of association. There are strong arguments for such a differentiated approach when workers experience persistent obstacles and disadvantages that require targeted protections. Given the special contribution of freedom of association to empowering

[69] *Unite the Union v United Kingdom* App. No 65397/13, 3 May 2016 [29].
[70] Ibid. [49].
[71] The judgment is criticised in Kalina Arabadjieva, 'Another Disappointment in Strasbourg: Unite the Union v United Kingdom' (2017) 46 Industrial Law Journal 289.
[72] *Unite* (n 69) [57] (emphasis added).
[73] Ibid. [66].

the disadvantaged, there is no equality objection to providing special protections to disadvantaged sectors and occupations. This is a situation where unequal treatment is aimed at substantive equality. And it is difficult to imagine a stronger set of facts for a positive obligation claim than *Unite* itself. As the English legal history demonstrates, the implementation of targeted sectoral measures is a special responsibility of legislatures and governments. Constitutional courts are not well placed to do this because it requires legislation and ongoing administrative support to ensure such schemes (like wages councils) are practical and effective. However, courts have an important subsidiary role either in preventing deregulation (at issue in *Unite*) or directing legislatures to consider positive intervention. After *Manole* and *Unite*, the scope for Article 11 positive obligations to improve the associational rights of the most disadvantaged workers has been severely curtailed.

IV. Freedom of Association and 'Personal Scope' under UK Law

The basic legal category for most trade union rights under UK law is the 'worker'.[74] In this respect, it is like most other statutory employment rights in UK law. There is nothing special about the group of statutory employment rights commonly described as freedom of association rights. 'Worker' is based upon a statutory definition, and its general legislative purpose is to be broader and more inclusive than the common law concept of employee.[75] This statutory definition requires (1) a contract whereby the worker undertakes to do or perform work for the other party, (2) the worker must undertake to do 'any' of the work personally, and (3) the status of the other party to the contract must not be as a 'professional client' of his.[76] This includes some self-employed persons in circumstances where the other party to the contract is an employer, as recognised by Lord Windlesham in the debates on the legal definition during the passage of IRA 1971.

The constitutionalisation of employment status in freedom of association in the UK has deployed two main legal techniques. The first technique

[74] There is a specific statutory definition set out in s. 296 TULRCA.

[75] See *Byrne Bros v Baird* [2002] ICR 667, EAT.

[76] There is a different definition of worker in the 'individual' consolidation statute, ERA1996, where the boundary is defined as a 'client or customer' of a 'profession or business undertaking': ERA 1996 s. 230(3)(b). For discussion of these textual differences, which are unlikely to be of practical significance, see discussion in Alan Bogg, 'Square Pegs in Round Holes? Collective Bargaining and the Self-Employed' (2021) 42 Comparative Labor Law and Policy Journal 409, 412–416. There is a wider statutory definition of worker in respect of secondary industrial action and the trade dispute immunity: see s. 224(6) and s. 224(5) TULRCA.

is the purposive application of the general legal definition of worker so that its legal boundary is more inclusive. This purposive jurisprudence is not specific to freedom of association rights, but it would include those rights. As a legal technique, it is 'internal' to labour law and entirely consistent with the autonomy of labour law.

The second technique is through the mechanisms in the Human Rights Act 1998 (HRA), adjusting the boundary of the worker category through interpretation so that it is aligned with the Article 11 concept of an 'employment relationship'. This has been most effective where there are occupational gaps or express statutory exclusions from the general worker category. While this is potentially more radical than 'ordinary' purposive interpretation, it is still properly described as consistent with the autonomy of labour law because the Article 11 'employment relationship' concept is itself a labour law category. It is very far from the 'rights for everyone' approach.

A. *Uber* and purposive interpretation

Let us begin with purposive interpretation. The leading case is now *Uber BV and others v Aslam and others.*[77] This did not involve trade union rights specifically, but Lord Leggatt proposed a 'purposive' and 'realistic' approach to worker status based upon the general legislative purpose of protecting vulnerable workers from unfair treatment.[78] The features of subordination, economic dependence, and unequal bargaining power were central to this statutory purpose. This would certainly encompass trade union rights, in addition to whistleblowing, unfair dismissal, and wages and working time protections. Following *Uber*, the task of the court is to scrutinise the real working practices and to apply the legal tests to ensure the inclusion of those work arrangements that Parliament intended to protect. While this 'purposive and realistic' enquiry is a 'labour law' development, the divergence from a human rights approach should not be over-emphasised. Many of these statutory employment rights, including trade union rights, are also human rights.[79] Lord Leggatt treats statutory employment rights as a genus with a common normative basis, protecting workers from exploitation in a subordinate, dependent, and unequal contractual relationship.

[77] [2021] UKSC 5.
[78] Ibid. [71].
[79] That is certainly true of statutory whistleblowing protections, which are human rights protections under Article 10 protecting freedom of expression.

This general concern with collective empowerment, and protecting workers from abuse of power, is central to the justification for freedom of association. In many cases involving the precarious self-employed seeking trade union protections under the legislation, the *Uber* approach is now likely to lead to their inclusion within the general worker category. In the much-lamented case of *O'Kelly v Trusthouse Forte Plc*, casuals working in hospitality events at a luxury Park Lane hotel alleged they had been dismissed for trade union reasons.[80] The Court of Appeal upheld the tribunal's findings that they were not employees because of the casual nature of the employment arrangements and the absence of 'mutuality of obligation'. Since they were independent contractors, the casual waiters were not protected from trade union victimisation. *O'Kelly* has been described as a 'landmark of legalism' by one leading scholar, since the focus was on the technicalities of contractual mutuality and the scope for appeals on points of law.[81] This technical approach obstructed the purposive dimension of the enquiry into employment status. It is very likely that *O'Kelly* would be decided differently today at first instance, applying *Uber*.[82]

B. Occupational exclusions: Parks police and foster carers

If the first technique falls short, the second technique is the use of the HRA to align the personal scope of statutory rights with an Article 11/ILO 'employment relationship'. Article 11 has also been used to scrutinise certain occupational exclusions from statutory rights. Where there is a misalignment in personal scope, the court will scrutinise the interference by reference to proportionality. This is an equality enquiry because the court considers if the difference in treatment is justified by relevant reasons.

Wandsworth London Borough Council v Vining is an occupational exclusion case. The parks police were excluded from collective redundancy consultation legislation because they were employed in the 'police service'.[83] This was subject to a statutory exclusion. The Court of Appeal concluded that this exclusion violated the Article 11 right to collective bargaining. Collective consultation on redundancies was within the broad scope of negotiations over

[80] *O' Kelly v Trusthouse Forte* Plc [1984] QB 90, CA.
[81] A.C.L. Davies, 'O' Kelly v Trusthouse Forte PLC: A Landmark of Legalism', in Jeremias Adams-Prassl and others (eds), *Landmark Cases in Labour Law* (Hart 2022) chapter 8.
[82] This involved a dismissal claim, which is still restricted to employees. The *Uber* purposive approach applies here too because it is based in the protective statutory right being claimed. This would include statutory employment rights restricted to employees.
[83] [2017] EWCA Civ 1092, [2018] ICR 499. See Philippa Collins, *Putting Human Rights to Work: Labour Law, the ECHR, and the Employment Relation* (OUP 2022) 120–122.

occupational matters. The state was under a positive obligation to ensure the effective enjoyment of this right.[84] Where the state had implemented a legislative scheme, as here, it needed to strike a fair balance between competing interests.[85] There was no universal entitlement of access to the statutory procedure. Indeed, this is scarcely coherent because there needs to be a party to consult *with* (i.e., an employer of some description). However, specific occupational exclusions of occupational groups still needed to be justified. Since no justification had been provided for the exclusion of parks police in this case, the Court of Appeal had little trouble in concluding that the parks police ought to be included within the legislation. It was 'read down' using the HRA s. 3 interpretative duty since the inclusion of the parks police did not contradict a fundamental feature of the legislation. In *Vining*, the parks police had no alternative mechanisms of legal protection. This was a simple case of legislative oversight. Even given the wide margin of appreciation for the government, it was an easy case. In other cases where there has been explicit democratic consideration and a rational basis for the exclusion, the justification enquiry might be more finely balanced.

In *Vining*, the Court did not consider the definitional scope of 'employment relationship' under Article 11 because it was clear that the parks police were in some kind of employment relationship. This was not the case in *National Union of Professional Foster Carers v Certification Officer (NUPFC)*, which considered the right of foster carers to form a trade union.[86] There was binding authority holding that foster carers did not provide work under a contract. Without the missing ingredient of a contract, they could not be workers under the statutory definition. This meant that the foster carers' trade union could not be 'listed', since a trade union is defined under s. 1 TULRCA as an organisation 'which consists wholly or mainly of workers'. The foster carers argued that, despite the absence of a contract, they were in an 'employment relationship' under Article 11 by reference to the criteria in the relevant ILO Recommendation. This would then form the basis of a Convention-compliant interpretation of the statute.

The Court of Appeal agreed with this analysis. The extensive supervision and disciplinary control of foster carers, and the remuneration of that work, were indicative factors pointing in favour of an 'employment relationship'. 'Contract' (or its absence) was not a conclusive factor in this holistic

[84] Ibid. [64].
[85] Ibid.
[86] [2020] ICR 607. The authority on the absence of a contract of foster carers is *W v Essex County Council* [2001] 2 AC 592.

assessment. The exclusion of foster carers from the right to form a trade union could not be justified under Article 11(2) since there was nothing in their occupational role that militated against them forming a trade union. Indeed, it was permissible for them to *join* other trade unions that were prepared to represent them. The Court emphasised that other Article 11 rights, such as the right to strike, would need to be considered separately.[87] The assessment of justification is likely to vary across the spectrum of trade union rights, given the range of impacts on those in foster care, especially in some forms of collective industrial action. Power imbalances are relevant both in justifying access to freedom of association through trade unions *and* in justifying its legitimate restriction given impacts on vulnerable service users.

C. Delivery riders in the gig economy

In *Independent Workers Union of Great Britain v Central Arbitration Committee and anoth*er, Deliveroo riders did not satisfy the 'personal work' element of the worker definition.[88] This was because of a wide substitution clause in their contracts, which allowed them to delegate the work to others. There were very few contractual restrictions on this power of delegation in terms of timing (the work could be delegated even once the rider had accepted a slot on the App), frequency of delegation, or even the identity of the substitute worker. Since this contractual power to delegate work to a substitute was not a sham, the Central Arbitration Committee concluded that they were not workers. The union was therefore unable to apply for statutory recognition under Schedule A1 and to seek collective bargaining on their behalf. The Supreme Court rejected the Article 11 challenge because it treated the personal work requirement as *essential* to the existence of an employment relationship. The Supreme Court did not regard the claimant's universal scope argument as persuasive:

> The category of persons who benefit from the right to form and join a trade union under article 11 is a smaller sub-class of those—described as 'everyone' in the opening of article 11(1) —who enjoy the right . . . to freedom of association . . . Although Lord Hendy initially argued on this appeal, as he had argued in the courts below, that the right to form and join a trade union was enjoyed by everyone, he

[87] Ibid. [131].
[88] [2023] UKSC 43.

> did not pursue this submission... This concession was, in our view, correctly made and compelled by the Strasbourg authorities considered above. We will refer to the class of people on whom article 11 trade union rights are conferred as 'article 11 workers'.[89]

While this analysis is broadly correct—it is embedded in the relational logic of rights and duties—the Supreme Court then adopted an unduly narrow interpretation of the ILO Recommendation. According to the Supreme Court judgment, the substitution clause was 'totally inconsistent with the existence of an obligation to provide personal service which is essential to the existence of an employment relationship within article 11'.[90] This erroneous analysis is contradicted by the structure of the ILO Recommendation, which states that there should be a 'broad range of means for determining the existence of an employment relationship'.[91] These factors are described as indicators. Indicative factors are not conclusive factors. For example, 'contract' was treated as an indicative rather than a conclusive factor in *NUPFC*. Its absence was counterbalanced by other factors pointing towards subordination and dependence. The Recommendation also provides for a presumption of employment relationship where there are any pro-indicators, as there were in this case.[92] The effect of the presumption was not considered by the Supreme Court in *Deliveroo*.

The *Deliveroo* judgment reveals the inherent limitations of the open-textured criteria in the ILO instrument. The national courts interpret and apply Convention rights constrained by the 'mirror' principle: it is not legitimate for national courts to exceed the ECtHR's interpretation of Convention rights.[93] The national court must stay aligned with them. In cases involving speculative consideration of how open-textured criteria *might* apply in novel fact situations, the UK courts may feel that their constitutional legitimacy is strained. This could explain the outcome in *Deliveroo*. Even on this charitable view, however, it is very difficult to reconcile its reasoning either with the language of the instrument itself or *NUPFC*.

[89] Ibid. [61].
[90] Ibid. [69].
[91] 11 (a).
[92] 11 (b).
[93] *R (on the application of Elan-Cane) v Secretary of State for the Home Department* [2021] UKSC 56, [87]. See further Lord Sales, 'The Developing Jurisprudence of the Supreme Court on Convention Rights', Scottish Public Law Group Conference, 5 June 2023. See also A.C.L. Davies, 'Article 11 in the Mirror: The Importance of Section 2 Human Rights Act 1998 in Understanding the Court's Approach to Article 11 of the European Convention on Human Rights' (2025) Industrial Law Journal advanced access https://doi.org/10.1093/indlaw/dwaf014.

There are fewer strains on constitutional legitimacy when the court is dealing with a narrow occupational exclusion, as in *Vining* or *NUPFC*. The issues raised by justification are also more tractable where the occupational parameters are closely defined. By contrast, where the relevant occupational group is more diffuse (as in *Deliveroo*), the social and economic consequences of a s. 3 interpretation are more speculative. These consequentialist concerns may lead courts to proceed more cautiously. It is also difficult to pin down the *Deliveroo* category with precision: food transportation? delivery riders? 'Gig workers'? Cases like *Vining* and *NUPFC* were relatively easy cases in that there was no rational justification for the exclusion. These were straightforward examples of legislative oversight. Where there has been proper democratic consideration and a conscientious attempt at rational justification, the outcome will depend upon the relevant standard of review. In *Gilham v Ministry of Justice*, which involved the exclusion of judicial office-holders from whistleblowing protections, Lady Hale did not regard the highly deferential standard of 'manifestly without reasonable foundation' approach as appropriate to the proportionality enquiry.[94] More exacting judicial scrutiny may be warranted in cases involving the distribution of access to fundamental rights (as compared with the resource distribution of welfare benefits).[95] On the other hand, it has been emphasised by the Strasbourg jurisprudence that there is often a wide margin of appreciation in Article 11 cases because implementation depends upon difficult judgements of social and economic policy. Deciding on the scope of statutory employment rights involves sensitive and controversial distributive judgements involving employers, those in the labour market, and unemployed people seeking access to the labour market.

The standard of review in *Gilham*-type cases will inevitably be shaped by background constitutional values such as the separation of powers and respect for parliamentary democracy.[96] Legislative distinctions will often reflect evaluation of complex labour market data which courts are not well-equipped to assess. This would certainly be true of democratic decisions not to extend freedom of association rights to everyone in the labour market but to restrict them to a narrower class of workers. Unless an employment status distinction is closely linked to a suspect ground, such as race or sex, constitutional arguments support a restrained role for judicial review where there is a rational basis for the legislative categorisation. Stricter review could apply where

[94] [2019] UKSC 44, [34].
[95] See Atkinson (n 8) 1194.
[96] See, e.g., *R (on the application of SC) v Secretary of State for Work and Pensions* [2022] AC 223.

the work in an excluded occupation tends to be performed predominantly by workers with a protected characteristic. There seems to be little constitutional warrant to insist that opting for a selective category (such as worker) in the first place requires justification because it deviates from a presumptively legitimate baseline of universal entitlement. The judges are already at sea on Neurath's boat.

Path dependence means that 'worker' is likely to persist as the fundamental organising category for trade union rights in British labour law. The courts have made some modest adjustments at the margins using Article 11 'employment relationship' to adjust the worker category in national law. They have also addressed discrete occupational gaps, as in *Vining*. More generally, purposive interpretation has extended the boundary of the worker so that it operates inclusively. Beyond this, it is unlikely that the courts will upend the labour law foundations of trade union rights through constitutional review. Instead, we are likely to see incremental adjustments to the worker paradigm using human rights arguments. That judicial caution is constitutionally fitting.

V. Freedom of Association and Personal Scope in Canada

Freedom of association for workers and trade unions in Canada is implemented primarily through statutory regimes in the provinces. As in the UK, these are usually based upon some kind of personal employment contract. In this respect, 'freedom of association' statutes in labour law are like any other kind of legislated employment right. Much of this collective bargaining legislation is also subject to specific occupational exclusions. As we have seen, there is a familiar pattern of inclusions and exclusions in labour law systems across the world. In this section, we will consider three examples: agricultural workers, managers, and the Royal Canadian Mounted Police (RCMP). For example, s. 3 of the Ontario Labour Relations Act (LRA) excludes domestic workers employed in private homes; persons employed in agriculture, hunting, or trapping; members of the police force; and provincial judges. In some provincial jurisdictions, there is a statutory exclusion of managers as in s. 1(1) of the Quebec Labour Code, which excludes from the scope of 'employee' any 'manager, superintendent, foreman or representative of the employer in his relations with his employees'. This exclusion of managerial employees is a particular feature of the North American model of adversarial collective bargaining. The RCMP were excluded from collective bargaining under s. 2 of the Public Service Labour Relations Act 2003 and covered by a bespoke staff representative regime.

Under s. 2(d) of the Charter, 'everyone' is guaranteed 'freedom of association' as a 'fundamental freedom'. This is subject to the general limitation clause in s. 1: 'such reasonable limits prescribed by law as can be demonstrably justified in a free and democratic society'. Unlike Article 11 ECHR, there is no explicit reference to 'trade unions' (or any other specific types of association) in s. 2(d). The Charter 'exclusion' cases have also considered arguments under s. 15(1): 'Every individual is equal before and under the law and has the right to equal protection and equal benefit of the law without discrimination and, in particular, without discrimination because of race, national or ethnic origin, colour, religion, sex, age or mental or physical disability.' While s. 15 arguments have a natural affinity with these exclusion cases, they are currently marginal to the SCC's approach. This marginalisation has been criticised strongly by Brian Langille for many years.[97]

There are some important differences between Article 11 and s. 2(d). The most basic difference is that, unlike Article 11, there is no 'employment relationship' requirement as a formal gateway to constitutional protection of s. 2(d) freedom of association. This is because the Charter freedom is a *general* constitutional freedom for *'everyone'*. However, it is important not to overemphasise the 'autonomy' of this general constitutional freedom. As emphasised by McLachlin CJ and LeBel JJ, the jurisprudential content of s. 2(d) has 'developed mainly with respect to labour relations'.[98] Indeed, some scholars have argued that, in effect, these s. 2(d) judgments have been 'constitutionalising' the labour relations statutes by integrating core statutory concepts into the constitutional jurisprudence.[99] In most of the cases to be considered, there is little doubt that these occupational groups are employees or workers. The exclusion results from a legislative choice to remove these workers from the general statutes that would otherwise apply. The constitutional focus is therefore more circumscribed in that they do not involve challenges to the baseline of employee or worker for trade union rights. Instead, the courts focus on the justification for the interference with s. 2(d) rights by considering the exclusion of groups from general legislative coverage.

[97] See, e.g., Brian Langille, 'The Freedom of Association Mess: How We Got into It and How We Can Get out of It' (2009) 54 McGill Law Journal 177.

[98] *Mounted Police Association of Ontario v Canada (Attorney General)* [2015] 1 SCR 3 (*M.P.A.O.*) [30].

[99] See, e.g., Benjamin Oliphant, 'The Nature of the Fundamental Freedoms and the Sui Generis Right to Collective Bargaining: The Case of Vulnerable and Precarious Workers' (2019) 21 Canadian Labour and Employment Law Journal 319; Brian Langille, 'Why are Canadian Judges Drafting Labour Codes—And Constitutionalizing the Wagner Act Model?' (2009–10) 15 Canadian Labour and Employment Law Journal 101.

A. The agricultural worker exclusion and *Dunmore*

In *Dunmore*, the exclusion of agricultural workers from the freedom of association provisions of the LRA was challenged.[100] For a short period, associative rights had been extended to agricultural workers in the Agricultural Labour Relations Act 1994, but this was repealed by s. 80 of the Labour Relations and Employment Statute Law Amendment Act 1995. It restored the long-standing statutory exclusion of Ontarian agricultural workers from the LRA. This exclusion was challenged by agricultural workers under s. 2(d) and s. 15 of the Charter. By a majority, the SCC concluded that the exclusion was unconstitutional. Bastarache J gave the lead judgment on behalf of six Justices. L'Heureux-Dube gave a separate judgment concurring in the result. At a minimum, it was necessary to introduce statutory rights that protected agricultural workers from interference, coercion, and discrimination in the exercise of their basic associational freedoms. This was, in essence, a right to organise. The constitutional remedy was to strike down the exclusion clause but suspend the invalidity for 18 months. This allowed democratic scope for the legislature to consider its legislative response, which might involve a tailored regime of trade union rights rather than full access to the LRA.

Bastarache J considered the distinction between negative and positive obligations under the Charter. In circumstances where the threat to Charter freedoms came from private parties, as in *Dunmore*, mere exclusion from a statutory scheme was not sufficient to engage s. 2(d). There was no free-standing constitutional right to inclusion in a statutory scheme.[101] Something more than mere exclusion was required to implicate the government in a private party's interference with a Charter freedom. Labour statutes 'instantiate' the right to organise because those in employment are exposed to tangible risks of retaliation by economically powerful actors: employers.[102] The suspect nature of exclusions is 'not simply to the extent that it discriminates against an unprotected class, but to the extent it substantially orchestrates, encourages or sustains the violation of fundamental freedoms'.[103] This was captured in Harry Arthurs' quotation, cited by Bastarache J, that without statutory protections from union discrimination, the freedom to organise amounts 'to no more than the freedom to suffer serious adverse legal and economic consequences'.[104]

[100] *Dunmore v Ontario (Attorney General)* [2001] 3 SCR 1016 (*Dunmore*).
[101] Ibid. 1046.
[102] Ibid. 1056.
[103] Ibid. 1049.
[104] Harry W. Arthurs and others, *Labour Law and Industrial Relations in Canada* (4th ed, Kluwer 1993) paragraph 431, cited ibid. 1045.

In this way, the application of the abstract s. 2(d) freedom was contextually sensitive to the specific labour context of the claims. In particular, it was sensitive to the dynamics of social and economic power in that labour relations context.

Bastarache J adopted a three-step framework: (1) are the claims grounded in a Charter freedom rather than demanding inclusion within a particular statutory regime? (2) did the exclusion have the purpose or effect of substantially interfering with the Charter freedom? (iii) is there a causal link between the exclusion and the substantial interference, such as to satisfy the constitutional threshold of state action? Given the especially vulnerable position of agricultural workers to employer reprisals, the exclusion from statutory protection substantially impaired their freedom to organise. This could not be justified as a minimal impairment under s. 1. Since the claimants succeeded under s. 2(d), Bastarache J did not consider the alternative s. 15 equality argument.

The concurring judgment of L'Heureux-Dube was more strongly focused on the structural vulnerabilities of agricultural workers. In considering the occupational exclusions in the LRA, she contrasted the 'legal and social recognition and respect' of the police force and provincial judges, with the social, legal, and economic disadvantages of agricultural workers.[105] She regarded the purpose of the statutory exclusion as unconstitutional because the point of it was to leave agricultural workers unprotected from employer interference in their organisational activities.[106] She also rejected the argument that s. 15(1) did not apply to this case. Agricultural workers 'generally suffer from disadvantage' and the effect of the statutory exclusion 'is to devalue them and marginalize them within Canadian society'.[107] This meant that agricultural worker status should be treated as an 'analogous ground' within the scope of s. 15.

In both judgments, the constitutional freedom under s. 2(d) was sensitive to the labour law context. *Dunmore* does not stand for the strong primacy of constitutional norms over labour law norms. Brian Langille has offered powerful arguments in favour of a s. 15 equality-based analysis in *Dunmore*-type cases. According to Langille, the s. 15 enquiry should consider whether the exclusion is amenable to principled justification by the legislature. The SCC has adopted a narrower approach to s. 15, and this s. 15 route is currently closed. In terms of the eventual political outcome following the *Dunmore* judgment,

[105] *Dunmore* (n 100) 1089–1090.
[106] Ibid. 1098.
[107] Ibid. 1112.

little turned upon this distinction between s. 2(d) and s. 15. The Ontario Legislature enacted a statutory provision that essentially included basic 'right to organize' protections in s. 2 of the Agricultural Employees Protection Act 2002. Since there is little scope for reasonable variation in defining the right to organise, this was definitionally similar to the right to organise in the general labour relations regime.

Nevertheless, we should not lose sight of an important difference which could be relevant in other cases. Section 15 ensures that the excluded group is given the *same protections* as the included group. By contrast, s. 2(d) has permitted the emergence of occupationally specific legislative regimes that are *less* protective than the general statute.[108] This has effectively facilitated the deregulation of freedom of association in specific occupations because these weaker statutory regimes meet the constitutional standard. This is especially problematic where excluded groups already experience significant social and economic disadvantages compared to 'standard' workers.

B. The manager exclusion and *Societe des casinos du Quebec inc.*

It is a long-standing feature of the North American Wagner Act model that managerial employees are excluded from its scope. The standard justification for this exclusion is to avoid conflicts of interest in an adversarial enterprise-based bargaining regime. As Brian Langille has explained, the exclusion of managers from the statutory bargaining framework preserves the loyalty of managers to the employer, and it protects the solidarity of non-managerial employees from erosion or dilution.[109] This exclusion may be justified in a pluralist system based on arms-length bargaining between an employer and a trade union with divergent interests. It is also controversial because, as 'employees', many managers and supervisors experience similar problems of subordination, economic dependence, and inequality of bargaining power. In *Societe des casinos du Quebec inc. v Association des cadres de la Societe des casinos du Quebec and others*, this statutory exclusion was challenged under s. 2(d).[110] The Charter challenge was dismissed by the SCC. As a relatively privileged group within the employee category, the managers always faced an

[108] This will be considered in Chapter 4 below on the right to collective bargaining.
[109] Brian Langille, 'Lost at Sea: The Managerial Exclusion after Casinos du Quebec' (2025) 48 Dalhousie Law Journal 897.
[110] 2024 SCC 13.

uphill struggle in demonstrating the *Dunmore* threshold. There was a strong contrast with the disadvantages typically experienced by agricultural workers.

The majority reasons were set out in Jamal J's judgment. Jamal J drew a distinction between the abstract Charter freedom and the legislative specification of that freedom in a labour relations statute. The statutory instantiation in the Quebec Labour Code did not exhaust the Charter freedom. This statute was simply one way of rendering the Charter freedom more determinate through legislative specification. It followed that this Charter freedom could be implemented in a variety of ways. There was no single 'correct' statutory model. It might even be possible to exercise freedom of association without access to any statutory regime. Jamal J applied the test of 'substantial interference', concluding that the exclusion of the managers from the statutory labour relations framework did not satisfy the constitutional threshold. The managers were able to engage in some organisational and bargaining activities, and there were other legal remedies available to the employees since they were employed by the government.[111] Given this evidence, it could not be demonstrated that 'the legislative exclusion orchestrates, encourages, or sustains a violation of the fundamental freedoms of the Association's members'.[112]

The concurring judgment of Cote J (with whom Wagner J joined) reached the same result but emphasised the distinctiveness of positive state obligation cases under s. 2(d) and the need to apply the three-step framework in the *Dunmore* decision carefully. This framework 'ensures that courts do not unduly interfere with the exercise of legislative power and the development of public policy . . . This point cannot be stressed enough. Only in exceptional circumstances can the courts require the state to legislate'.[113] The casino managers failed to demonstrate that there was a substantial interference with their s. 2(d) rights either in purpose or effect. Cote J also suggested that 'the special vulnerability of the excluded group may be indicative of state responsibility' in establishing a causal connection between the statutory exclusion and private interference with associative activities.[114] There was no 'special vulnerability' here beyond the ordinary subordination experienced by employees. This restrained approach to exclusion cases was also affirmed by Rowe J, reflecting a constitutional concern with separation of powers and the limits of the judicial role.[115]

111 Ibid. [52]–[57].
112 Ibid. [56].
113 Ibid. [150].
114 Ibid. [187].
115 Ibid. [218]–[219].

After *Societe des casinos du Quebec inc.,* the scope for a successful s. 2(d) challenge to a legislative exclusion has diminished significantly. While Jamal J did not endorse the 'special vulnerability' analysis of Cote J, it seems likely in practice that something like this will be necessary for a successful s. 2(d) challenge in the future. The alternative rights and remedies available to the casino managers reflect what Eric Tucker has described as a 'liberal voluntarist' settlement.[116] It lacks the full protective features of the standard statutory model, such as full organisational rights, a duty to bargain in good faith, majoritarian exclusivity, and so forth. On Langille's preferred approach, there is a simple constitutional question here: is the legislative differentiation amenable to principled justification?[117] The answer in this case may well have been that there was a principled justification because the inclusion of managers is inconsistent with the adversarial bargaining model in the statute. That would be preferable to the reasoning in this case, which has led to s. 2(d) giving implicit constitutional endorsement to clearly defective legal protections. This could have deregulatory implications for other excluded groups of workers.

C. The RCMP exclusion and *M.P.A.O.*

In *M.P.A.O.*, the majority found that the exclusion of the RCMP from the federal collective bargaining regime, coupled with the imposition of a Staff Relations Representative Program that failed to satisfy requirements of independence and choice, infringed s. 2(d).[118] Like *Dunmore*, it represented a successful Charter challenge to a legislative exclusion. The majority judgment of McLachlin CJ and LeBel J shed important light on the purposive nature of s. 2(d) and its basis in empowerment. The judgment is strongly rooted in a labour law approach.

The majority judgment develops the earlier arguments on constitutional purpose in Dickson CJ's celebrated dissent in the *Alberta Reference*. On this approach, s. 2(d)

> functions to protect individuals against more powerful entities. By banding together in the pursuit of common goals, individuals are able to prevent more powerful entities from thwarting their legitimate goals and desires. In this way, the

[116] Eric Tucker, 'Société des casinos du Québec inc. v. Association des cadres de la Société des casinos du Québec: The Supreme Court of Canada Gambles on Liberal Voluntarism to Provide Meaningful Access to Collective Bargaining' (2025) All Papers 420 advanced access https://digitalcommons.osgoode.yorku.ca/all_papers/420.

[117] Langille (n 97).

[118] *M.P.A.O.* (n 98).

> guarantee of freedom of association empowers vulnerable groups and helps them work to right imbalances in society. It protects marginalized groups and makes possible a more equal society.[119]

The judgment adopts a broad view of disempowerment. For example, there are references to the oppositional potential of civil society in respect of women's suffrage, gay rights, racial minorities, and religious groups.[120] This list is not limited to subordination and dependence in the employment relationship. The empowerment rationale also has implications for the limits of s. 2(d): 'the flip side . . . is that the guarantee will not necessarily protect all associational activity. Section 2(d) is aimed at reducing social imbalances, not enhancing them.'[121] The judgment gives the extreme example of violent conspiracies. Other examples might include concerted price-fixing by well-organised professions.

The judgment implicitly affirms a conventional 'labour law' view of the personal scope of collective bargaining. So, purposive interpretation 'required constitutional protection for the right of *employees* to engage in a process of collective bargaining'.[122] Or again, this right to meaningful collective bargaining is 'in pursuit of *workplace* goals'.[123] Without this right, 'workers may be left essentially powerless in dealing with their *employer* or influencing their *employment conditions*'.[124] This is not the same as *Pastoral Cel Bun*, where the ECtHR specified 'employment relationship' as a necessary threshold for Article 11 rights. However, the choice of language in *M.P.A.O.* reflects the reality that in collective bargaining situations, the relevant duty-bearer will usually be an employer, because the subject-matter of the right (i.e., collective bargaining) is concerned with terms and conditions of employment. For these reasons, the scope will tend to align with some kind of personal employment contract and their trade unions. Given the nature of the right, how could it be otherwise?

M.P.A.O. does not establish a formal 'employee' threshold for the constitutional right to collective bargaining. After all, the employee category was not itself at issue in the case: the constitutional challenge was addressed to a specific legislative exclusion *from* the general category. In an interesting recent

119 Cited in *M.P.A.O.* at [57].
120 Ibid. [56]–[57]. On the relations between civil society and democracy, see Andrew Arato and Jean L. Cohen, *Civil Society and Political Theory* (MIT 1994).
121 *M.P.A.O.* (n 98) [59].
122 Ibid. [44] (emphasis added).
123 Ibid. [45] (emphasis added).
124 Ibid. [68] (emphasis added).

paper, Bakan and Choudhry pose the question whether digital platform workers in the gig economy might use s. 2(d) if they do not meet the employee or worker threshold.[125] They argue that the implicit exclusion of such individuals, because they do not meet the general legal test of employee, could lead to a successful s. 2(d) challenge. Ultimately, this would depend upon the constitutional test of substantial interference. It is plausible that the particular vulnerabilities of these platform workers mean that the 'liberal voluntarist' model does not meet the s. 2(d) standard. In terms of vulnerability and inequality, platform workers are closer to the agricultural workers in *Dunmore* than the managers in *Societe des casinos du Quebec inc.* According to the authors, 'the Court has avoided formalistic and classification-based reasoning in its decisions, focusing instead on workers' need for collective labour rights due to vulnerabilities inherent to workplace power imbalances'.[126]

The reasoning in *M.P.A.O.* is equivocal in terms of this proposed next step. On the one hand, the judgment considers vulnerabilities and power imbalances in a broad way to include different forms of marginalisation and exclusion. On the other hand, it appears to assume in its language that the right to collective bargaining is a right for *employees*. Many gig workers fail to satisfy the formal legal definition of worker or employee, but they do display the substantive vulnerabilities of a group in need of collective empowerment through a trade union. Unlike *Dunmore*, it is not a simple task to envisage the appropriate legislative response. A successful s. 2(d) challenge would represent a more fundamental challenge to the entire basis of legal ordering in Canadian labour law, currently based on the employee or worker. As we have seen, this may explain the caution of the UK Supreme Court in *Deliveroo.* Constitutional courts have sought to avoid fundamental challenges to the autonomy of labour law. The scrutiny of specific occupational exclusions provides a more circumscribed mechanism for tailored constitutional review, allowing for the incremental adjustment of the existing legislative categories.

The strongest example of a substantive inequality analysis as a direct challenge to the formal categories of labour law is in a recent decision of the European Committee of Social Rights (ECSR) under the ESC. The ECSR considered the treatment of certain self-employed workers under Irish competition law, and it found that competition law restrictions constituted a violation of their right to collective bargaining. The constitutional norm challenged the labour law norm of personal scope, and this prompted a reconfiguration

[125] Joel Bakan and Sujit Choudhry, 'Constitutional Labour Rights in the Gig Economy: Digital Platform Workers and Section 2(d) of the Charter' (2025) 70 McGill Law Journal 443.

[126] Ibid. 21.

of established categories. This case was distinctive in that it involved a direct state interference with the freedom to engage in collective bargaining. It was not a case like *Dunmore*.[127]

VI. Personal Scope under the European Social Charter

Competition law or 'antitrust' is an important source of constraint on the collective bargaining activities of non-employees. In circumstances where undertakings are fixing prices through collusion, this kind of empowerment could create risks of abuse of power over vulnerable consumers and service users. As the SCC observed in *M.P.A.O.*, a fundamental purpose of freedom of association is to empower the disadvantaged. It follows that freedom of association should not be used as a means to oppress the weak by economically powerful groups.

Anticompetitive collusive wrongs represent the dark side of freedom of association. European competition law has been predicated on the binary division between 'employees' and 'undertakings'. The bargaining coordination of employees through trade unions is shielded from competition law through a labour exemption. The coordination of undertakings is subject to competition law. In Ireland, this boundary caused difficulties for 'freelance' self-employed, including doctors, journalists and photographers, session musicians, and voice-over actors.[128] Some of these 'freelancer' groups experienced significant disadvantages in individual bargaining, and they needed collective empowerment. On a conventional labour law approach, they failed to meet the formal classification of employee or worker. They are characterised as undertakings. To what extent could the human rights approach challenge the binary division between employees and undertakings? The Irish decision under the ESC provides a promising and distinctive approach.

In *Irish Congress of Trade Unions (ICTU) v Ireland (ICTU)*, the ECSR considered a complaint arising out of the Irish Competition Authority's treatment of freelance voice-over actors as 'undertakings' subject to the Competition Act 2002.[129] This decision had a wider chilling effect on the bargaining activities

[127] Langille has emphasised the distinction between 'vertical' and 'horizontal' interferences in freedom of association cases. See Brian Langille, 'Why the Right-Freedom Distinction Matters to Labour Lawyers—And to All Canadians' (2011) 34 Dalhousie Law Journal 143.

[128] For a full account of the friction between Irish labour law and Irish competition law, see Michael Doherty, 'Competition Law, Cartels and Collective Bargaining', in Sanjukta Paul and others (eds), *The Cambridge Handbook of Labor in Competition Law* (Cambridge UP 2022) chapter 18.

[129] European Committee of Social Rights, *Irish Congress of Trade Unions (ICTU) v Ireland* (Complaint No. 123/2016).

of other freelancer groups in the Irish labour market. In 2017, legislation was passed in the Competition (Amendment) Act 2017, which provided automatic exemptions from competition law for certain defined occupational groups: self-employed voice-over actors, journalists, and session musicians. The legislation also created mechanisms for Ministerial exemptions for categories of 'false self-employed worker' and 'fully dependent self-employed worker'. In many labour law systems, the former category would usually be included in the standard labour law tests through 'sham' doctrines or purposive interpretation. The 'fully dependent' category is a more significant extension of the boundary. It includes self-employed workers who are dependent on not more than two main purchasers of their labour power for their main income. The ECSR considered the Irish law under the ESC both before and after the 2017 legislative changes.

The starting point for the Committee was that the self-employed were within the personal scope of the Article 6 right to collective bargaining unless the context indicated a limitation to employed persons.[130] This established a legal default favouring inclusion. The context did not support a limitation, and this was reinforced by reference to ILO standards and relevant committee decisions.[131] Any exclusion of the self-employed would therefore need to be justified under the proportionality standard set out in Article G. The ECSR recognised that competition law goals could constitute legitimate aims for the purpose of justification.[132]

The ECSR adopted a contextual method for its analysis. This contextual method focused on the distribution of economic power, adopting a realistic approach to contractual arrangements. This enabled it to examine the substance of power relations rather than the contractual form. The ECSR observed that 'the world of work is changing rapidly and fundamentally with a proliferation of contractual arrangements, often with the express aim of avoiding contracts of employment under labour law, of shifting risk from the labour engager to the labour provider'.[133] This meant that some people in need of collective empowerment were excluded because they were unjustifiably exposed to competition law. Given this labour market context, and the realities of economic power in fissured labour markets,[134] the ECSR adopted an inclusive approach to personal scope:

130 Ibid. [35].
131 Ibid. [39].
132 Ibid. [98].
133 Ibid. [38].
134 On the dynamics of fissuring, which encompass the fragmentation and disintegration of bilateral work relations between a single employer and a dependent employee, see David Weil, *The Fissured Workplace* (Harvard UP 2017).

> In establishing the type of collective bargaining that is protected by the Charter, it is not sufficient to rely on distinctions between worker and self-employed, the decisive criterion is rather whether there is an imbalance of power between the providers and engagers of labour. Where providers of labour have no substantial influence on the content of contractual conditions, they must be given the possibility of improving the power imbalance through collective bargaining.[135]

In focusing on market power rather than contract-type, substance over form, the ECSR concluded that a complete prohibition of self-employed collective bargaining would be disproportionate.[136] The relevant boundary would need to be specified by more discriminating criteria that identified markers of bargaining power, such as having several clients, the ability to exercise strategic control over the direction of an independent business, and the ability to hire staff. This meant that the pre-2017 restrictions on specific freelancer occupations were excessive and could not be justified. Many of these freelancers experienced an imbalance of power relative to the engagers of their labour. The ECSR was not prepared to conclude that the 2017 categories of 'false' and 'dependent' self-employment were too narrow; that would depend upon how they were interpreted and applied by the national competition authorities.

The *ICTU* decision is the strongest example of a human rights approach, presenting an important challenge to the autonomy of labour law. The ECSR noted that economic inequalities and precarious work are significant issues for many self-employed people, and these vulnerabilities justified the need for access to collective empowerment. These self-employed workers needed the rights to organise and bargain collectively, even though they were formally excluded because of contractual form. The ESC is a social and labour rights instrument. Yet it has provided the clearest example of a constitutional conception of freedom of association disrupting the labour law conception of personal scope. By contrast, the ECHR and the Canadian Charter have more readily integrated some kind of employment relationship paradigm into their jurisprudence. The Irish ESC decision may also reflect the distinctive value of expert committees rather than courts. Courts may be more attracted to the rule of law virtues of stable and defined legal categories. Finally, since this involved a vertical state interference with collective bargaining activities, concerns with identifying duty-bearers (i.e., employers) were not necessary to the resolution of the case.

135 *ICTU* (n 129) [38].
136 Ibid. [40].

Even the ECSR approach presupposes *some* kind of boundary. Its approach has nothing to do with linguistic arguments about universal rights for 'everyone'. The dividing line is 'imbalance of power' rather than formal contractual classification. 'Imbalance of power' is too imprecise to be used directly by courts as a test for identifying access to trade union rights. It requires legislators in member states to formulate rules to distinguish genuinely independent entrepreneurs from other types of vulnerable self-employment. This may require something different from the standard contractual categories of employee or worker, but many of the social and economic factors relevant to the conventional boundary will continue to be relevant to any power-adjusted boundary.

VII. The Enduring Autonomy of Personal Scope

The autonomy of labour law has endured, reflecting the deep social and legal roots of the worker category. In many cases, the worker category still encompasses those individuals in need of trade union empowerment because of inequality of bargaining power. These case studies reveal the variety of ways in which constitutional norms have been used to adjust or refine that basic category. Sometimes, this has led to the inclusion of occupational groups within the scope of general labour legislation (such as with the foster carers and parks police in the UK). Other cases have prompted legislators to introduce legislation specifically for the excluded group, though this has sometimes been an attenuated version of the fully protective general labour statute (as with the agricultural workers in Ontario). For all their differences, there is an underlying theme of equality before the law. The court is concerned to ensure that there is a relevant justification for the legislative differentiation of occupational groups or contract types.

The most radical challenge to the existing binary divide has been through the ESC, prompting a reconfiguration of standard labour law categories to include some self-employed within the scope of competition law exclusions. The ILO Committee on Freedom of Association has recently considered the UK *Deliveroo* case, and the Committee was critical of the assumption that an 'employment relationship' was necessary for freedom of association protections.[137] ILO norms required a more encompassing scope to include all those

[137] Committee on Freedom of Association, Case No. 3455 Complaint against the Government of Great Britain and Northern Ireland presented by the Independent Workers Union of Great Britain (IWGB) (10–20 March 2025).

who sold their labour on a market and to include all workers without distinction. And yet in the Committee's recommendations, it noted (and endorsed) the Government's impending consideration of a new legal test distinguishing workers from the genuinely self-employed. Even this is not a boundaryless right, then. It is just that the class of right-holders needs to broaden so that it includes more self-employed workers who are in need of protection. Personal scope will persist for as long as legal rights are correlative to legal duties.

Constitutional litigation has been less successful in securing stronger legislative protections for highly precarious occupational groups. As scholars like Valerio de Stefano have argued, inclusion in general labour legislation may not be sufficient to protect freedom of association for disadvantaged groups like non-standard workers.[138] The general rules may need to be tailored to their specific needs and vulnerabilities. There are many historical legislative examples of this, like the system of wages boards in the UK. In *Unite*, the ECtHR adopted a highly deferential approach so that the repeal of special legislation for agricultural workers was within the state's margin of appreciation. The general statutory framework was effectively closed off to unions and agricultural workers because no employer in the UK agricultural sector would meet the 21-worker threshold specified in the general legislation. Such cases only have the appearance of equality of treatment. Substantive equality will sometimes require tailored legislative interventions to ensure that workers have an effective and realistic opportunity to exercise trade union rights. This reinforces the constitutional importance of recognising the shared responsibilities of courts and legislatures in protecting freedom of association. It is not a task that can be left to courts alone.

[138] Valerio de Stefano, 'Non-Standard Work and Limits on Freedom of Association: A Human Rights-Based Approach' (2017) 46 Industrial Law Journal 185.

4

Freedom of Association and the Right to Collective Bargaining

I. Introduction

We have been considering Kahn-Freund's two social and legal functions of freedom of association: its guise as a civil liberty or human right and as a labour right supporting the operation of collective labour relations. How do these two elements fit together in the law of collective bargaining, and what is the proper constitutional role of the courts in delimiting the boundary between the two legal functions?

The very idea of a civil liberty to collective bargaining is puzzling and somewhat obscure. Collective bargaining is so deeply embedded in the social and legal histories of most labour law systems that it is not very clear what a separate and distinct civil liberty to collective bargaining might mean. There are huge comparative variations in the law and practice of collective bargaining across legal systems. The pattern of legal intervention may also change radically within a single legal system over time. These changes are highly sensitive to shifts in the political ideologies of governments and shaped by the social history of trade unions and employers in the development of bargaining practices. Collective bargaining is perhaps the most 'political' of the labour rights in its regulatory variety. The quest for a core of universal standards may be elusive. It is constituted by laws, administrative practices, and social norms at the epicentre of labour law. The right to bargain collectively is so deeply connected to the very identity of labour law itself that it is difficult to imagine what an autonomous constitutional standard might look like.

In these respects, collective bargaining can be contrasted with the right to strike. The right to strike is linked to fundamental human rights such as the freedom from forced labour, freedom of assembly in picketing cases, and freedom of expression.[1] These connections mean that it is easier to conceive of

[1] For a civil liberty-style justification for the right to strike, drawing upon republican theories of non-domination, see Alan Bogg and Cynthia Estlund, 'The Right to Strike and Contestatory Citizenship', in Hugh Collins and others (eds), *Philosophical Foundations of Labour Law* (OUP 2018) chapter 13.

Freedom of Association. Alan Bogg, Oxford University Press. © Alan Bogg 2026. DOI: 10.1093/9780191831690.003.0004

a right to strike as an individual civil liberty. By contrast, it is more conceptually difficult to do the same for collective bargaining. What could it be, separate from its labour law instantiation?

This chapter begins by outlining the challenge of incommensurability and the extensive variation in the laws and social practices of collective bargaining. This contextualises the basic difficulty for constitutional courts: how to formulate constitutional standards that are meaningful without (1) being so general as to be vacuous, (2) replicating the detailed statutory rules in labour law, or (3) being so divergent from existing labour law norms that they are excessively disruptive of reasonable political compromises.

It then examines two leading scholarly reflections on the right to collective bargaining as derived from freedom of association, by Brian Langille and Benjamin Oliphant, and Sheldon Leader. These arguments reveal the constitutional challenges and tensions in the elaboration of a right to collective bargaining. For Langille and Oliphant, constitutional courts should proceed very cautiously because of the constitutional values of democracy, the rule of law, and the separation of powers. For Leader, by contrast, there is a fundamental right to members-only bargaining, which would require radical overhaul of many existing labour law systems. It is fair to say that the constitutionally cautious arguments of Langille and Oliphant have had much stronger predictive power than Leader's arguments in tracing the constitutional trajectory of collective bargaining.[2]

The second part of the chapter considers the jurisprudence on collective bargaining and freedom of association under the ECHR, in the UK, and in Canada. This case law reveals some common patterns. In particular, there is a bifurcation between 'individual' and 'collective' cases. The courts have been scrupulous in safeguarding individual rights against non-discrimination, reflecting the fundamental status of the right not to be discriminated against for trade union reasons. This is often described as the 'right to organise'. The scope for reasonable variation in fundamental norms on non-discrimination is narrow, and democratic arguments in favour of judicial deference are far weaker.

In 'collective' cases involving controversial political determinations—for example, defining which unions are representative, the requirements of a duty to bargain, or the design of auxiliary interventions to support collective bargaining—the courts have proceeded more cautiously. These determinations are often political matters that vary in reasonable ways, and legislatures

[2] In fairness to Leader, Langille and Oliphant were writing while the judicial developments were underway, whereas Leader was writing long before the explosion in constitutional litigation.

have been accorded a wide discretionary margin to specify the right to bargain collectively in concrete terms through legislation. In the Canadian context, the Supreme Court of Canada (SCC) has developed constitutional principles that are intermediate between the abstract right to freedom of association and the detailed legislative schemes. These principles leave legislators with a wide (but not unlimited) democratic freedom to select between incommensurable legal models that are each compatible with the abstract principle. This gives democracy its due while providing for meaningful judicial supervision.

II. The Right to Collective Bargaining as a Fundamental Human Right: The Cchallenge of Incommensurability

The right to collective bargaining is a fundamental human right in the international legal order.[3] For example, it is constitutionalised in the International Labour Organisation (ILO) in the 1944 Declaration of Philadelphia[4] and the ILO Declaration on Fundamental Principles and Rights at Work 1998. It is also protected in a broad range of international human rights treaties, for example, Article 6 of the European Social Charter. The leading ILO instrument ILO Convention 98 on the Right to Organise and Collective Bargaining (1949). Article 4 provides that

> Measures appropriate to national conditions shall be taken, where necessary, to encourage and promote the full development and utilisation of machinery for voluntary negotiation between employers or employers' organisations and workers' organisations, with a view to the regulation of terms and conditions of employment by means of collective agreements.

This envisages 'measures' which must be 'appropriate to national conditions'. It does not appear to be formulated as a *right* (whose right is it? what is it a right to?) that is correlative to *duties* on employers or employers' organisations (and a duty to do what? Are duties compatible with voluntary collective bargaining?). It is presented as an open-textured normative standard addressed to governments and their positive obligations to 'encourage and promote'. We should not jump to the hasty conclusion that the right to collective bargaining is therefore not a *real* right, with determinate duties imposed on others. As

[3] Patrick Macklem, 'The Right to Bargain Collectively in International Law: Workers' Right, Human Right, International Right?', in Philip Alston (ed), *Labour Rights as Human Rights* (OUP 2005) chapter 3.
[4] III e.

Webber and others have argued, 'it might be thought that human rights such as the freedom of expression, assembly, and religion are Hohfeldian liberties. The problem with classifying them as such, however, is that their two-term structure does not describe any particular relationship between persons'.[5] As the authors explain, these abstract freedoms are like directive guides to legislators, indicating that a certain kind of activity (i.e., collective bargaining) is of such importance that it is something citizens have by right. These 'broad goal-oriented' two-term formulae require further specification and translation into three-term rights through legislation and case law.[6] The implementation of a constitutionalised right to collective bargaining therefore requires that 'a series of acts and arrangements—a combination of Hohfeldian relationships—must be selected from among more or less reasonable alternatives and authoritatively established'.[7] The formulation as a directive guide in international instruments is important, given the diversity of collective bargaining models.

The right to collective bargaining is so challenging as an object of constitutionalisation because these 'reasonable alternatives' in legal implementation display a dazzling variety. The legal models defy reduction into familiar categories like 'common law versus civil law' legal systems.[8] They are strongly shaped by diverse social histories, ideologies, and structures of trade union movements and employers' associations.[9] From a comparative perspective, the concept of 'collective bargaining' and its legal regulation is so varied that the relevant phenomena sometimes appear only to be distant relatives. Within a national legal order, the legal techniques for supporting collective bargaining have often shifted flexibly in response to changing political and economic circumstances. Many of these legal techniques do not involve the enforcement of a 'duty to bargain'. For most of the 20th century, for example, the British system did *not* impose a general legal duty to bargain at all on employers or employers' associations.[10] Yet this absence of a legal duty to bargain was consistent with strong state support for collective bargaining coverage and decent

[5] Gregoire Webber and others, *Legislated Human Rights: Securing Human Rights through Legislation* (Cambridge UP 2018) 127. In other words, 'the two-term structure of rights signifies the importance of the subject matters x (life, liberty, security, privacy, etc) that persons (P) have by right, but does not identify which measures will realise everyone's right by identifying duty-holders and the content of their duties that correlate to the right(s) in question' (at 21).

[6] Ibid. 21.

[7] Ibid. 42.

[8] Paul Davies and Mark Freedland (eds), *Kahn-Freund's Labour and the Law* (3rd ed, Stevens & Sons 1983) 72.

[9] Antoine Jacobs, 'Collective Labour Relations', in Bob Hepple and Bruno Veneziani (eds), *The Transformation of Labour Law in Europe* (Hart 2009) 202–203.

[10] Alan Bogg, *The Democratic Aspects of Trade Union Recognition* (Hart 2009) chapter 1.

economic outcomes for many workers. This avoidance of direct sanctions and legal duties was even considered to be a mark of its 'maturity'.[11]

This context is important because it isolates a difficulty that is not so acute for other freedom of association rights, such as the right to strike: when we are seeking to constitutionalise the right to collective bargaining, what precisely are we asking the courts to constitutionalise? And how do these constitutionalised norms relate to the detailed specification of collective bargaining laws in ordinary legislation?

A. The right to collective bargaining in comparative perspective

The point of this thumbnail sketch is to identify the multiplicity of ways in which collective bargaining systems vary across different legal systems. Recognising the scale of this variation in collective laws and institutions is a commonplace of comparative labour law.[12] This variety reveals the significant normative challenge of constitutionalisation, especially for supranational courts. It is difficult to determine which elements should be entrenched in a right to collective bargaining while accommodating reasonable national variations, because no single feature seems to recur universally.

As early as 1954, in his famous essay in *The British Journal of Sociology*, Kahn-Freund postulated a basic distinction between 'static' and 'dynamic' models of collective bargaining.[13] The 'static' model envisaged a process of regular negotiation of collective agreements, which were often reduced to writing like standard commercial contracts. These collective agreements, renewed periodically through periods of negotiation when the agreement expired, crystallised the substantive rights and duties. This was characteristic of the North American systems and some European models of collective bargaining. The 'dynamic' model was more focused on joint procedures and institutions, such as negotiation boards and joint industrial councils. Any negotiated standards were more amenable to adjustment, as conflicts over 'interpretation' shaded into conflicts of interest and the negotiation of new standards. For much of the 20th century, this 'dynamic' model was characteristic of many British collective agreements and Belgian collective agreements.[14] These 'dynamic' models

[11] Otto Kahn-Freund, 'Intergroup Conflicts and their Settlement', in Otto Kahn-Freund, *Selected Writings* (Stevens & Sons 1978) 41, 54.

[12] See, e.g., Kahn-Freund (n 8) chapter 3.

[13] Kahn-Freund (n 11) 52–55. As Kahn-Freund noted, many legal systems displayed features of both models, albeit in differing degrees of magnitude.

[14] Kahn-Freund (n 8) 70–71.

were themselves variable, ranging from highly formalised institutions to more informal and spontaneous modes of shop floor bargaining between managers and shop stewards.[15] A constitutionalisation project for an international right to collective bargaining would need to allow space for both models, though the dynamic model is more difficult to translate into the juridical categories of rights and duties.

Another fundamental distinction, which cuts across the 'static' and 'dynamic' spectrum, is the level of bargaining and the extent of collective bargaining decentralisation. In the North American 'Wagner Act' legal models and the UK system, collective bargaining is generally focused on the individual enterprise or plant, and negotiation occurs between a trade union and a single employer.[16] In many European countries, collective bargaining has tended to occur on a sectoral basis (either regionally or nationally) between large trade unions or federations of trade unions and employers' associations.[17] This could be supplemented by various forms of 'neo-corporatism', which was sometimes institutionalised, and which engaged 'social partners' in the economic and industrial policy-making at the national level.[18] The line between collective bargaining and public regulation/legislation tended to blur as negotiation processes operated at higher levels of centralisation. In most labour law systems, collective bargaining operates at multiple levels, which then requires rules on the prioritisation of sources where there are conflicts of norms.[19]

Then there is the matter of a legal 'duty to bargain', which is often taken to be the conceptual touchstone of the correlative right. This intersects with static/dynamic and centralised/decentralised bargaining in unpredictable ways. The legal duty to bargain, administered by a labour board and enforceable through federal courts, was introduced in the US in 1935.[20] This developed within a highly juridified system based upon enterprise or plant-level bargaining units. However, this was not restricted to common law countries. In the posthumous third edition of his *Hamlyn Lectures*, for example, *Kahn-Freund's Labour and the Law* pointed to the recent introduction of a legal duty to bargain in France from 1982, which applied to both enterprise and industry-level bargaining.[21]

[15] Hugh Clegg, 'Otto Kahn-Freund and British Industrial Relations', in Lord Wedderburn, Roy Lewis, and Jon Clark (eds), *Labour Law and Industrial Relations: Building on Kahn-Freund* (OUP 1983) chapter 2.
[16] Kahn-Freund (n 8) 79.
[17] Jacobs (n 9) 208–210.
[18] Ibid. 211.
[19] Simon Deakin, 'Why There is Not Yet (But Could be Soon) a Principle of Favourability in British Labour Law', in Alan Bogg and Paul S. Davies (eds), *Private Law and the Employment Contract* (Hart 2025) chapter 2.
[20] Kahn-Freund (n 8) 90.
[21] Ibid. 92.

This French duty was enforced through criminal penalties, which set it apart from parallel models of the duty to bargain in the US and the UK. There was also a long-standing duty to bargain concept in Swedish labour law, which operated within a highly centralised bargaining structure involving unitary trade unions.[22] By contrast, the Italian *Statuto dei lavoratori* (Workers' Statute) of 1970 did not implement a legal duty to bargain, and yet it was regarded by comparative scholars as promoting strong workplace collective bargaining.[23] This reflected a deliberate choice by the Italian legislator to avoid the problems that had vexed the US 'duty to bargain' concept.[24] Instead, the *Statuto* protected the union activities of workers in the enterprise through strong remedies and a sympathetic judiciary.[25] This was underpinned by a constitutional culture that prized autonomous collective bargaining. As Lord Wedderburn observed, 'by not intervening in regard to the duty to bargain, and the many correlative difficulties about bargaining parties and their conduct, the *Statuto* paradoxically achieved an intervention which has been stronger and more lasting'.[26] The constitutional entrenchment of a 'duty to bargain' seems difficult to justify when its very absence appears to have been critical in some national systems to strong legal support for collective bargaining.

Where a collective agreement results from collective bargaining, there are also wide comparative variations in the normative effects of that agreement on individual employment contracts. Lord Wedderburn famously coined the term 'inderogability' to describe these legal phenomena.[27] In some countries, such as France, Spain, Germany, and the Netherlands, there is 'extension' machinery available which can give representative collective agreements binding *erga omnes* effect.[28] By contrast, such extension machinery would not be acceptable in Italy, Sweden, or Denmark because it contradicts fundamental civil law or constitutional principles. There are also variations in how collectively agreed terms bind individual employment contracts. In France and Sweden, for example, the terms operate as imperative norms through law rather than (as in the English case) through a contractual mechanism of 'incorporation'.[29] In Wedderburn's terms, 'the agreement binds as reglement'.[30] The collective

[22] Howard F. Gospel, 'Trade Unions and the Legal Obligation to Bargain: An American, Swedish and British Comparison' (1983) 21 British Journal of Industrial Relations 343.

[23] Lord Wedderburn, 'The Italian Workers' Statute: British Reflections on a High Point of Legal Protection', in Lord Wedderburn, *Employment Rights in Britain and Europe* (Lawrence and Wishart 1991) chapter 9.

[24] Ibid. 246–247.

[25] Ibid. 240–243.

[26] Ibid. 247.

[27] Lord Wedderburn, 'Collective Bargaining at European Level: The Inderogability Problem', in Lord Wedderburn, *Labour Law and Freedom* (Lawrence and Wishart 1995) chapter 6.

[28] Ibid. 221.

[29] Ibid. 222.

[30] Ibid. 222–223.

agreement in these different systems, varied in such intricate ways, is a form of public regulation, more akin to legislation than to private contract. Yet there is no single legal model for achieving this, and these divergences were compatible with strong collective bargaining and effective legal support.

Finally, all legal systems use criteria of 'representativeness' to determine which associations should be accorded negotiation rights or privileges. As Jacobs explained, 'There were numerous instances in which a selection had to be made, either as regards public law institutions or in labour relations under private law. It appeared to be impossible to treat all trade unions and employers' associations equally.'[31] We might even say that 'representativeness' approximates to a universal element in the right to collective bargaining. However, there are huge differences in how 'representativeness' is defined in different systems.[32] These include majority support in a bargaining unit ballot, levels of membership density in industrial sectors, affiliation to representative federations, and capacities for engaging in effective collective bargaining.[33] These variations tend to reflect diverse histories and structures of industrial relations and politics rather than rational ethical choices.

Overall, these significant variations in the constitution of the right to collective bargaining can be described as trans-systemic incommensurability. These legal models represent different and incompatible legislative choices, though each model may be reasonable in its own terms. It means that there are significant challenges for any transnational constitutionalisation of the right.

There is one important respect in which something like a universal legal standard might be identified. In his general reflections on comparative law, Kahn-Freund contrasted Article 1 and Article 4 of ILO Convention 98.[34] As we have seen, Article 4 is formulated through open-textured promotional obligations. By contrast, Article 1 dealing with acts of anti-union discrimination against workers 'is expressed in strict legal terms'.[35] This 'right to organize', which appears as a counterpart to the right to collective bargaining in ILO Convention 98, is more amenable to being defined and enforced as a universal legal standard. In comparative terms, it is also a strong candidate for

[31] Jacobs (n 9) 211.

[32] This point is developed in a perceptive article by Guy Mundlak, 'On Labour Representativeness: The Hidden Components of the Human Right to Freely Associate in Trade Unions' (2020) 36 International Journal of Comparative Labour Law and Industrial Relations 445.

[33] For a comparative review of these different typologies of representativeness, see Bruno Veneziani, 'The Intervention of the Law to Regulate Collective Bargaining and Trade Union Representation Rights' (1999) 5 Transfer: European Review of Labour and Research 100.

[34] Otto Kahn-Freund, 'On Uses and Misuses of Comparative Law', in Otto Kahn-Freund, *Labour Law* (Stevens & Sons 1978) 313–315.

[35] Ibid. 314.

entrenchment as a constitutionalised right with correlative duties on employers. The definition of an individual right not to be victimised or discriminated against for trade union reasons, while variable to some degree, is not variable to the same extent as the right to collective bargaining. Its fundamental character is reflected in its treatment as a basic protective standard in constitutional norms. It is not linked instrumentally to the existence or pursuit of collective bargaining in the workplace. The individual right to join a trade union and to participate in its activities is fundamental and intrinsic. It is protected regardless of whether the individual union activities are linked to recognition or collective bargaining, and as we shall see, this has been reflected particularly in the ECHR jurisprudence.

B. The right to collective bargaining in national perspective: the case of collective laissez-faire

The challenges in identifying a constitutional core to the right to collective bargaining are not simply a consequence of wide comparative variations. Even within national legal systems, there are often significant changes over time to 'auxiliary' labour law interventions supporting collective bargaining.[36] In the British context, the term 'collective laissez-faire' was used to describe the distinctive pattern of state involvement in collective bargaining.[37] This emphasised the primacy of voluntary bargaining practices and respect for the industrial autonomy of trade unions and employers. Under collective laissez-faire, the most significant modes of intervention were often implemented through governmental policies rather than legislation. Given the prominence of the executive, the line between law and politics in the development of 'auxiliary' supports could be very blurred. Changes in government policy were also highly charged politically. This was a conflictual space. These changes could be responses to wage inflation, the incidence and pattern of strike action, and other contested matters of industrial politics. Given the dynamic and evolutive quality of the legal framework of collective bargaining, which of these political measures should be constitutionally entrenched? Where does the constitutionally protected 'right to collective bargaining' end and the inherent flexibility of ordinary legislative politics (and executive practices) begin?

[36] For an authoritative and comprehensive account, see Lord Wedderburn, *The Worker and the Law* (3rd ed, Penguin 1986) chapter 4.

[37] Otto Kahn-Freund, 'Labour Law', in Otto Kahn-Freund, *Selected Writings* (Stevens & Sons 1978) 1, 8.

The British example of collective laissez-faire is illuminating because of the relative absence of a legal duty to bargain for much of the 20th century. Yet in juridical terms, this duty is the natural correlative counterpart of a 'right' to bargain collectively.[38] Paradoxically, the absence of this legal duty reflected the strength and maturity of British collective bargaining. As Kahn-Freund observed,

> British collective labour law is in on respect unique among the legal systems of the larger industrial countries. Trade union 'recognition' was achieved in this country by purely industrial as distinct from political and legislative action. No Wagner Act, no Weimar Constitution, no Front Populaire legislation has imposed upon British employers the duty to enter into negotiation with trade union representatives.[39]

This British reticence around a directly enforced legal duty to bargain did not reflect ambivalence about collective bargaining as a valuable democratic practice. For example, Lord Wedderburn was deeply engaged with the political debates concerning the enactment of a British duty to bargain in the 1960s and 1970s. He had noted the reservations of the Donovan Commission on this specific proposal, and the risk of 'the importation of regulation by the back door and the mass of legalistic hair-splitting which surrounds the "duty to bargain in good faith" in the USA'.[40] By the late 1970s, he did not regard the recent legal experimentation with a duty to bargain as a successful intervention to support collective bargaining.[41] These 'direct' interventions, based upon legal duties to bargain in good faith, had been subverted by unsympathetic judicial meddling and weak remedies.[42]

By contrast, there was strong and effective state support for collective bargaining for much of the 20th century. This positive state support was channelled through institution-building led by the Ministry of Labour, encouraging the voluntary formation of Joint Industrial Councils.[43] This institution-building relied upon the administrative power of the executive rather than legislation. There was also a panoply of 'indirect' legal supports

[38] As I have argued elsewhere, this led Lord Wedderburn to be somewhat cautious about the terminology of a right to bargain collectively during some periods of his intellectual development: Alan Bogg, 'The Hero's Journey: Lord Wedderburn and the "Political Constitution" of Labour Law' (2015) 44 Industrial Law Journal 299, 326–327.

[39] Otto Kahn-Freund, 'Collective Agreements under Wartime Legislation' (1943) 6 Modern Law Review 112, 143.

[40] K.W. Wedderburn, *The Worker and the Law* (2nd ed, Penguin 1971) 23.

[41] Lord Wedderburn, 'The New Structure of Labour Law in Britain' (1978) 13 Israel Law Review 435, 456.

[42] Bogg (n 10) chapter 2.

[43] K.D. Ewing, 'The State and Industrial Relations: "Collective laissez-faire" Revisited' (1998) 5 Historical Studies in Industrial Relations 1.

to voluntary collective bargaining practices. These 'indirect' techniques could be contrasted with the 'direct' method of the duty to bargain as a correlative to the right to bargain collectively:

> There is a difference between saying to the employers: 'You act unlawfully if you refuse to recognise unions and to bargain with them in good faith' (the American attitude) and saying to them 'It is for you to decide whether or not you wish to bargain collectively, but if you do not we may impose upon you terms and conditions of employment which you must observe.[44]

Even within this broad category of 'indirect' methods, there were significant variations in legal technique. Some recognition problems arose out of the failure of employers to observe applicable collective agreements. This was addressed through measures such as the Fair Wages Resolution 1946, which restricted public contracts to employers which observed recognised terms and conditions. Other measures to support the normative effect of established collective agreements included section 8 of the Terms and Conditions of Employment Act 1958. There were also problems in certain industries where trade union organisation had not taken root, such as agriculture or catering. The absence of adequate collective bargaining machinery in an industry was addressed through the system of Trade Boards and Wages Councils, which (in different guises) involved the creation and support of wage-setting institutions as a stimulus to voluntary collective bargaining.[45] These indirect measures were rationalised by Kahn-Freund as a framework 'for organized persuasion . . . Persuasion and indirect sanction, that is promise of benefits and threat of disadvantages, are the ways by which in this country the law traditionally exercises its function as an auxiliary to collective bargaining'.[46] The appraisal of this diverse regulatory framework by scholars such as Kahn-Freund and Wedderburn was highly positive in terms of its social effects on collective bargaining practices.

Now, in one sense, the 'right to collective bargaining' could be viewed as sufficiently broad to accommodate this entire legal structure in its detail and its manifold changes. The 'right' simply encompasses the broad range of positive state measures enacted to support collective bargaining from time to time. In this usage, it is a mode of rhetoric, signalling that collective bargaining is

[44] Otto Kahn-Freund, 'Legal Framework', in Allan Flanders and Hugh A. Clegg (eds), *The System of Industrial Relations in Great Britain* (Blackwell 1954) 42, 55.

[45] Frederic J. Bayliss, *British Wages Councils* (Blackwell 1962).

[46] Otto Kahn-Freund, 'Industrial Relations and the Law: Retrospect and Prospect' (1969) 7 British Journal of Industrial Relations 301, 304.

valuable and the state ought to promote it as effectively as possible. Yet in circumstances where the right is being invoked as a justiciable legal entitlement, more precision is needed. For example, if government support of bargaining institutions is so vital, can courts direct governments to allocate budgetary resources to this? Is the state under a positive duty to maintain wages councils for disadvantaged agricultural workers? Is it a violation of the right to collective bargaining to fail to enact (or to repeal) a general statutory duty to bargain? Did the United Kingdom violate the right to collective bargaining prior to 1971 before the introduction of statutory recognition machinery? Is it relevant to that assessment that 'indirect' legal supports were remarkably effective in supporting strong collective bargaining?

There are considerable constitutional sensitivities around these matters. In adjudicating upon them, judges have been keenly aware of deference factors such as institutional competence, expertise, and democratic legitimacy. This has often been reflected in a cautious judicial approach to constitutional claims based upon the right to bargain collectively. This may be described as intra-systemic incommensurability. It reflects the scope for reasonable yet incompatible regulatory approaches to collective bargaining even within the logic and history of a single national system.

III. Collective Bargaining as Freedom of Association: Two Theoretical Arguments

This section will consider two major theoretical arguments deriving collective bargaining from freedom of association. The first set of arguments was developed in the Canadian context by Brian Langille and Benjamin Oliphant. They are sceptical about the prospects for a constitutionalised right to collective bargaining because this would lead constitutional courts to trespass on matters that are properly allocated to democracy and legislatures. They do envisage a narrower constitutional remit for core rights protecting workers from anti-union discrimination. Their arguments reflect a strong commitment to the autonomy of legislated labour law from constitutional intervention, while leaving scope for a core of individual anti-discrimination protections.

The second argument was developed by Sheldon Leader. Leader offered a radical argument for a constitutionalised right to members-only bargaining derived from the individual right to freedom of association. In contrast to Langille and Oliphant, this envisaged a highly interventionist role for courts. Its realisation would require a radical overhaul of many well-functioning collective bargaining systems, which produce decent outcomes for most workers.

This would have uncertain economic and social consequences for those workers. On Leader's approach, the constitutional right has strong primacy over the legislated model.

A. Langille and Oliphant and the Distinction between Rights and Freedoms

Brian Langille is one of our leading thinkers on freedom of association in constitutionalised labour law jurisprudence. While his arguments have been developed within the Canadian context, they are of wider theoretical importance. Langille has been particularly critical of constitutional overreach in freedom of association cases, which for him reached its unhappy zenith in the constitutionalisation of a *right* to collective bargaining. This entailed the constitutionalisation of a *duty* to bargain collectively.[47] This escalating constitutionalisation of rights and duties attracted a battery of criticisms. The nature of these criticisms has shifted between early and later work (this later work is based on a very fruitful collaboration with Benjamin Oliphant).[48] The later work is less categorical in its rejection of constitutionalised labour rights, and its criticisms are more measured. Let us begin with the early critique, which was addressed to the constitutional recognition of a right to collective bargaining in *Health Services and Support-Facilities Subsector Bargaining Association v British Columbia*.[49]

In 'The Freedom of Association Mess: How We Got into It and How We Can Get out of It', Langille emphasised the basic juridical distinction between freedoms and rights.[50] Rights are correlative to duties on others. Freedoms are not correlative to duties. This means that the interest of a right-holder inevitably restricts the freedom of the duty-bearer, because the duty restricts her freedom of action.[51] However, freedom of association, like freedom of expression or freedom of religion, is formulated as a freedom, not a right. For Langille, this is not a linguistic accident. It reflects the fact that it would be 'crazy' to constitutionalise rights and duties because the duty curtails the

[47] Brian Langille, 'The Freedom of Association Mess: How We Got into It and How We Can Get out of It' (2009) 54 McGill Law Journal 177, 198–204.

[48] Brian Langille and Benjamin Oliphant, 'The Legal Structure of Freedom of Association' (2014) 40 Queen's Law Journal 249.

[49] [2007] 2 SCR 391.

[50] Langille (n 47).

[51] Langille is scrupulous in applying Hohfeld's work on the juridical nature of rights: Wesley Newcomb Hohfeld. See Wesley Newcomb Hohfeld, 'Fundamental Legal Conceptions as Applied in Judicial Reasoning' (1917) 26 Yale Law Journal 710.

freedom of the duty-bearer.[52] It might mean that a duty-bearer is compelled to listen to your speech, to join your religious community and worship with you, and so forth. That would be a negation of the duty-bearer's own constitutional freedoms. The enactment of rights and duties is the province of ordinary legislation and the legislature. Labour legislation specifies the rights and duties of employees and employers, and these can be modified from time to time through the democratic process. This includes duties not to victimise or dismiss trade unionists, duties to bargain with trade unions in good faith, duties not to penalise strikers, and duties to allow union organisers to access the employer's property. This is exactly what legislated labour codes should be regulating, but it would be illegitimate to constitutionalise these duties because to do so would disregard the employer's constitutional freedoms. It would also curtail the legislator's democratic freedom to alter the law.

For Langille, this does not mean that collective bargaining should not be recognised as a fundamental constitutional matter. But it must be recognised in such a way as to respect everyone's equal constitutional freedoms. Each worker has the freedom to negotiate their contractual bargain with an employer. Freedom of association protects the freedom to do that collectively with others. By treating it as a constitutional *freedom*, this ensures that legislatures can enact (and change) the detailed rights and duties in ordinary labour legislation. There are virtues in this democratic flexibility. The 'duty to bargain' is only one legal model. As the British historical experience might suggest, it may not even be the most effective auxiliary intervention. It would seem odd to limit the legislator's freedom in this way and to treat the 'Wagner Act' model as constitutionally required, because this would curtail the scope for reasonable legislative variation of collective bargaining laws.

Langille's early concerns about constitutional overreach raised serious points. However, the categorical exclusion of rights and duties from the constitutional domain rested upon two controversial claims: (1) the linguistic formulation of constitutional *liberties* and (2) the equivalence of individual and collective bargaining. Both claims are too reductive. For these reasons, 'early' Langille must be rejected.

To begin with constitutional liberties, Webber and others have argued that it is a mistake to view constitutional formulae as Hohfeldian liberties simply because of their linguistic use of 'freedom'.[53] These general formulae indicate that certain activities—that is associating or expressing—are of such importance that they must be protected through the further determinate specification of

[52] Langille (n 47) 200.
[53] Webber and others (n 5) 127.

rights, liberties, powers, and immunities. What we call 'freedom of association' (or indeed any other fundamental constitutional freedom) is in fact a complex 'molecular' phenomenon composed of a range of juridical relationships.[54] This would certainly include some rights and their correlative duties. The real enquiry is to assess *which* pattern of rights and duties should be constitutionally entrenched and which should be devolved to legislatures for concrete specification in labour statutes. This would require a fuller argument about the relative expertise and competence of courts and legislatures and the proper role of democracy in specifying legal rights.

The second point, the equivalence between individual and collective bargaining, also presents a misleading picture of what is being constitutionalised. According to Langille, collective bargaining is nothing more and nothing less than the aggregated individual freedom to negotiate a contractual bargain. In this respect, Langille's approach reflects the classical market-based conceptualisation of collective bargaining offered by the Webbs:

> In short, for the Webbs, collective bargaining was exactly what the words imply: a collective equivalent and alternative to individual bargaining. Where workmen were willing and able to combine, they preferred it to bargaining as individuals with their employer because it enabled them to secure better terms of employment by controlling competition among themselves.[55]

As we saw in Chapter 2, this market-based formulation was dominant in the 19th-century English law and practice of freedom of association. It has been criticised by Flanders because the Webbs 'were not comparing like with like . . . collective bargaining is not collective bargaining'.[56] Individual bargaining is an exchange-based relationship negotiating the price for the sale of labour. Collective bargaining is not a collective analogue of this individual bargaining, even in its decentralised enterprise-based forms. It is 'essentially a rule-making process, and this is a feature which has no proper counterpart in individual bargaining'.[57] This disparity is especially marked in sectoral and national collective bargaining, where the formulation of industry-wide standards is more analogous to (public) law-making than (private) market

[54] This 'molecular' argument is set out in Alan Bogg and K.D. Ewing, 'A (Muted) Voice at Work? Collective Bargaining in the Supreme Court of Canada' (2012) 33 Comparative Labor Law and Policy Journal 379. 397. It draws upon Leif Wenar, 'Rights', Stanford Encyclopaedia of Philosophy, Rights (Stanford Encyclopedia of Philosophy).

[55] Allan Flanders, 'Collective Bargaining: A Theoretical Analysis', in Allan Flanders, *Management and Unions: The Theory and Reform of Industrial Relations* (Faber & Faber 1970) 213, 215.

[56] Ibid. 215.

[57] Ibid. 216.

exchange. In fact, the constitutionalisation of the market-based model would contradict Langille's proper concern to avoid constitutionalising (and ossifying) legal models that restrict the scope for democratic experimentation. It would entrench a restrictive conception of a process that is much more varied.

In 'The Legal Structure of Freedom of Association', co-authored with Benjamin Oliphant, the constitutional critique is more nuanced.[58] The authors still counsel caution on the constitutional entrenchment of duties imposed by the government on private actors, but they also accept that in certain circumstances such 'derivative rights' may be warranted. In so doing, they do not pursue the earlier linguistic argument about constitutional 'freedoms'. The authors identify *Dunmore v Ontario (Attorney General)* as an example of the justified constitutional recognition of derivative rights.[59] *Dunmore* involved the exclusion of agricultural workers from the basic legal protections against unfair labour practices, such as the discriminatory victimisation of trade unionists. The SCC directed the legislature to introduce legislation that protected agricultural workers from interference and discrimination in the exercise of their basic associational freedoms. In other words, this was constitutionalising the 'right to organise'. This was not very different to an equality-type remedy, because the remedial legislation would (in effect) extend the general statutory protections from anti-union discrimination available to other workers in the labour code.

There are several arguments that justify this limited recognition of derivative rights in a *Dunmore*-type case.[60] The specification of the rights and duties in targeting individual discrimination wrongs is relatively precise compared with the definitional ambiguities of a 'duty to bargain in good faith'. Given this feature of the right to organise, the scope for usurping the legislator's democratic role is also more limited. The protection of workers from acts of discriminatory victimisation lies at the core of the right to organise. Unlike the wide comparative variations in legal models of collective bargaining, individual protections from discrimination seem to be universal elements recurring across legal systems. Given their determinate content, the specification of these rights is not as politically controversial as a duty to bargain. Most importantly, for Langille and Oliphant, this approach also emphasises the exceptional nature of 'derivative rights'. In *Dunmore*, it was all but impossible for this disadvantaged group of workers to organise without basic legal protections from employer discrimination. The absence of legal protections would

[58] Langille and Oliphant (n 48).
[59] [2001] 3 SCR 1016.
[60] Langille and Oliphant (n 48) 290–293.

have rendered the agricultural workers' constitutional freedoms illusory. By contrast, the freedom of agricultural employers to victimise trade unionists was of no value at all and provided a weak argument against imposing a duty.

This basic distinction between 'collective' and 'individual' rights has been reflected in the case law under the ECHR, the UK, and Canada. This is unsurprising. There is a compelling *moral* case for judicial protection of workers against discriminatory victimisation. These derivative rights have constitutional priority. This is not because they are easy or simple to define, but because it is a distinctive judicial responsibility to enforce norms against wrongful discrimination. Beyond this right to organise, I will argue that there is scope for constitutionalising the right to collective bargaining without thereby constitutionalising the Wagner Act model. As we shall see, the SCC has developed constitutional *principles* which provide guidance to legislators while leaving creative space for a range of compliant legislative schemes. This provides a response to Langille and Oliphant's reasonable concerns that constitutional norms might ossify a specific statutory model of labour relations.

B. Sheldon Leader and the constitutional right to members-only bargaining

Proceeding from a similar basic concept of freedom of association—the freedom to do collectively that which one is at liberty to do as an individual—Sheldon Leader reaches a radically different outcome from Langille and Oliphant.[61] Leader also focuses on individual rights, defending an individual right that the worker's chosen trade union should be able to negotiate on her behalf. Leader starts from the proposition that workers have a *duty* to join a trade union.[62] As a complement to this duty, Leader also defends the *right* to join a trade union of the individual's choice. This enhances the freedom of workers by providing them with a range of representational options. Given the right to join a trade union of one's choosing and be a trade union member, this facilitation of free choice also extends to the representational activities of the trade union. Union membership without union representation negates the value of joining a union. This includes the right that the union should be able to negotiate on the member's behalf: 'Respect for the right to freedom

[61] Sheldon Leader's book on freedom of association has been the foundational monograph for nearly thirty years. Sheldon Leader, *Freedom of Association: A Study in Labor Law and Political Theory* (Yale UP 1992).

[62] Ibid. chapter 10.

of association demands both freedom of choice of union membership and the right of unions representing significant minority interests to negotiate on the same terms as majority unions do.'[63] This is a norm of equal treatment as between majority and minority trade unions in the bargaining unit. Where the employer is subject to a duty to negotiate with a majority trade union, the equality norm would require the duty to negotiate to extend to all minority unions as well.

In some respects, Leader's arguments reflect the logical implications of the individual right/duty to be a trade union member. They also reflect his pluralistic account of the diversity of needs and conflicts of interests *between* workers.[64] These considerations are a product of the heterogeneity of workers' needs and interests in modern labour markets, and the disintegration of the 'standard' employee.[65] Part-time workers, casual workers, women workers, older and younger workers, black and other minority ethnic workers, all have their own needs and experiences. Unions with monopolised exclusive bargaining rights will inevitably tend to favour the interests of the majority. This could lead to the interests of marginalised groups within the workforce being devalued or even ignored in collective negotiations. The advantage of a constitutionalised right to members-only bargaining is that conflicts between groups of workers can be more effectively mediated through negotiation. Unions would be free to coordinate their bargaining demands in appropriate cases, but they would also have the freedom to represent the distinctive interests of their own members when needed.

Recall Jacobs' comparative law observation on union representativeness that 'It appeared to be impossible to treat all trade unions and employers' associations equally.'[66] Yet this impossibility is precisely what Leader's argument would seem to demand. From a comparative perspective, members-only bargaining is relatively rare, and in some legal systems it may even be illegal.[67] Most legal systems settle upon some kind of priority rule for representative trade unions. This is to avoid excessive fragmentation of bargaining units, weakened bargaining power for workers, and inefficient bargaining practices for employers. A particularly strong example is the exclusive bargaining agent model in the US system. In most labour law systems, however, minority unions

[63] Ibid. 178.

[64] A.C.L. Davies, 'Identifying "Exploitative Compromises": The Role of Labour Law in Resolving Disputes between Workers' (2012) 65 Current Legal Problems 269.

[65] Sheldon Leader, 'Review of *Labour Law and Freedom: Further Essays in Labour Law* by Lord Wedderburn' (1996) 25 Industrial Law Journal 83.

[66] Jacobs (n 9) 211.

[67] Wedderburn (n 27) 223.

will usually experience some disadvantages where there are legal criteria of representativeness. Unequal treatment is the corollary of representativeness.

As with any equality argument, the critical normative question is always: can the unequal treatment be justified? If it can, it is not wrongful. Leader's constitutionalised right to members-only bargaining would be radically disruptive of many well-functioning systems of collective bargaining. Most legal systems use some criteria of representativeness, and these inevitably disadvantage minority unions. Many of these systems developed in ways that reflected the social histories of trade union movements. Legal criteria of representativeness reflected democratic choices by legislatures, usually in consultation and dialogue with the social partners. The ubiquity of representativeness, and its importance as an object of democratic choice, should lead us to be sceptical about Leader's argument on members-only bargaining. While the practical feasibility of a constitutional principle is not decisive to its application, it surely matters that a significant number of otherwise decent labour law systems would infringe the fundamental constitutional right to members-only bargaining.

This individualised right could also lead to the fragmentation of collective bargaining and weaken the bargaining strength of workers. The case of *UKAPE v ACAS*, discussed by Leader, is interesting in this respect.[68] In the Court of Appeal, Lord Denning upheld a judicial review challenge against a decision of ACAS not to award recognition to a smaller union under the statutory recognition procedure in force at that time. This judgment was eventually overruled by the House of Lords, which affirmed the administrative discretion and expertise of ACAS. The effect of the Court of Appeal's intrusive judicial review of ACAS in this (and other cases) effectively disabled ACAS, and this led in part to the repeal of the recognition procedure in 1980.[69] It is difficult to view this repeal as a beneficial legal development for workers' freedom of association. The judiciary had undermined democratically enacted legislation in pursuit of an individualistic conception of freedom of association. It would be surprising if this removal of auxiliary legislation improved the bargaining power of workers in 1980.

The functional evaluation of bargaining models—does it improve the bargaining power of workers overall?—is a relevant consideration in assessing the attractiveness of the individual right to members-only bargaining. It is also highly relevant to constitutional issues around judicial intervention. If the legislature has adopted criteria of representativeness leading to the unequal

[68] *United Kingdom Association of Professional Engineers (UKAPE) and another v ACAS* [1979] ICR 303.
[69] R.C. Simpson, 'Judicial Control of ACAS' (1979) 8 Industrial Law Journal 69.

treatment of different unions, a measure of judicial self-restraint is warranted. Where those differences in treatment can be justified, in part by considering the overall social and economic outcomes of the bargaining system, it would not be constitutionally appropriate for the courts to intervene.

We now move on to consider the judicial treatment of collective bargaining under the ECHR, the UK, and Canada. In different ways, each of these legal contexts demonstrates that the courts have discharged their constitutional responsibilities with due restraint. In this respect, many of the cautionary arguments of Langille and Oliphant have been reflected in the case law.

IV. Article 11 and the Right to Collective Bargaining

A. The early case law: *Swedish Engine Drivers' Union* and *National Union of Belgian Police*

Let us begin with two of the earliest Article 11 cases on trade union rights. They were not concerned directly with the 'right to collective bargaining'. It would be over three decades before such a right was recognised explicitly by the Strasbourg Court. However, it is instructive to consider them because there is an underlying factor—I will call it 'constitutionalising voluntarism'—that has been remarkably enduring in the modern law on Article 11. Both cases considered 'representativeness' criteria for trade unions in national legal systems. This is perhaps the neuralgic point in the clash between labour law and civil liberties, because representativeness is inherently exclusionary in its effects. Inevitably, some trade unions benefit, whereas others do not. Indeed, that is the very point of the criterion.

In *Swedish Engine Drivers' Union v Sweden*, the ECtHR examined the highly centralised Swedish collective bargaining model under Article 11.[70] This early Article 11 case was centrally concerned with the issue of representativeness in a national context. The Swedish National Collective Bargaining Office only concluded collective agreements with the three major trade union federations. This policy favouring federated unions meant that the public negotiator was not presented with an excessive number of bargaining partners, and this facilitated the efficient negotiation of collective agreements.[71] The Office refused to conclude a collective agreement with the smaller non-federated

[70] (1979-80) 1 EHRR 617.
[71] Ibid. [46].

Swedish Engine Drivers' Union (the Union). Inevitably, non-federated unions were disadvantaged by this unequal treatment because it rendered membership of smaller unions less attractive. It also meant that the Union could not appoint safety inspectors and representatives on the Central Works Council of the Swedish State Railways.

The Court concluded that there was no interference under Article 11(1) and that the difference in treatment between federated and non- federated unions was justified by relevant reasons under Article 14. There was no right to conclude a collective agreement, and in any event, this would be inconsistent with the voluntary nature of collective bargaining. Limiting the conclusion of collective agreements to federated unions also enabled more efficient collective bargaining, and according to the Court, there were no 'ill-intentioned designs in the matter'.[72] This no doubt reflected the fact that the rules on representativeness were aimed at *supporting* effective collective bargaining, not undermining it. The Court also set down propositions that would be canonical in the decades that followed. The Convention 'leaves each State a free choice of the means to be used' in ensuring that the members of a trade union have a right, to protect their interests, that the trade union should be heard by an employer.[73] While the negotiation of a collective agreement was one such means, there were others available in this case. What was required was that 'under national law trade unions should be enabled, in conditions not at variance with Article 11, to strive for the protection of their members' interests'.[74] This envisaged a consideration of the totality of measures in a legal system, to assess the general ability of unions to defend the occupational interests of members.

It was also relevant in this case that the Union was not *prevented* from seeking negotiations with the Office and its members were protected from acts of individual prejudicial discrimination for trade union reasons.[75] These fundamental rights were protected under the Swedish 1936 Act on the Right to Organise and Negotiate. These rights ensured that trade unions could pursue voluntary negotiations supported by legal protections for employees against acts of anti-union discrimination. If either of these elements had not been guaranteed under Swedish law, it seems very likely that this would have constituted an interference. It was implicit in *Swedish Engine Drivers' Union* that there were two fundamental and necessary elements under Article 11. The

[72] Ibid.
[73] Ibid. [40].
[74] Ibid.
[75] Ibid. [41].

first was that the union was not *prevented* from seeking voluntary negotiations with the employer (the 'voluntary principle'). The second was that individual employees were protected from discrimination and victimisation for trade union reasons (the 'individual non-discrimination principle'). This constitutionalised the basic preconditions of a voluntary system of collective bargaining. It also left the state with a significant discretionary margin to choose the form of its bargaining institutions beyond that voluntarist baseline.

The *National Union of Belgian Police v Belgium* case was also concerned with legal criteria of representativeness, which had the effect of excluding the National Union of Belgian Police from consultation with the Ministry of the Interior.[76] These representativeness rules accorded preferential access to unions open to all staff, which inevitably disadvantaged unions with a narrower occupational focus. The Court concluded that there was no interference under Article 11 and the difference in treatment of unions was justified under Article 14. As in *Swedish Engine Drivers' Union*, the ECtHR emphasised that the union in this case was able 'to present claims and to make representations for the protection of the interests of its members or certain of them'.[77] Individual trade union members were also protected in their right to join the trade union.[78] While the representativeness criteria indisputably led to unequal treatment of trade unions, this difference was justified by reference to avoiding 'trade union anarchy' and promoting a cohesive staff policy.[79] Since representativeness was aimed at supporting a system of efficient consultation, not undermining it, this was not wrongful discrimination under Article 14. As with *Swedish Engine Drivers' Union*, this case could also be viewed as constitutionalising voluntarism.

It is little surprise that these early engagements should emphasise the primacy of labour law's autonomy. 'Representativeness' is a universal element of the right to bargain collectively. It is integral to the concrete definition and realisation of the right in national legal orders. It is inevitable that there should be winners and losers, because to define representativeness is necessarily to include some and exclude others. The ECtHR emphasised the importance of the government's justifying reasons: were they relevant reasons or were they 'ill-intentioned'?

These judgments also point to a fundamental baseline under Article 11 that we have described as 'constitutionalising voluntarism'. These early cases

[76] Application no. 4464/70, 27 October 1975.
[77] Ibid. [40].
[78] Ibid. [41].
[79] Ibid. [48].

indicated a collective and an individual dimension. The collective dimension focused on whether the association was prevented from making representations to an employer (let us call this the voluntary principle). The individual dimension considered whether there were adequate individual non-discrimination protections inherent in a right to organise (let us call this the individual non-discrimination principle). These dimensions have proved to be remarkably enduring and still provide the core of Article 11 in the modern case law.

B. The watershed: *Wilson v UK*

Wilson v UK still stands as a landmark judgment in the development of trade union rights under Article 11, not least because the applicant trade unions succeeded in their Article 11 claims.[80] It arose out of two separate cases under UK law, which involved the derecognition of trade unions by employers in the journalism and ports sectors. Under UK law at that time, trade union recognition was voluntary in nature. To facilitate derecognition, the employers used financial inducements to persuade employees to sign new 'personal' contracts that excluded collective bargaining and union representation. At the collective level, the employers were fully entitled to withdraw recognition because there was no legal duty to recognise or negotiate under UK law at that time. At the individual level, the litigation was focused on whether withholding pay increases from employees who wished to continue with union representation was statutory 'action short of dismissal' with the purpose of deterring, penalising, or preventing trade union membership. There were many twists and turns in the domestic litigation, but eventually the House of Lords concluded that there was not 'action short of dismissal' because of trade union membership.[81] The failure to give benefits was an omission, not an act. And the discrimination was targeted at union representation, not the protected category of union membership.

The ECtHR concluded that there had been a violation of Article 11. It is tempting to read *Wilson* as a fundamental shift from *Swedish Engine Drivers' Union* and *National Union of Belgian Police*. That would be a mistake. The issue in *Wilson* was not discrimination between trade unions. It was discrimination

[80] [2002] 35 EHRR 20 (*Wilson*). For a biographical account of this litigation, see Alan Bogg, 'Wilson and Palmer: A Biographical Portrait of a Landmark Case', in Jeremias Adams-Prassl and others (eds), *Landmark Cases in Labour Law* (Hart 2022) chapter 10.
[81] *Associated Newspapers Ltd v Wilson; Associated British Ports v Palmer* [1995] 2 AC 454.

targeted at individuals. Individual discrimination was not an issue in those older cases. The Court in *Wilson* recognised that these facts engaged the state's positive duty to protect Article 11 rights of trade unions and workers. It observed that

> it is of the essence of the right to join a trade union for the protection of his interests that employers should be free to instruct or permit the union to make representations to their employer or to take action in support of their interests on their behalf. If workers are prevented from so doing, their freedom to belong to a trade union, for the protection of their interests, becomes illusory. It is the role of the State to ensure that trade union members are not prevented or restrained from using their union to represent them in attempts to regulate their relations with employers.[82]

The statutory framework 'permitted employers to treat less favourably employees who were not prepared to renounce a freedom that was an essential feature of union membership. Such conduct constituted a disincentive or restraint on the use by employees of union membership to protect their interests'.[83] There are four aspects of this judgment that should be emphasised. First, the description in terms of 'less favourable treatment' indicates that this was analogous to a core direct discrimination wrong. *Wilson* did not involve coercive interference or the imposition of penalties by the employer. The failure to give benefits was sufficient to trigger liability under Article 11. Second, the ECtHR did not consider whether the legal framework permitting individual discrimination was justified under Article 11(2). It moved directly to a finding that there had been a violation. Nor did the Court make any reference to the state's margin of appreciation, presumably because there was no margin in relation to individual discrimination. This reinforces the fact that this is a serious intrinsic wrong. Third, *Wilson* involved a private sector employer, and this did not register as a matter of any significance for the Court in the application of a strict legal standard. Finally, there is no suggestion that the freedom of the unions to seek voluntary negotiations with the employers (the unions were not *prevented* from doing so) was sufficient to outweigh the potential for individual discrimination. The robust individual protection from trade union discrimination is an *essential* Article 11 requirement. It is not merely a relevant factor to be considered in the overall totality.

In relation to the collective aspects of *Wilson*, such as the absence of a legal duty to recognise or negotiate, the ECtHR pursued a more orthodox line. In

[82] *Wilson* (n 80) [46].
[83] Ibid. [47].

these matters, the state enjoyed a 'wide margin of appreciation', given 'the sensitive character of the social and political issues involved in achieving a proper balance between the competing interests and the wide divergence between the domestic systems in this field'.[84] The voluntary framework for union recognition was within that permissible range:

> Compulsory collective bargaining would impose on employers an obligation to conduct negotiations with trade unions. The Court has not yet been prepared to hold that the freedom of a trade union to make its voice heard extends to imposing on an employer an obligation to recognise a trade union. The union and its members must however be free, in one way or another, to seek to persuade the employer to listen to what it has to say on behalf of its members.[85]

This was entirely consistent with the 1970s case law. Provided that the union was not *prevented* from seeking to represent its members' occupational interests (what we have called the voluntary principle), this feature of UK law was consistent with Article 11. The significance of *Wilson* was in clarifying this Article 11 bifurcation between individual discrimination (no margin of appreciation) and collective regulation (wide margin of appreciation). I have argued that this was already implicit in the earlier case law. *Wilson* clarified it. The post-*Wilson* case law developed these distinctions further.

C. After *Wilson:* the right to organise and the right to bargain collectively

The explicit recognition of the right to collective bargaining as an essential element came in *Demir and Baykara v Turkey*.[86] This was a 'collective' case concerning the legal framework regulating public sector trade unions and collective bargaining. It was also an extreme case on its facts, and this has been important in the subsequent treatment of the case by other courts. Under Turkish law, the union had not acquired legal personality, which meant that its collective agreement was annulled because it was of no legal effect. This required the reimbursement of sums that had been secured through the annulled collective agreement. These facts engaged two elements of Article

[84] Ibid. [44].
[85] Ibid.
[86] *Demir and Baykara v Turkey* [2009] 48 EHRR 54.

11: the right to form and join trade unions by municipal civil servants; and the right to engage in collective bargaining.

The Grand Chamber concluded that the right to collective bargaining should now be recognised as an essential element, reflecting developments in international law and comparative national law and practice.[87] The annulment of the collective agreement was a significant interference with Article 11, and it could not be justified as 'necessary' under Article 11(2). Following *Demir*, there were high expectations for the progressive development of trade union rights under Article 11.[88] Later cases have certainly disappointed those expectations. We have already identified the 'voluntary principle' as an element in the implicit constitutional bedrock of Article 11 from those early cases in the mid-1970s. This collective enquiry examines the totality of measures to ascertain if the union can represent its members' occupational interests effectively. On the extreme facts in *Demir*, the non-recognition of legal personality and the annulment of a collective agreement *prevented* the union from pursuing its activities in any way.

After *Demir*, the bifurcation between 'individual' and 'collective' cases can now be seen more clearly. Starting with the post-*Demir* 'individual' cases, the ECtHR has pursued a strong protective approach in cases concerned with individual trade union discrimination, victimisation, and the right to organise.[89] The cases have examined substantive rights in national law which should protect workers from discrimination in respect of union membership, union activities, and union representation.[90] The ECtHR has also emphasised the importance of effective remedies and accessible enforcement procedures. In *Danilenkov v Russia*, there had been extensive anti-union victimisation in the aftermath of a strike at the Kalingrad seaport.[91] This included a reduction of earnings, penalising union members by the allocation of work duties, and mass redundancies. The legal protections under national law were based in criminal liability, and the high evidential burden for criminal liability meant that it was difficult for claimants to secure effective redress. According to the ECtHR, 'real and effective' protection required accessible redress in the civil courts, rather than relying on public prosecutorial agencies to pursue criminal charges. In cases of alleged anti-union discrimination, where there is a prima facie case of discrimination, the burden should shift onto the employer

[87] Ibid. [153]–[154].
[88] K.D. Ewing and John Hendy, 'The Dramatic Implications of Demir and Baykara' (2010) 39 *Industrial Law Journal* 2.
[89] This has also been reflected in the Article 11 jurisprudence on the right to strike. See Chapter 5 below.
[90] *Straume v Latvia* [2022] IRLR 802, [91]–[93].
[91] [2009] ECHR 1243.

to prove innocent intent.[92] This would address some of the difficulties for claimants in proving a mental state of discriminatory intent. It is likewise important that remedies for trade union discrimination are calibrated to have a dissuasive and deterrent effect on wrongdoers.[93] This would not be satisfied by low levels of financial compensation that allow discriminating employers to pursue union exclusion as a cost of doing business. It might require the reinstatement of trade unionists to restore the visible presence of the trade union in the workplace and even punitive damages. Given the intrinsically wrongful nature of trade union discrimination, even 'minimal sanctions dissuade trade union members from freely engaging in their activities'.[94] This 'right to organise' is protected as an intrinsic matter. It is not necessary for the union activities to be linked instrumentally to collective bargaining. Discrimination against individual workers is a core wrong, regardless of any consequential effects on union strength in the workplace.

In the post-*Demir* 'collective' cases, by contrast, the ECtHR has continued to emphasise the wide margin of appreciation for states. In *UNITE the Union v UK*, the union challenged the abolition of Agricultural Wages Boards by the Enterprise and Regulatory Reform Act 2013.[95] This framework was first introduced in 1917 to provide a mechanism to set minimum wages and conditions in the agricultural sector, and it provided a substitute for voluntary collective bargaining. Without this strong auxiliary intervention, conditions in the agricultural sector meant that union organisation and collective bargaining was unlikely to sustain itself. Unions in the agricultural sector were not prevented from applying for recognition under the general legal procedure in Schedule A1 Trade Union and Labour Relations (Consolidation) Act (TULRCA) 1992. However, this legal procedure was practically inaccessible because no agricultural employer satisfied the statutory threshold of employing at least 21 workers. This excluded almost all agricultural workers from the general recognition machinery because they were employed in smaller enterprises. Despite this, the ECtHR concluded that the application was manifestly ill-founded. The key matter for the Court was that unions were not 'prevented' from seeking negotiations and securing collective agreements with employers.[96] This could be contrasted with the situation in *Demir*, where the union was prevented through non-recognition of legal personality and annulment of the collective agreement. Given the diversity of collective bargaining models

[92] *Hoppen and Trade Union of AB Amber Grid Employees v Lithuania* [2023] ECHR 46, [230].
[93] *Tek Gida Is Sendikasi v Turkey* [2017] ECHR 318, [55]–[56].
[94] *Straume* (n 90) [92].
[95] *Unite the Union v United Kingdom* App. No. 65397/13.
[96] Ibid. [65].

across Europe, the ECtHR is likely to have been very wary of constitutionalising specific auxiliary interventions. It was also relevant that the 2013 legislation had been preceded by a public consultation (although the parliamentary debates were ex post facto). After *UNITE*, the prospect for a successful positive duty claim in an Article 11 collective bargaining case is likely to be severely limited. The facts in *UNITE* were extreme and amounted to the *de facto* prevention of collective bargaining, even if not its *de jure* prevention.

The Article 11 case law in the mid-1970s had its origins in constitutional challenges to the rules establishing the representative status of trade unions. This continues to be a source of friction between labour law and constitutional norms. In *Association of Civil Servants and Union for Collective Bargaining and Others v Germany*, the ECtHR considered the legal prioritisation of collective agreements negotiated by the most representative unions in the German system.[97] This unequal treatment of smaller and minority unions meant that it was more difficult for them to negotiate and apply their own collective agreements. Unsurprisingly, the ECtHR held that 'States remained free to organise their collective bargaining system so as, if appropriate, to grant special status to representative trade unions.'[98] What counts as 'representative' displays significant and reasonable variation across different European systems. The ECtHR also regarded it as important that the rules were designed to support rather than undermine a strong system of collective bargaining. The treatment of these 'representativeness' issues by the Court has remained remarkably consistent since the 1970s.

In sum, the right to collective bargaining under Article 11 has been sensitive to the autonomy of labour law, especially in 'collective' cases. The recent development of the legal principles has been less dramatic than it first appeared. *Demir* certainly signalled an important shift in giving explicit recognition to the right to collective bargaining. Yet the underlying norms (and their application) have been remarkably stable and consistent.

To conclude, there are two fundamental norms under Article 11. The first is where the union is *prevented* from engaging in voluntary collective bargaining, considering the totality of the measures (what I have called the voluntary principle). The second is where the legal framework does not provide effective legal protections for individual workers from anti-union discrimination and victimisation (what I have called the individual non-discrimination principle). These non-discrimination protections are categorical and cannot be mitigated by pointing to the factual abilities of the union to pursue its

[97] [2022] ECHR 543.
[98] Ibid. [60].

activities. In this respect, the right to organise is not connected instrumentally to recognition or collective bargaining. This also has significant consequences for the margin of appreciation.

This bifurcation of the 'collective' and 'individual' is demonstrated perfectly in *Tek Gida v Turkey*.[99] In relation to the union's challenge to the representativeness rules in Turkish law, the ECtHR (predictably) did not find a violation on the facts. This reflects a consistent pattern of strong deference to 'collective' legal concepts in national law, and this is obviously relevant to legal criteria of representativeness. In relation to the mass dismissal of trade unionists, by contrast, the remedies under Turkish law were not sufficiently dissuasive of discriminatory behaviour. The ECtHR adopted a very stringent approach with a narrow margin because this involved individual discrimination against trade unionists and the need for effective judicial protection.

V. The Right to Collective Bargaining and UK Law: Democracy and Deference

There is an extensive statutory framework regulating the right to organise and the right to collective bargaining in UK law. In respect of the right to organise, the statutory rights in TULRCA 1992 provide workers and employees with extensive protection from anti-union discrimination in respect of access to employment, detriment, financial inducements, and dismissal. These provisions generally protect union membership (and non-membership), taking part in the activities of an independent trade union at an appropriate time, and the use of union services.[100] Together, they establish a norm of individual non-discrimination. There has been relatively little domestic recourse to Article 11 in respect of these statutory provisions, which are already fairly comprehensive in scope. In *Jet2.com Ltd v Denby*, the Employment Appeal Tribunal (EAT) considered the scope of discrimination protections for union membership in a refusal of employment case.[101] Unusually, s. 137 refers only to trade union membership, and it does not extend to union activities or the use of union services. In this case, the claimant had been a trade union activist during his previous employment with Jet2.com. The EAT supported a purposive interpretation of union membership to encompass those union

[99] *Tek Gida* (n 93).
[100] For a human rights analysis of these statutory provisions, see Alan Bogg and others, *Human Rights at Work: Reimagining Employment Law* (Hart, 2024) 71–75.
[101] UKEAT/0070/17/LA.

activities and services that are integral to membership. This conclusion was supported by Article 11. There has been more extensive domestic engagement with Article 11 in relation to the statutory instantiation of the 'right to collective bargaining'.

A. Representativity and human rights

In the UK, most recognition is still 'voluntary' in that it is negotiated between employers and trade unions through persuasion, threats to use a statutory recognition procedure, or to pursue strike action. The main auxiliary statutory prop to the right to collective bargaining in the UK is contained in Schedule A1 TULRCA. Introduced in 2000, this sets out a lengthy and detailed legal procedure which provides an independent trade union with the opportunity to seek a legal declaration of recognition from the Central Arbitration Committee (CAC). Schedule A1 is based upon a specific conception of representativity—majority worker support in the bargaining unit—and this is assessed by the CAC either through membership checks or a ballot process. An important feature of the Schedule A1 model is its prioritisation of voluntary agreements over statutory recognition. The CAC cannot accept an application where there is an existing voluntary recognition agreement covering any part of the union's proposed bargaining unit. This reflected a political judgement that voluntary arrangements were more likely to be durable and efficient. There was also a desire to avoid legal resources being wasted on damaging inter-union disputes, which had been a particular feature of the 1970s experience with statutory union recognition.[102]

In fact, this primacy of voluntary arrangements was rooted in collective laissez-faire. It reflected a distinctive conception of 'representativeness' that had emerged over long historical development. The legal determination of recognition should always be subsidiary to the parties' own negotiated arrangements, because direct legal enforcement should be a last resort. There was also a strong historical aversion to judicial interference in collective labour relations. As in Strasbourg, contestation over 'representativeness' has been the constitutional flashpoint for the autonomy of labour law in the domestic courts. The wide margin of appreciation in 'collective' cases like *Demir* and *UNITE* has effectively insulated Schedule A1 from domestic Article 11

[102] For an early analysis of Schedule A1 in its historical context, Bob Simpson, 'Trade Union Recognition and the Law, a New Approach—Parts I and II of Schedule A1 to the Trade Union and Labour Relations (Consolidation) Act 1992' (2000) 29 Industrial Law Journal 193.

challenge. This is because of the 'mirror principle' and the fact that national courts will not exceed the scope of Convention rights as interpreted by the ECtHR.[103] If a matter is treated by the ECtHR as within the margin of appreciation, as legal criteria of representativity usually are, there is no Article 11 violation. If there is no Article 11 violation in Strasbourg, the mirror principle means that there is no violation in an English court either.

The first of these cases was *R (Boots Management Services Ltd.) v Central Arbitration Committee*.[104] It involved a voluntary recognition agreement with a non-independent association, the Boots Pharmacists' Association (BPA), which blocked a competing statutory application by the independent union, the Pharmacists' Defence Association Union (PDAU). The agreement with the BPA did not encompass core issues such as pay. The only statutory mechanism for displacing the existing voluntary agreement was by an application of an individual worker to trigger a statutory derecognition ballot. The PDAU argued that this convoluted process for displacing the voluntary agreement violated its Article 11 rights. Underhill LJ undertook a thorough review of the Strasbourg authorities. He acknowledged the possibility, in light of *Demir* and *UNITE*, 'that the absence of a statutory mechanism for compulsory collective bargaining might in particular circumstances give rise to a breach of Article 11'; though he also indicated that such a claim 'may face an uphill struggle'.[105] Given the extremity of the facts in *UNITE* itself, that assessment seems fair. If the agricultural workers in *UNITE* didn't make it up the hill, it is difficult to know who would.

Underhill LJ then considered the relationship between the abstract Article 11 right to collective bargaining and its concrete statutory instantiation in Schedule A1:

> it does not follow . . . that article 11 confers a universal right on any trade union to be recognised in all circumstances. It is self-evident that any right to be recognised conferred by domestic law will have to be defined by rules which identify which unions should be recognised by which employers in respect of which workers and for what purposes.[106]

[103] *R (on the application of Elan-Cane) v Secretary of State for the Home Department* [2021] UKSC 56, [87]. See further Lord Sales, 'The Developing Jurisprudence of the Supreme Court on Convention Rights', Scottish Public Law Group Conference, 5 June 2023. See A.C.L. Davies, 'Article 11 in the Mirror: The Importance of Section 2 Human Rights Act 1998 in Understanding the Court's Approach to Article 11 of the European Convention on Human Rights' (2025) Industrial Law Journal advanced access https://doi.org/10.1093/indlaw/dwaf014.

[104] [2017] IRLR 355 (*Boots*). For a human rights analysis, see Alan Bogg and Ruth Dukes, 'Article 11 ECHR and the Right to Collective Bargaining' (2017) 46 Industrial Law Journal 543.

[105] *Boots* (n 104) [47].

[106] Ibid. [54].

The legislative specification of any right is inevitably exclusionary because it is circumscribing specific juridical relationships between defined parties. The idea of 'universal' rights makes no sense at the level of legislative implementation. One of the core concepts in giving concrete legal form to the right to collective bargaining is representativeness. In this case, the option of seeking a derecognition ballot through the petition of an individual worker meant that there was a 'reasonably practicable route' for the PDAU to seek recognition.[107] There was a wide range of legislative choices that might have been made by the legislature in specifying the right and the conditions for its exercise, but these were matters for a democratic legislature.[108] It might have been preferable to give the PDAU itself a legal route for seeking a derecognition ballot of the incumbent union. Ultimately, Underhill LJ concluded that these legislative choices were within the legislature's margin of appreciation. It was not relevant that the court itself might have favoured a different legislative scheme. The effect of this was to insulate the concrete statutory instantiation of the right to collective bargaining from Article 11 challenge except in extreme cases.

Boots is a case that affirmed the primacy of labour law's autonomy. It leaves very little normative space, if any, between the abstract Article 11 right and its legislated definition in Schedule A1. Underhill LJ did however leave open the tantalising possibility that the nuclear option—the complete repeal of Schedule A1 (as distinct from suboptimal choices of statutory definition)—might violate Article 11.

Boots involved a case of a non-independent association, and there was a procedure in the legislation to displace it. *R (Independent Workers Union of Great Britain) v Central Arbitration Committee* involved a judicial review challenge by the IWGB.[109] The IWGB was locked out of Schedule A1 because of a subsisting voluntary agreement between the employer and UNISON. UNISON is a large and well-resourced independent union operating mostly in the public sector. There is no equivalent mechanism for derecognition where the recognised union is independent, as it was in this case. The leading judgment was given by Bean LJ, who concluded that there was no violation of Article 11 on these facts. Bean LJ's judgment contains some interesting reflections on the role of Article 11 and its relationship with legislation specifying its determinate content.

First, Bean LJ considered that the Article 11 right to collective bargaining is correlative to a legal duty on the employer to recognise it once the wishes of

107 Ibid. [66].
108 Ibid. [68].
109 [2021] ICR 729.

the workforce had been ascertained.[110] This is a controversial claim. Earlier in the chapter, we noted that the 'duty to bargain' concept is by no means a universal feature of collective bargaining systems across the world. Indeed, it has only been an intermittent feature of the British system in historical perspective. There is a wide range of ways in which collective bargaining can be promoted effectively through 'indirect' auxiliary mechanisms. For much of the 20th century, this was the position in the UK. It is highly unlikely that the Strasbourg Court would treat the absence of a legal duty to bargain as outside the state's margin of appreciation where there are other supportive state measures in place. The 'wishes of the workforce' is itself only one of the many ways in which representativity can be established, although it has been prominent in Anglo-American enterprise-based legal models. For all these reasons, the mirror principle is unlikely to support the proposition that a legal duty to bargain is an essential requirement of Article 11.

Second, Bean LJ perceptively traced the differences between conceptions of representativity.[111] One model would facilitate competition between different trade unions so that different worker constituencies were represented effectively. This conception has strong affinities with Sheldon Leader's arguments on freedom of association. Another model favours stability and unity by prioritising majority rule and exclusive bargaining rights. This was the model adopted by the legislature in Schedule A1. Bean LJ regarded this as a policy choice that was within the scope of legitimate democratic decision for the legislature. Underhill LJ agreed with this assessment and reiterated the 'very wide margin of appreciation to national legislatures in this area'.[112]

In *IWGB v Central Arbitration Committee and another*, the UK Supreme Court considered the argument that Article 11 required the state to maintain a legal recognition procedure like Schedule A1.[113] Strictly speaking, this was not necessary for the decision because the Court had concluded that Deliveroo Riders were not in an 'employment relationship' and so not entitled to trade union rights under Article 11 in the first place. This aspect of the decision has already been considered in Chapter 3. Based on a review of the Strasbourg jurisprudence and domestic cases, the Supreme Court considered that Article 11 did not include 'a right to compulsory collective bargaining'.[114] This was based upon the fact that in *UNITE* the *formal* ability of unions to seek voluntary negotiations was sufficient to avoid a violation of Article 11.[115]

110 Ibid. [64].
111 Ibid. [66].
112 Ibid. [73].
113 [2023] UKSC 43 (*Deliveroo*).
114 [133].
115 [133]–[134].

Given the mirror principle, it was not permissible for the national courts to go further than Strasbourg had gone in *Demir* and *UNITE*.[116] This reading of the Strasbourg case law is probably correct. I have argued that the Strasbourg Court has not yet gone beyond 'constitutionalising voluntarism'. However, *Deliveroo* is not a *UNITE*-type case. The critical difference is that the agricultural workers in *UNITE* were very likely to be in an 'employment relationship', but they were held not to be in *Deliveroo*.

Why does this matter? It matters because without 'worker' status, the riders in *Deliveroo* were legally unprotected from the most basic forms of anti-union discrimination under s. 146 TULRCA. Section 146 is a right for 'workers'. Non-worker riders are now exposed to the risk of discriminatory union victimisation, and they would have no legal remedies under the legislation. The definition of a trade union in s. 1 TULRCA also depends upon the organisation consisting wholly or mainly of 'workers'. This means that the riders would be unable to form their own 'trade union' as a precursor to seeking voluntary collective bargaining. The trade dispute immunity for strike action is limited under s. 244 TULRCA to a dispute 'between workers and their employer'. If the riders are not workers, this would expose organisers of strike action to liabilities in tort. There is also the uncertain ambit of competition law liabilities. In sum, it would not be legally safe either for a newly formed union to seek voluntary collective bargaining or for the riders to join or be active in a trade union. This violates the fundamental baseline of 'constitutionalising voluntarism'. The exclusion from union discrimination protections in s. 146 violates the individual norm. The exclusion from the statutory definition of a 'trade union' under s. 1 violates the collective norm. *Deliveroo* must be regarded as wrongly decided on the ambit of Article 11 duties.[117]

By way of final postscript on Article 11 in the UK, it is instructive to consider some recent developments on s. 145B TULRCA. This was the statutory provision introduced in 2004 to address the violation identified in *Wilson v UK*. The provision highlights the interesting ambiguities around individual non-discrimination and 'collective' matters. Under s. 145B TULRCA, an employer is prohibited from making offers to members of an independent trade union that is recognised (or seeking recognition). These offers must have the 'prohibited result', which is defined as a result whereby acceptance of the offers by multiple workers would mean that the term or terms are not or no longer determined by a collective agreement. It must also have been the 'sole or main

[116] [130].

[117] These arguments were set out following the High Court decision in *Deliveroo* but evidently fell on deaf ears: Alan Bogg, 'Taken for a Ride: Workers in the Gig Economy' (2019) 135 Law Quarterly Review 219.

purpose' of the employer. This statutory provision is far wider than *Wilson* itself, as demonstrated by the leading judgment in *Kostal UK Ltd v Dunkley and others.*[118] *Kostal* did not involve any discriminatory treatment of trade unionists but the making of offers during an ongoing collective bargaining negotiation prior to exhaustion of procedures and impasse. The UK Supreme Court unanimously held that this was a violation of s. 145B, and (unsurprisingly) they did not need to use Article 11 to get to that result. In many legal systems, this would be treated as a 'collective' issue, perhaps as an unfair labour practice because of a breach of good faith bargaining duties. Section 145B had evolved from its origins in tackling intrinsically discriminatory conduct in *Wilson* itself. The 'collective' nature of s. 145B means that it will usually be amenable to a wide margin under Article 11. Yet labour disputes constantly throw up new and challenging scenarios, and in a recent dispute, the employer appeared to restrict financial offers to non-members specifically to avoid s. 145B liability.[119] There can be no doubt that allocating contractual offers based upon union membership is a clear violation of Article 11. In fact, it is a more extreme case of individual discrimination than *Wilson* itself, where the offers there did not differentiate between members and non-members. This is a reminder of the ever-porous boundary between the 'individual' and the 'collective' in this context, which has significant implications for margin of appreciation.

VI. The Right to Collective Bargaining under the Canadian Charter: From Rights to Principles

The SCC has been in the vanguard of the constitutionalisation of the right to collective bargaining. There are important differences between the SCC and the ECtHR in terms of constitutional role and institutional limits. The ECtHR must contend with a wide comparative variety of European collective bargaining models in developing its normative standards, which we have described as trans-systemic incommensurability. It is sensitive to these national variations through its margin of appreciation doctrine. The SCC, by contrast, develops constitutional standards within a concrete legal tradition, relatively settled parameters for Canadian collective bargaining, and extensive statutory regulation. This does not mean that concerns around deference and democracy are irrelevant in national contexts. As we have seen, Langille

[118] [2021] UKSC 47.
[119] See Livv Housing strikers find solidarity at community conference | News | News | UNISON National.

and Oliphant's most persuasive challenge to the SCC's constitutional recognition of the right to collective bargaining is a deference concern.[120] They point to the risk of constitutionalising a specific legal model—the majoritarian Wagner Act model. According to the authors, this ossification would inhibit democratic experimentation with other legal models. This could prevent improvements to the existing statutory law. We can certainly acknowledge the authors' concerns. Even within national labour law systems, the 'duty to bargain in good faith' is not a universal element. It may not even be the most effective auxiliary legal support for collective bargaining.

The central question is whether the SCC has charted that delicate constitutional path between recognising the right to collective bargaining while respecting the democratic scope for legislators to instantiate it in incommensurable ways. Has the SCC avoided constitutionalising the Wagner Act model? If so, how has the constitutional standard interacted with the labour law formulation of the right to collective bargaining?

Although the legal contexts are very different, there are parallels in the sequences of constitutionalisation under the ECHR and the Charter. This has been reflected in three broad waves of constitutional collective bargaining cases that unfolded chronologically. The first wave of constitutionalisation occurred in the judicial concern to protect individual workers from acts of anti-union discrimination and victimisation. It was not sufficient to recognise a *freedom* to organise. This freedom was meaningless without a protective perimeter of rights and correlative duties not to dismiss, not to penalise, and so forth. The SCC took this step in *Dunmore*, and this was recognised by scholars like Langille and Oliphant as a legitimate instance of what they aptly describe as 'derivative rights'.[121] Almost contemporaneously, the ECtHR recognised the fundamental position of individual non-discrimination norms in *Wilson v UK*. There is now a solid constitutional entrenchment of the *right* to organise (and correlative duties not to penalise or discriminate).

The second wave of constitutionalisation occurred in the protection of collective bargaining and collective agreements from *direct acts of governmental interference*. This has arisen particularly in public sector collective bargaining contexts. In Canada, it was addressed in *Health Services & Support-Facilities Subsector Bargaining Association v British Columbia (B.C. Health Service)*.[122]

[120] Langille and Oliphant (n 48). See also Brian Langille and Benjamin Oliphant, 'From Rand to Rothstein: Labour Law, Fundamental Values and the Judicial Role', in Ivo Entchev and Lisa M. Kelly (eds), *Judicious Restraint: The Life and Law of Justice Marshall E. Rothstein* (LexisNexis 2016) 251.

[121] Langille and Oliphant (n 48) 270–272.

[122] [2007] 2 SCR 391 (*B.C. Health Services*).

This could be viewed as Canada's *Demir* moment, since in *Demir*, the ECtHR also considered a direct state interference with a public sector collective agreement. In so doing, it recognised the fundamental right to collective bargaining as an essential element under Article 11. The issue of institutional competence is less problematic in this type of case because the court is not constitutionalising a specific legal model. Instead, the focus is on assessing the justification for the governmental interference with the collective bargaining process. That collective bargaining process is already operating within the parameters set by the legal framework of collective bargaining. The court is not defining a specific model for collective bargaining.

The third wave raises the most difficult constitutional issues. In the Canadian context, it has arisen specifically in the context of occupational groups excluded from the general labour relations legislation, such as agricultural workers (as in the *Fraser* case)[123] or the police (as in the *Mounted Police Association of Ontario* [*M.P.A.O.*] case).[124] As discussed in Chapter 3, the most direct challenge to these occupational exclusions would be through a s. 15 equality argument, examining if the exclusion is justified by relevant reasons. The SCC has adopted a different route in these exclusion cases. It has evaluated the specific labour relations legislation for these occupational groups by reference to constitutional standards on collective bargaining developed under s. 2(d). I argue that the SCC has managed to avoid constitutionalising the Wagner Act model.

This has been achieved using two constitutional techniques. Let's describe these as 'basic floor' review (in *Fraser*) and directive constitutional principles (in *M.P.A.O.*). In *Fraser*, the SCC effectively endorsed what could be described as a 'basic floor' approach to the right to collective bargaining.[125] This identifies a basic constitutional floor of entitlements as a minimum representational guarantee for excluded workers. This approach provides a representational safety net for the agricultural workers, albeit one that falls short of the full range of 'Wagner Act' statutory rights and duties. In *M.P.A.O.*, the SCC articulated general constitutional principles that were more determinate than the abstract 'right to collective bargaining' but less specific than the statutory rules in the Wagner Act model. These principles were sufficiently general to accommodate a range of compliant statutory models, while also providing some guidance to legislators.

[123] *Ontario (Attorney General) v Fraser* [2011] 2 S.C.R. 3 (*Fraser*).

[124] *Mounted Police Association of Ontario v Canada (Attorney General)* [2015] 1 SCR 3 (*M.P.A.O.*).

[125] There are some affinities with 'minimum core' review in social rights adjudication. For a critical account of 'minimum core' review, see Jeff King, *Judging Social Rights* (Cambridge UP 2012) 114–115.

While both techniques have sometimes been criticised as a dilution of full-blooded collective bargaining as instantiated in legislation, this flows from the limits of constitutional adjudication in a democracy. The constitution should provide a floor rather than a developed system of collective bargaining rights. This allows legislators to build on this constitutionalised floor of rights.

Before considering these two techniques, we should begin with *B.C. Health Services*, which elucidated the constitutional right to collective bargaining under s. 2(d) of the Charter. This case involved a direct interference with sectoral collective bargaining in the B.C. health sector. In response to concerns about the financial sustainability of health care, the legislator enacted the Health and Social Services Delivery Improvement Act 2002. It did so after minimal consultation with the affected trade unions. The legislation invalidated existing provisions in collective agreements on a range of matters, and it pre-emptively barred any future agreements. This subject-matter included provisions on job security, layoffs, and bumping rights. The SCC found that there had been a 'substantial interference' with the right to collective bargaining and that this interference was not justified under s. 1 of the Charter.

In certain respects, the position of the SCC in recognising the right to collective bargaining involves different constitutional dilemmas to the ECtHR. The SCC was not faced with a multiplicity of collective bargaining models across many countries. It was considering the *Canadian* right to collective bargaining in light of *Canadian* constitutional values and *Canadian* history. There are two features of the argumentation in McLachlin CJ and LeBel J's judgment that warrant emphasis.

The first feature was that s. 2(d) should be approached purposively as a contextualised freedom specifically for trade unions. Obviously, this is consistent with a contextualised and purposive approach to other types of association too. This avoids the worry that other associations are disfavoured: they are treated in accordance with principles relevant to their own specific needs. In the terminology of equality before the law, any variation in treatment is justified by relevant differences. By contrast, 'generic' or decontextualised interpretation of s. 2(d) as a general associative freedom 'ignored differences between organizations. Whatever the organization—be it trade union or book club—its freedoms were treated as identical. The unfortunate effect was to overlook the importance of collective bargaining—both historically and currently—to the exercise of freedom of association in labour relations'.[126] A decontextualised interpretation will necessarily lead to a thinner set of constitutional norms

[126] *B.C. Health Services* (n 122) 417.

because the norms will need to be apt for a wide variety of different types of association: trade unions, political parties, churches, social clubs, and book clubs. Note there is nothing here to suggest that trade unions are any more intrinsically valuable than other types of association. The underlying point is that different associations instantiate a plurality of goods, they encounter distinctive challenges in civil society, and they may therefore need different packages of rights and liberties.[127] Collective bargaining is unlikely to be relevant to religious associations and learned societies; the freedom of collective worship is unlikely to be relevant to trade unions. This contextualisation also pointed towards constitutional values, especially the Charter values of equality and democracy. The traditional labour law justification for collective bargaining was to alleviate inequality of bargaining power and to provide workers with a collective voice to shape their working lives. This labour law justification was aligned with Charter values, and it gave those abstract values concrete content in the *B.C. Health Services* case.[128]

The second feature concerns the idea of *autochthony* in fundamental rights jurisprudence.[129] The term describes a situation where the specific content of rights is shaped by the thick ethical, constitutional, and cultural goods in a national context. Of all the rights considered in this book, the right to collective bargaining is deeply entwined in localised norms, histories of economic struggle, and social practices. The right to collective bargaining is described as 'a fundamental Canadian right',[130] and the judgment of McLachlin CJ and LeBel J elucidates it through its specific legal history in Canada.[131] This avoids some of the legitimacy challenges faced by supranational courts developing norms that must accommodate a range of incommensurable legal models. The SCC is working within the parameters set by Canadian social practices, long-standing legislation on collective bargaining, and national constitutional values. Where there is stability in the legal culture, this could allow a national court to develop more elaborate constitutional principles of representativity, for example, where these are embedded in long-standing legal and social practices. That would be far less legitimate for the ECtHR.

Does it follow from this contextualisation that the SCC was effectively drafting a labour code or constitutionalising the Wagner Act model? The SCC

[127] For an interesting defence of a contextualised approach to freedom in freedom of association, see Guy Davidov, 'Judicial Development of Collective Labour Rights—Contextually' (2010) 15 Canadian Labour and Employment Law Journal 235.

[128] *B.C. Health Services* (n 122) 440–441.

[129] Paul Craig, *UK, EU and Global Administrative Law: Foundations and Challenges* (Cambridge UP 2015) 272.

[130] *B.C. Health Services* (n 122) 420.

[131] Ibid. 420–433.

emphasised that the constitutional right to collective bargaining did not 'guarantee access to any particular statutory regime'.[132] It is obviously vital that there is constitutional space between s. 2(d) and the statutory schemes because of the separation of powers. Nevertheless, the abstract content of the constitutional right to collective bargaining was certainly shaped by this legislative context. This was reflected in the correlative linking of the right to collective bargaining with a duty to consult and negotiate in good faith.[133] McLachlin CJ and LeBel J elucidated this in terms of core features of the North American legal model: that it was procedural in nature, required a willingness to seek explain positions and seek an agreement, did not preclude 'hard bargaining' in pursuit of economic self-interest, and so on.[134] It would not have been legitimate for the ECtHR to have articulated constitutional standards with such precision because many European systems do not adopt a 'duty to bargain in good faith'.

There also needed to be 'substantial interference'. To establish this, the restrictions must strike at bargaining matters that are sufficiently important (and this may well be narrower than statutory subjects of bargaining). They must have a serious negative impact on the collective bargaining process. While this constitutional minimalism has been criticised by some scholars,[135] the SCC may simply have been signalling the proper limits of constitutional adjudication. As in *Demir*, the function of the constitutional court is to provide remedies for serious abuses that strike at the core of constitutional rights. This leaves the legislator free to build upon the constitutionally protected basic floor and to enact more generous statutory rights.[136]

This cautious approach has been reflected in the subsequent SCC case law on the right to collective bargaining. It has been supported by the elaboration of general constitutional principles which provide some determinate guidance to legislators while leaving a measure of creative freedom to select between different legislative schemes. In *Fraser*, the SCC considered the constitutionality of the Agricultural Employees Protection Act 2002 by reference to the s. 2(d) right to collective bargaining.[137] This provided a discrete statutory framework for agricultural workers, which conferred less extensive rights and duties than the general Labour Relations Act. It gave agricultural workers

[132] Ibid. 412.
[133] Ibid. 447.
[134] Ibid. 449.
[135] Judy Fudge, 'The Supreme Court of Canada and the Right to Bargain Collectively: The Implications of the *Health Services and Support* case in Canada and Beyond' (2008) 37 Industrial Law Journal 25, 40–41.
[136] For an elegant theoretical defence of this style of approach, see David Doorey, 'Graduated Freedom of Association: Worker Voice beyond the Wagner Model' (2012) 38 Queen's Law Journal 515.
[137] *Fraser* (n 123).

a right to make representations on terms and conditions of employment, and this was coupled with a duty on the employer to listen to those representations. Once again, the majority emphasised that s. 2(d) did not require a single or uniform statutory model. The constitutional standards were potentially compatible with a range of statutory schemes. In *Fraser*, the SCC evaluated the statutory scheme by reference to the general principle of a 'meaningful process' to pursue workplace goals. This required the employer's duty to be interpreted as requiring good faith consideration of those representations. While this standard is not empty, it did involve a retreat from the more substantial good faith negotiation norms elucidated in *B.C. Health Services*.[138] Abella J dissented on this basis, pointing out that there was no evidence of a single collective agreement having been negotiated under the 2002 legislation.[139] The open-textured nature of principles such as 'meaningful process' means that there is likely to be some disagreement in their application in hard cases like *Fraser*.

In *M.P.A.O.*, the SCC considered the imposition of a 'Staff Relations Representative Programme' in the Royal Canadian Mounted Police Service (RCMP) by reference to s. 2(d) of the Charter.[140] It found that there was a violation of s. 2(d) because the imposed scheme did not meet the constitutional principles protected under s. 2(d). This representative structure had been introduced as a substitute mechanism because RCMP members were not permitted to unionise or engage in collective bargaining. The majority in the SCC based its reasoning on constitutional principles of 'choice' and 'independence'. The workers' freedom to choose a representative facilitated accountability and empowered workers to shape the collective goals pursued by their association: it ensures that '*their* voice will be conveyed to the employer by the people *they* choose'.[141] The principle of 'choice' meant that a constitutionally compliant legal framework would need to protect 'the ability to form and join new associations, to change representatives, to set and change collective workplace goals, and to dissolve existing associations'.[142] Independence complements choice by ensuring that the association and its collective goals are autonomously chosen by the workers themselves. This would necessitate 'the freedom to amend the association's constitution and rules, the freedom

[138] See Bogg and Ewing (n 54) 380–388. Judy Fudge, 'Constitutional Rights, Collective Bargaining and the Supreme Court of Canada: Retreat and Reversal in the *Fraser* Case' (2012) 41 Industrial Law Journal 1.
[139] *Fraser* (n 123) [334].
[140] *M.P.A.O.* (n 124).
[141] Ibid. [87].
[142] Ibid. [86].

to elect the association's representatives, control over financial administration and control over the activities the association choose to pursue'.[143]

These may be understood as constitutional principles of trade union representativity. They reflect the ideal of a contextualised s. 2(d) freedom. Independence and choice are not salient for all associations, at least to the same degree. For example, it is not clear how independence would apply to religious associations. The principle of 'choice' might be controversial if adopted by the Strasbourg court because it is less easy to translate into European sectoral collective bargaining contexts. It is deeply embedded in the law and practice of Canadian collective bargaining and so fits with the idea of autochthony. As with 'meaningful process', these principles allow for a range of implementing statutory rules. For example, 'choice' can be implemented or measured in different ways, and it is consistent with a variety of specified support thresholds for collective bargaining rights. It is not tied to the majoritarian Wagner Act model.

VII. Conclusion

The right to collective bargaining as a civil liberty does have meaningful content. Across these three legal orders, there is a strong judicial emphasis on the fundamental individual right of non-discrimination, reflected in cases like *Wilson* and *Dunmore*. The 'right to organise' as an individual right is more amenable to judicial elaboration and protection than the 'right to collective bargaining' as a collective right. The relevant rights and duties can be defined with relative precision, and they are now underpinned by a clear basic norm of effective judicial protection and remedies in the ECHR system.

The parameters of a 'collective' right to collective bargaining are more politically contested and reveal a wide variety of regulatory models. Inevitably, the courts have proceeded more cautiously here. They have been sensitive to their limitations of expertise and the value of democracy in defining collective bargaining legislation. Constitutional standards have been permeable to labour law's definitions and justifications of the right to collective bargaining. Indeed, it is difficult to see how constitutional courts could derive a 'right to collective bargaining' from first principles, detached from a labour law anchoring. In terms of the fundamental constitutional core of this right, the direct state prevention of voluntary bargaining has triggered constitutional intervention.

[143] Ibid. [89].

The jurisprudence around positive duties to promote collective bargaining has been more cautious.

The SCC has developed intermediate constitutional principles to provide guidance to legislators, such as 'meaningful process' or 'choice', which limit the scope for judicial overreach. Yet these principles do provide legislators with determinate guidance. In cases like *B.C. Health Services*, this is formulated as a *Canadian* right to bargain collectively. By contrast, the UK courts have struggled to articulate a 'British' right to collective bargaining because of the domestic mirror principle. English courts must have regard to the margin of appreciation in Strasbourg cases, so that if a measure is within the Strasbourg margin of appreciation, it cannot then provide the basis for a legal challenge under the HRA. That margin is influenced by the wide range of European models of collective bargaining, which is less relevant when UK courts are evaluating national legislation. The diversity of European standards on collective bargaining is not an issue for the UK courts. The mirror principle has inhibited a British-style autochthony in the domestic Article 11 jurisprudence, and this contrasts with the freedom of the SCC to develop constitutional principles sensitive to national context.

At a minimum, the universal core of a right to collective bargaining requires that individual workers should be protected from employer discrimination and that their trade union should not be prevented from seeking to persuade an employer to listen to its representations. In this respect, the UK Supreme Court judgment in *Deliveroo* represents a failure to comply with Article 11, even accounting for the limiting effect of the mirror principle.

5
Freedom of Association and the Right to Strike

I. Introduction

This chapter will now consider the position of the right to strike in freedom of association. In most legal systems, the right to strike is a complex amalgam of ordinary legislation and private law doctrines such as contract and tort. It may also be protected as a constitutional right. When there is no specific textual reference to the right to strike in a constitutional document, this protection will often be based upon its derivation from the general right to freedom of association.

The issue to be addressed in this chapter is the nature of this interaction between the constitutionalised human right to strike and its concrete instantiation in labour law legislation. Most fundamentally, when there is a disagreement about the specific content of the right to strike, between the legislature and the constitutional court, how should the ambit of the right be determined? These issues are often more concerned with the appropriate allocation of public decision-making power between constitutional actors as they are with any first-order normative theory of a right to strike. This resolution of 'who decides?' is centred on the autonomy of labour law (especially statutes) and its relationship to general constitutional norms.

As comparative labour lawyers know, there are profound variations across different national systems. Comparative strike law is, in Lord Wedderburn's vivid formulation, 'kaleidoscopic' in terms of the right-holders (trade unions? Individual workers?), procedural requirements such as ballots and strike notices, the linkages with collective bargaining and collective agreements, peace obligations, the timing of strikes, the scope for sympathy and political strikes, and so forth.[1] The national specification of this right will often

[1] Lord Wedderburn, 'The Right to Strike: Is there a European Standard?', in Lord Weddeburn, *Employment Rights in Britain and Europe* (Lawrence & Wishart 1991) 276, 334.

Freedom of Association. Alan Bogg, Oxford University Press. © Alan Bogg 2026. DOI: 10.1093/9780191831690.003.0005

reflect reasonable yet incommensurable legislative choices. The 'organic' right of trade unions in the German system of industrial unions based on sectoral collective bargaining would be unthinkable in the pluralistic French system, where unions are organised on ideological and confessional lines and the right to strike is an individual constitutional right.[2] Given this reasonable incommensurability in strike laws, what are the constitutional limits of the autonomy of labour law? These challenges are more pronounced still for supranational courts grappling with wide variations in national laws and practices.

The chapter begins by considering three leading scholarly treatments of the right to strike and freedom of association. Some of these accounts were critical of what they regarded as excessive deference by constitutional courts to the legislated right to strike in labour legislation. To the critics, this deference leaves the right to strike vulnerable to popular democratic discontent, given the social and economic consequences of strikes. It is fair to say that the right to strike may sometimes not be a popular right, especially for those whose lives are disrupted by its exercise. Experience also suggests that it is easier for legislatures to enact restrictions than to enlarge freedoms in this domain. There is a problem if courts defer too quickly and too readily to populist measures in the heat of an industrial dispute. To some extent, the courts are immune to these short-term political pressures.

Over the last couple of decades, there has been a transformation in the constitutional life of the right to strike. It has been recognised as an element in freedom of association by the European Court of Human Rights (ECtHR), the United Kingdom Supreme Court (UKSC), and the Supreme Court of Canada (SCC). The chapter will examine how these different courts have grappled with the frictions between labour law and constitutional law, and with the interaction between legislatures and courts.

The main argument of this chapter echoes that of the previous chapter on collective bargaining: there is a fundamental bifurcation between 'individual' and 'collective' strike cases. In 'individual' cases involving sanctions against strikers participating in lawful industrial action, the courts are less inclined to defer to the legislature. This is because these discriminatory actions are intrinsically wrongful. When citizens are exposed to sanctions for exercising a fundamental right, this is analogous to wrongful direct discrimination. This reflects a deeper concern with equality before the law. By contrast, in 'collective' cases involving legislative choices about lawful purposes or democratic

[2] Alan Bogg, 'The Right to Strike, Minimum Service Levels, and European Values' (SSRN Working Paper Series, 2003).

procedures such as ballots, the courts have tended to give a very wide democratic latitude to legislatures. These matters vary widely across different legal systems, and this reflects reasonable incommensurability in the specification of the right. On this approach, the legislature defines the collective perimeter of lawful strike action, subject to light-touch judicial review. Within that perimeter, sanctions imposed on strikers attract vigorous judicial protection. This bifurcation between the individual and the collective has been reflected very strongly in the jurisprudence of the ECtHR. I shall argue that this basic constitutional distinction is sound, while also recognising that there has sometimes been excessive deference in some 'collective' cases under the European Convention on Human Rights (ECHR).

II. Freedom of Association and the Right to Strike: Three Leading Theorists

Before examining the case law on the right to strike and freedom of association, we will first consider three leading theoretical arguments on the right to strike. Each of them was written before the huge developments in constitutional courts deriving the right to strike from freedom of association. It is interesting to consider them in their own terms, and then to see how far these theoretical arguments have been reflected in later judicial reasoning. The arguments of Sheldon Leader and Keith Ewing were (in different ways) concerned to identify a much stronger role for constitutional norms. By contrast, Brian Langille is more cautious about the scope for a constitutionalised right to strike. His account is more sympathetic to the 'autonomy' of labour law, and constitutional respect for a *right* to strike enacted in ordinary labour legislation. This is consistent with Langille's approach to collective bargaining, considered in Chapter 4. The chapter will then consider the case law in the ECHR, the UK and Canada in light of these theoretical arguments.

A. Sheldon Leader and the 'independent' right to strike

In Sheldon Leader's important work on freedom of association, he developed an 'independent' argument for the right to strike.[3] The right to strike was rooted directly in freedom of association. If one is free to withdraw labour as

[3] Sheldon Leader, *Freedom of Association: A Study in Labor Law and Political Theory* (Yale UP 1992) 199–205.

an individual, one should be free to do it collectively with others. Freedom of association makes its distinctive contribution by shielding the collective exercise of those things that we are at liberty to do as individuals. This is freedom of association understood as the basic freedom to do collectively that which one is at liberty to do as an individual. It has nothing to say, by definition, on the individual freedom.

He contrasts this with an 'indirect' or 'instrumental' argument for the right to strike. This alternative argument is based either in the right to strike's indirect derivation from collective bargaining[4] or in its instrumental contribution to the trade union's effective pursuit of workers' occupational interests.[5] Leader's defence of the 'independent' over the 'instrumental' approach is concerned with the autonomy of labour law, a theme that is central to my own arguments in this book. In essence, his 'independent' argument is based upon the primacy of a constitutionalised right to strike. The 'independent' right to strike in the constitutional order may be very different to the legislated 'labour law' version of it. Where they diverge without justification, the constitutional right should trump the statutory right. This 'independent' right to strike might be highly disruptive of the 'labour law' right to strike as enacted in labour legislation. By contrast, the 'instrumental' or 'indirect' argument leads constitutional courts to defer in most cases to the existing legislation. There would be a strong default in favour of the labour law conception. According to Leader, this would marginalise the role of constitutional courts in right to strike cases unduly. Why is this so? And why is it a problem?

This marginalisation occurs because the 'indirect' or 'instrumental' argument is vulnerable to judicial concerns about 'deference' or 'judicial self-restraint'.[6] 'Deference' or 'judicial self-restraint' describes the set of considerations that curtail the legitimate role of the courts in constitutional review. These have already been considered in Chapter 1. These might include the democratic legitimacy of elected representatives or the relative expertise of courts compared with other institutions. The 'instrumental' argument depends upon the judicial characterisation of strike activity as an *essential* trade union activity. According to Leader, this kind of argument 'is vulnerable to a particular sort of judicial scruple: the aim to be politically impartial'.[7] The choices about the most appropriate mechanisms for facilitating trade union

[4] Sheldon Leader, 'Can You Derive a Right to Strike from the Right to Freedom of Association?' (2009–10) 15 Canadian Labour and Employment Law Journal 271, 273.

[5] Leader (n 3) 195–199.

[6] For an excellent account of judicial self-restraint, and its role in public law and labour law, see A.C.L. Davies, 'Judicial Self-Restraint in Labour Law' (2009) 38 Industrial Law Journal 278.

[7] Leader (n 3) 197.

activities are politically controversial. In sensitive matters of social and economic policy, courts tend to defer to legislatures. Strikes are disruptive, and electorates often favour restricting them. Deference reinforces these restrictive political forces. Courts do not have the social science expertise to evaluate legal effects on the relative bargaining power of employers and unions. As Leader argues, 'the instrumental argument forces courts into too close and too debatable a calculation of what healthy trade union activity calls for: a calculation of whether or not the right to strike should in any given case form part of the package of rights allowing for the right level of activity, or whether its absence is compensated for by other factors.'[8]

The 'independent' conception of the right to strike is based upon a version of equal protection or equality before the law arguments.[9] The basic equality claim is that individuals should be at liberty to do collectively with others that which they are each free to do as individuals. This would certainly block the imposition of special legal disabilities or penalties imposed on group activities simply because they are collective in nature. As our discussion of 19th-century labour law in Chapter 2 demonstrates, liberty does not always extend from the individual to the collective in a simple aggregative way. The laws on conspiracy and combination are testament to the law's repressive role in respect of collective activities. The 'independent' conception provides a powerful argument against the direct legal prohibition of strikes *because* they are collective in nature. The 'independent' argument holds that there should be symmetry between the individual and collective counterparts of freedom.[10] The key issue is the *equivalence* of collective and individual exercises of the same freedom.

The 'independent' conception, based in a norm of equal treatment, is a simple and powerful idea. Leader's main arguments were presented in his 1992 monograph, long before the explosion in constitutional litigation. As we shall see, his 'independent' conception has not influenced constitutional courts. Instead, the 'instrumental' argument has been much more influential. Why might this be so?

I think there are two main reasons why this 'instrumental' argument has been favoured by constitutional courts. First, the 'independent' argument is normatively thin. It cannot explain *why* individuals should have a liberty or right to strike in the first place. Without this supplementing argument,

[8] Ibid. 198–199.

[9] Ibid. 202.

[10] This is described by Benjamin Oliphant as the 'parallel liberty' standard. See Benjamin Oliphant, 'Exiting the Freedom of Association Labyrinth: Resurrecting the Parallel Liberty Standard Under 2 (D) and Saving the Freedom to Strike' (2012) 70 University of Toronto Faculty Law Review 36, 62.

however, the 'freedom to do collectively that which one is at liberty to do as an individual' is formal and empty. Secondly, it accords too little respect to legislation and politics, particularly when labour law systems have adopted more 'collective' approaches to the right to strike. Paradoxically, then, the 'independent' argument has too little to say on the political morality of striking and too much to say about well-functioning labour law systems based on collective rights and institutions. Each of these points should be elaborated.

On the first point, equality of treatment is a fragile basis for a right to strike because it is highly dependent on the existing state of positive law. Under English law, for example, the individual striker is usually committing a repudiatory breach of contract.[11] At common law, the individual striker can be sued for damages and summarily dismissed. To protect trade unions and strike organisers from the tort liabilities that flow from this individual baseline of repudiatory breach, there is a statutory 'trade dispute' immunity in tort for organising strike action.[12] Like all formal equality arguments, the 'independent' right to strike is vulnerable to levelling down. Symmetry can be achieved by limiting individual freedoms as well as by expanding collective freedoms: the 'independent' argument is itself silent on this matter. If the criminal law was to criminalise *individual* acts of striking, as with the 19th-century Master and Servant legislation, the 'independent' argument would have no foothold at all. Leader suggests that legal 'coherence' would push for consistency in favour of levelling up, not levelling down.[13] The permissive legal regime of (collective) immunities in tort would be replicated in the law of contract, even extending to support for a doctrine of contractual suspension during a strike.[14] This legal coherence argument is obscure. By abstaining from the direct normative case for the value of striking as an individual activity, it is simply not clear why we should level up (in favour of protections) or level down (in favour of prohibitions). Symmetry is achieved either way. The advantage of the 'instrumental' conception is that it tells us which kind of symmetry we should prefer: the one that empowers groups that would otherwise experience inequality. Striking is not like taking a day off work to go

[11] See *Simmons v Hoover Ltd* [1977] ICR 61.

[12] See Alan Bogg and Cynthia Estlund, 'The Right to Strike and Contestatory Citizenship', in Hugh Collins and others (eds), *Philosophical Foundations of Labour Law* (OUP 2018) 236. There are a wide variety of legal approaches to the individual striker, ranging from criminal liability to contractual breach through to a full suite of statutory protections from discriminatory victimisation. While there are strong arguments favouring full legal protections, there is little in the 'independent' conception that speaks directly to this question.

[13] Leader (n 3) 204.

[14] Ibid., where he suggests that the 'proper result' would be the adoption of a French-style doctrine of contractual suspension during a strike.

to the cinema. It is an expressive act, exercised collectively, and aimed at imposing economic damage on another party with a view to reaching an agreement.[15] It is especially valuable in unequal bargaining situations as a means of equalising bargaining power.

On the second point, the balance between judicial deference and intervention, the 'independent' right to strike could be highly disruptive of existing 'labour law' models of the right to strike. This would include systems that provide strong legal protections and good economic outcomes for workers. Here are some specific implications of the 'independent' right to strike indicated by Leader: (1) it is an individual right that belongs to everyone irrespective of their contractual status;[16] (2) 'wildcat' or unofficial strikers should be protected equally and the right should not be channelled through trade unions as collective right-holders;[17] (3) the right may be exercised for any purpose chosen by the right-holders so that it is not restricted to disputes about conditions of employment (and may presumably include purely political strikes).[18] The following further implications may also follow: (4) the right should not be restricted by democratic procedures such as mandatory ballots; (5) the right cannot be waived by collective 'peace obligations' in collective agreements; (6) it encompasses all forms of secondary or sympathy action. Now, Leader concedes that states may impose restrictions to protect the rights of others.[19] However, this will be subject to a strict proportionality assessment by the court. And it is not clear that some of these restrictions, such as restrictions on lawful strike purposes or ballot requirements, can be justified easily by reference to the rights of others. For example, some restrictions seem to flow from the *internal* normative rationale for the right to strike, such as the prioritisation of official trade union channels, which avoid fragmentation and promote collective empowerment and solidarity.

Imagine that the ECtHR adopted this 'independent' conception of the right to strike under Article 11. Each element is antithetical to the settled features of 'organic' models of the right to strike, such as in Germany.[20] It would entail extensive judicial intervention. Every aspect of the German right to strike would be open to intensive scrutiny under a strict proportionality standard. Despite its distinctive political and industrial history, it might be required to

[15] Bogg and Estlund (n 12).
[16] Leader (n 3) 206.
[17] Ibid. 206–207.
[18] Ibid. 208.
[19] Ibid.
[20] On the nature of 'organic' models such as Germany, which focus on the trade union as right-holder, see the comparative analysis in Lord Wedderburn (n 1) 297–304.

align its legal system with an 'individualist' model, such as France or Spain. These changes may lead to the disruption of a well-functioning industrial relations system, and the weakening of strong industrial unions and sectoral collective bargaining. By contrast, the 'instrumental' conception is sensitive to these wider systemic issues, and it would counsel far greater caution before courts interfered with legislated labour rights and the complex political compromises they reflect. This is wise judging in an area of sensitive economic and social policy.

Leader's arguments were developed before the explosion in constitutional development of the right to strike. Interestingly, it is the 'instrumental' conception that now holds constitutional sway. Leader was surely correct in arguing that excessive deference by constitutional courts was a potential problem. However, recent judicial developments reveal how these considerations, such as democracy and relative expertise, can be given appropriate weight even in the 'instrumental' conception.

B. Brian Langille and the 'gone fishing' argument

Brian Langille is sympathetic to Leader's general approach to freedom of association as the freedom to do collectively that which one is at liberty to do as an individual. He has developed his own arguments on the relationship between freedom of association and the right to strike in the Canadian context.[21] These arguments were developed prior to the SCC's recognition of a constitutional right to strike. As with Leader's arguments, judicial deference and equality are central themes in Langille's approach.[22] However, these themes are elucidated in a distinctive way with radically different implications for the right to strike. Langille avoids some of the objections to Leader's arguments, particularly the failure to take deference seriously. Ultimately, I think that Langille's account suffers from too much agnosticism on the special value of the strike weapon.[23]

Langille begins with a disarmingly simple question: what is a strike? He rejects the 'objective' definition under Canadian labour board jurisprudence that it is simply the concerted stoppage of work. A group of workers might

[21] Brian Langille, 'What is a Strike?' (2009-2010) 15 Canadian Labour and Employment Law Journal 355.

[22] These themes have been developed in an extensive body of work on freedom of association in the constitutional order. See, e.g., Brian Langille, 'The Freedom of Association Mess: How We Got Into It and How We Can Get Out of It' (2009) 54 McGill Law Journal 177.

[23] On the 'thinness' of Langille's constitutional arguments, see A. Bogg and K.D. Ewing, 'A (Muted) Voice at Work? Collective Bargaining in the Supreme Court of Canada' (2012) 33 Comparative Labor Law and Policy Journal 379.

decide to leave work and go fishing.[24] That would be a concerted stoppage, but it would not be a strike. A strike is a concerted stoppage for a particular purpose. Under Canadian law, this purpose is the first negotiation or renegotiation of a collective agreement, and the work stoppage is to impose economic pressure on the employer to induce it to agree to the union's terms. The common law recognises a liberty or freedom to strike, which is the lawful termination of the contract with notice to place economic pressure on the employer to reach a collective agreement. Freedom of association is simply the collective exercise of that individual contractual liberty. According to Langille, this is exactly what should be constitutionalised by the courts under s. 2(d) of the Charter: nothing more, and nothing less.

For Langille, this is a *liberty* or *freedom* to strike. These words (and the concepts) matter. It is not a *right* to strike, because it does not entail any correlative *duties* on employers.[25] Indeed, employers enjoy their own contractual liberties, which may include refusing to rehire strikers. Under labour legislation in Canada, however, employees are protected from victimisation and dismissal for participating in lawful trade union activities, which would include striking. This is a supervening layer of statutory rights-based protections, which sets a protective perimeter around the liberty. It is correlative to duties on the employer not to victimise, not to dismiss, and so forth. It is distinct from the liberty because it involves a distinctive juridical relationship between rights and duties, right-holders and duty-bearers. Langille argues that it is the liberty, not the right, that should be constitutionalised. Constitutions protect freedoms, and statutes protect rights. This is the nature of the division between the 'constitutional' freedom to strike and the 'labour law' right to strike. It envisages a more limited remit for constitutional courts compared with Leader. The constitutionalised liberty is not empty, of course. For example, it would provide a basis for judicial scrutiny of state prohibition of strikes, such as back-to-work legislation.

Given the critical importance of the individual *right* not to be victimised for participating in a lawful strike, its exclusion from the constitutional sphere seems surprising. How does Langille justify this? His first general argument is that constitutionalising rights inevitably leads judges into an unavoidable spiral of drafting comprehensive labour codes. The court must delimit the category of right-holders, define which forms of victimisation are prohibited,

[24] This fishing trip example was originally posed by Chief Justice MacKeigan of Nova Scotia, cited in Langille (n 21) 358.

[25] Langille's deployment of these conceptual distinctions is indebted to Hohfeld, of course. Wesley Newcomb Hohfeld. See Wesley Newcomb Hohfeld, 'Fundamental Legal Conceptions as Applied in Judicial Reasoning' (1917) 26 Yale Law Journal 710.

decide if this is restricted to certain types of strike, for certain purposes, and so it goes on. These are political tasks for legislators, not interpretive tasks for constitutional courts. Only legislators have the democratic legitimacy and expertise to draft detailed labour codes. By contrast, the more limited constitutionalisation of the liberty or freedom ensures that constitutional courts do not trespass on matters that are properly within the domain of legislation (and labour law).

The second argument concerns the role of constitutional equality. According to Langille, the core constitutional problem will usually be the unjustified statutory exclusion of certain occupational groups, such as managers or public sector employees, from the statutory perimeter of rights. The role of the constitutional court should be to scrutinise these statutory exclusions under the Charter's equality guarantee in s. 15. This ideal of equality before the law is particularly amenable to judicial consideration. This does not lead the court into drafting complex legislative schemes. The task for the court is more circumscribed: *given* the legislative scheme that already exists, is there a justification for the exclusion of this group?

This provides a neat constitutional vision. It is also a less disruptive constitutional vision than Leader's. Beginning with Langille's concerns about the escalating intervention of judges, this must be taken seriously. Many years ago, Lord Wedderburn articulated similar concerns about the cascading policy questions prompted when judges are developing a doctrine of contractual suspension.[26] This led him to change tack on the doctrine of suspension, initially favouring it but eventually arguing that it should be left to the legislature to define the specific circumstances of application (unofficial strikes? All forms of industrial action short of a full withdrawal of labour? What about misconduct during a strike?). One answer to this is to argue that the doctrines of individual protection (including suspension) apply *within the collective parameters as defined in legislation*. This means that the courts defer to the legislature on controversial policy judgements while ensuring robust individual protections. Once the strike is collectively lawful, *then* the contract should be treated as suspended.

The equality technique undoubtedly provides a powerful mechanism requiring governments to justify exclusions from general labour statutes. Ultimately, this equality technique is limited by the existing statutory baseline. In a situation where there are no statutory rights (and duties) protecting employees from discriminatory victimisation for striking, the equality

[26] See Alan Bogg, 'The Hero's Journey: Lord Wedderburn and the "Political Constitution" of Labour Law' (2015) 44 Industrial Law Journal 299, 337–341.

argument has nothing to say. This is another version of the levelling-down problem that we have already considered in Leader's work. What if the individual striker is governed purely by the common law? The striker could be sued in damages for breach of contract if effective notice to terminate is not given to the employer. The striker could be dismissed or demoted. Where there is no protective legislation, challenging this would depend upon the constitutional recognition of rights, not liberties. This cannot be addressed by pointing to any *difference* in treatment between protected and non-protected groups when everyone is exposed equally to the common law regime.

C. Keith Ewing and 'Laws Against Strikes'

The final piece was written by Keith Ewing, one of the world's leading scholars on the right to strike, in a *festschrift* for another leading scholar, Bob Hepple.[27] It was focused on the limitations of labour law in protecting the right to strike and the potential for human rights law to provide an effective alternative: 'With the expansion of human rights law, labour lawyers can no longer lay a proprietary claim to the right to strike. Indeed, it is a matter about which labour law has failed to provide effective or enduring protection. Human rights law may provide a more secure and lasting alternative.'[28] This argument is very explicitly framed as a constitutional challenge to the autonomy of labour law and the need for a human rights perspective to salvage the right to strike from a hostile political environment. Governments had tended to restrict the right to strike, and ordinary legislation was an insecure basis for this specific human right.

Like Leader, Ewing rejects the 'instrumental' case for the right to strike linked to recognised trade unions and collective bargaining. As a labour law rationale, this 'instrumental' case is too bound up with the fate of collective bargaining which has been in serious decline across many countries. The human rights argument is intrinsic to personhood, not instrumental to collective bargaining. According to Ewing, certain normative implications follow from the human rights framing. These reflect the general properties of human rights: (1) it is an individual right; (2) it is a universal right; (3) it is inalienable; (4) it is inappropriate to restrict the purposes of strike action 'just in the same way that we do not censor the purposes that may be promoted by

[27] Keith Ewing, 'Laws against Strikes Revisited', in Catherine Barnard and others (eds), *The Future of Labour Law: Liber Amicorum Sir Bob Hepple QC* (Hart 2004) 41.

[28] Ibid. 59.

the exercise of the right to freedom of assembly';[29] (5) it is not permissible to subject striking to procedural preconditions such as notices or ballots; and (6) waiver of the right to strike through peace obligations is illegitimate. It is possible to impose restrictions on the right to strike to protect the rights of others in very narrow circumstances and subject to proportionality. It follows that a human right to strike would be radically different to the circumscribed statutory 'trade dispute' form of the right to strike in UK labour law. These arguments also imply that the distinction between official and unofficial strike action should be irrelevant to the human right to strike (though this may be relevant to proportionate restrictions).

The radicalism of Ewing's argument is both a strength and a weakness. The argument's strength is in its clear identification of a core of protection for individual strikers from victimisation and discrimination: 'the individual worker would not be subjected to restraints or penalties when taking strike action . . . Those who exercised what is a human right would not be subject to other forms of discrimination as a result, for example in the way in which state welfare benefits are allocated.'[30] This right is correlative to duties on employers and governments to ensure that the individual is not exposed to any sanction, penalty, or disincentive. This would have significant legal consequences for the individual protection of striking workers. For example, it would require full detriment and dismissal protections, statutory immunity from individual damages claims for breach of contract, suspension of the contract, and no temporal limits on protections from victimisation so that it extends to the full duration of the dispute.

Yet there are risks of undesirable judicial overreach on 'collective' issues. As with Leader's argument, Ewing's argument has the potential to be constitutionally disruptive. Most well-functioning labour law regimes integrate some of the features included in the list of suspect elements (i.e., peace obligations, ballots, restrictions on political strikes). The value of the 'instrumental' perspective is in its broader consideration of whether the totality of the legal structure leads to decent outcomes for trade unions and workers. For example, the peace obligation may be a constitutive element in a strong system of collective bargaining that delivers security and decent wages for workers. If it is part of a broader package that works well and is supported by many trade unions and employers, is it right that constitutional courts disrupt it?

[29] Ibid. 53.
[30] Ibid. 50.

D. An alternative conception

Underlying these various arguments (and the criticisms of them), there is a basic distinction between 'individual' and 'collective' counterparts of the right to strike. The distinctive role of courts is to ensure that individual strikers are given strong and effective protection from discriminatory victimisation for participating in lawful and official strike action. The individual right to strike is correlative to duties on employers not to sanction, victimise, penalise, dismiss, and so on. Direct discrimination against trade unionists for exercising their human rights in a lawful manner is a core equality wrong. The exposure to private punishment is demeaning. It treats adults as children, and it violates their equal moral standing. There is no room at all for judicial deference here. These individual protections should be recognised as constitutional entitlements, and they should extend equally to everyone who participates in a lawful strike as defined by the legislature. It is a particular strength of Leader's and Ewing's accounts that they critique excessive judicial deference and highlight the importance of these fundamental individual protections. It is a weakness of Langille's freedom-based approach that these matters are left to statute when they should be matters of overriding constitutional concern.

By contrast, on 'collective' matters, such as the legitimate purposes of strike action or procedural requirements such as notice or ballots, the courts ought to give wide democratic scope to legislators. This would permit a broad variety of reasonable (yet incommensurable) legislative schemes for the right to strike. There is no single right answer on the scope for secondary action, the regulation of public sector strikes, the implementation of ballot and notice requirements, or the scope for socio-political strikes. This is particularly important for the ECtHR, given the wide variation of the right to strike across European labour law systems. The primacy of labour law (and legislation) should hold sway in collective matters, and the constitutional courts should accord due deference. Where the interlocking elements of a system seem to be well-functioning, securing decent social and economic outcomes for workers, and the system is supported by representative social partners, the involvement of constitutional courts may well be counterproductive. It is a particular strength of Langille's approach that he is sensitive to these institutional legitimacy factors. It is a difficulty with Leader's and Ewing's accounts that there is no clear stopping point for judicial intervention on collective issues.

In the following section, we consider the ECHR conception of the right to strike. While the Strasbourg court has not always articulated its approach in terms of this bifurcation, it is suggested that this captures the key elements of its jurisprudence.

III. The ECHR and the Right to Strike: The Individual, the Collective, and the Limits of the Judicial Function

A. The early years: *Schmidt and Dahlstrom v Sweden*[31]

The first significant ECHR case to consider the right to strike was *Schmidt and Dahlstrom v Sweden*. This was an unusual case because of the great strength of centralised collective bargaining in the Swedish labour law system at that time.[32] On an 'instrumental' approach to freedom of association, the prospects were not promising because Swedish unions enjoyed significant bargaining strength despite the restrictions being challenged in this case. The Swedish right to strike was also 'organic' in that it was channelled through union federations conducting centralised bargaining. Given the collectivist logic of the Swedish system, this would not be an easy national context for the application of an 'independent' right to strike. It is little surprise that the ECtHR pursued an 'instrumental' argument.

The applicants, one of whom (Folke Schmidt) was a leading labour law professor in Sweden, were members of two public sector union federations (known as SACO and SR). These federations had engaged in selective strike action during the negotiation of a new collective agreement. There was a divergence in tactics between different federations because of a state policy favouring larger wage increases for lower-paid workers. After the comprehensive agreement had been signed with the two other federations that supported the equalisation policy, retroactive benefits were denied to members of the belligerent unions. This reflected a fundamental principle in the Swedish industrial relations system, 'a strike destroys retroactivity'. Non-retroactivity was justified by the Swedish government in terms of the freedom of employers to impose their own economic sanctions in free collective bargaining.[33] These benefits were granted retrospectively to members of the non-belligerent unions and non-members who had not struck. The applicants (who had not themselves been called on to strike but were members of belligerent unions)

[31] Application no. 5589/72, 6 February 1976.
[32] See Michael Forde, 'The European Convention on Human Rights and Labor Law' (1983) American Journal of Comparative Law 301, 330.
[33] Ibid. 312.

argued that this denial of benefits violated their Article 11 rights and constituted unjustified discrimination under Article 14. Their claims were rejected.

The balance of analysis in the judgment reflected the caution of the Strasbourg court in these early cases. The major part of the judgment (up to paragraph [27]) is devoted to a careful elucidation of the legal and industrial relations characteristics of the Swedish system. It set out the historical basis of the centralised model, the structure of the Swedish union federations, and the long-standing nature of the Swedish legislation supporting centralised bargaining. It reads today like a Court that is very sensitive to its own limitations of industrial relations expertise and anticipating reasonable democratic variations in the national-level specification of trade union rights.

The Court adopted an 'instrumental' approach to freedom of association. While trade union freedom was protected as a special aspect of general freedom of association, 'the Article does not secure any particular treatment of trade union members by the State, such as the right to retroactivity of benefits'.[34] Such a right was not 'indispensable' for the 'effective enjoyment' of trade union freedoms. Since there had been no decline in union membership of the affected unions, it could not be said that retroactive benefits were instrumentally essential.[35] Furthermore, states must permit and make possible 'freedom to protect the occupational interests of trade union members by trade union action'.[36] While 'the grant of a right to strike represents without any doubt one of the most important of these means, there are others'.[37] The task of the Court was to assess whether there had been a negation of the unions' *general* capacity to protect its members' occupational interests. This is a high threshold. The denial of retroactivity to belligerent unions was a deeply rooted principle of Swedish labour law, and it pursued a legitimate aim in a proportionate manner. It did not therefore constitute unjustified discrimination against the members of striking unions.

This strongly 'instrumental' reasoning of the ECtHR, focused on the means-end efficacy of strike action, sealed the fate of an Article 11 challenge in a well-functioning system. While the ECtHR in these early cases was sometimes criticised for its 'individualistic' or 'formalistic' approach under Article 11,[38] *Schmidt and Dahlstrom* cannot be analysed sensibly in these terms. The

[34] *Schmidt and Dahlstrom* (n 31) [34].
[35] Ibid. [35].
[36] Ibid. [36].
[37] Ibid.
[38] Lord Wedderburn, 'Freedom of Association or Right to Organise? The Common Law and International Sources', in Lord Wedderburn, *Employment Rights in Britain and Europe* (Lawrence & Wishart 1991) 142, 150–151.

dilemma for the Court was captured by Michael Forde in an early scholarly engagement with this first wave of Strasbourg case law:

> The principal question . . . is the appropriateness of judges, many of whom possess relatively little industrial relations expertise, laying down common standards for collective bargaining systems of great complexity that often differ fundamentally from each other.[39]

This is appealing to judicial deference, a set of considerations that are particularly acute for general human rights courts compared with specialist labour courts. The deference arguments are also stronger for supranational courts adjudicating across different national labour law systems. *Schmidt and Dahlstrom* represents the strong affirmation of the autonomy of (national) labour law. In limiting judicial interference with statutory rights and well-established bargaining practices, *Schmidt and Dahlstrom* was entirely consistent with the mainstream academic pluralist view of courts and constitutional law in the post-war period.[40] However, it is also important not to overlook the problems of judicial underreach too. There was a latent danger in *Schmidt and Dahlstrom* that was obscured by its specific facts. Forde's analysis of *Schmidt and Dahlstrom* considered the arguments of the parties on whether the discriminatory denial of benefits should be treated as *intrinsically* wrongful, regardless of their consequential effects on trade union strength or membership. The Swedish Government had argued that 'a distinction should be drawn between action that is discriminatory and countervailing industrial action'.[41] While the point was not addressed by the ECtHR, the outcome in the case no doubt reflected an assumption that the denial of retroactive benefits was 'countervailing industrial action' within a broadly well-functioning system. It was not an instance of wrongful individual discrimination.

But what if the individual applicants had been dismissed, or demoted, or their wages reduced, as a retaliatory measure against belligerent unions? Should it matter at all that this occurred within the context of a well-functioning collective bargaining system? Or that the union could still pursue effective strike action regardless? Perhaps a defender of limited judicial review might still insist upon a distinction between retaliatory measures *against the*

[39] Forde (n 32) 332.

[40] Alan Bogg, 'Can We Trust the Courts in Labour Law? Stranded between Frivolity and Despair' (2022) 38 International Journal of Comparative Labour Law and Industrial Relations 103.

[41] Forde (n 32) 312.

union (as in *Schmidt and Dahlstrom*) and retaliatory measures *against an individual striker* because of his own industrial action. That seems like an elusive distinction. In later ECHR cases, the imposition of sanctions against individual strikers is effectively treated as intrinsically wrongful. While the Court in *Schmidt and Dahlstrom* demonstrated a laudable concern on the part of European judges not to 'tinker' as well-meaning 'amateurs' with industrial relations systems,[42] the facts in *Schmidt and Dahlstrom* strayed very close to the kind of discriminatory wrong that warrants intensive judicial scrutiny.

The fundamental constitutional distinction between intrinsic wrongs (against individuals) and democratic latitude for reasonable variation in defining the (collective) parameters of a lawful strike began to clarify only in the 2000s. In the realm of protecting individuals from sanctions for participating in lawful trade union activity, the state's margin was limited. In the realm of defining a lawful strike, such as scope for secondary action or strike notices, the state's margin was much wider. Although the ECtHR has not yet taken the step of formulating its approach explicitly in these terms, it is implicit in the case law. It also reflects an attractive normative theory of democracy, deference, and the equal moral standing of citizens.

B. Judicial limits and the individual/collective distinction

There is now no doubt that the right to strike is clearly protected under Article 11.[43] Before examining this bifurcation between 'individual' and 'collective' strike cases under Article 11, it is helpful to set out the general structure of reasoning under Article 11. Interestingly, there are two fundamental principles that have been applied in the 'collective' cases but are less prominent in the 'individual' cases. This supports the idea that there is a bifurcation in the character of legal reasoning between these two types of case.

These are the two fundamental principles relevant to 'collective' trade union cases:

> 144. . . . [T]he evolution of case-law as to the substance of the right of association enshrined in Article 11 is marked by two guiding principles: firstly, the Court takes into consideration the totality of the measures taken by the State concerned in order to secure trade-union freedom, subject to its margin of appreciation; secondly, the Court does not accept restrictions that affect the essential elements of

[42] Ibid. 332.
[43] *RMT v UK* [2014] IRLR 467.

> trade-union freedom, without which that freedom would become devoid of substance. These two principles are not contradictory but are correlated. This correlation implies that the Contracting State in question, while in principle being free to decide what measures it wishes to take in order to ensure compliance with Article 11, is under an obligation to take account of the elements regarded as essential by the Court's case-law.[44]

The 'totality' principle is especially important because it is sensitive to the cumulative effects of legal restrictions in labour law systems. A legal rule imposing a restriction, taken singly, may be easy to justify. For example, a legal duty to issue a strike notice to the employer could be readily amenable to justification as proportionate and pursuing a legitimate aim. Where there are multiple restrictions considered in 'totality', this could have the overall cumulative effect of negating trade union freedoms. For example, the UK labour law system has developed through the slow accretion of legal restrictions on strike action over many decades. In comparative terms, it is uniformly restrictive in relation to notice requirements, ballots and ballot thresholds, restrictions on secondary and political strikes, and individual protection of strikers.[45]

The 'devoid of substance' principle is 'correlated' with the 'totality' principle. This is because it requires the court to consider if the restriction prevented a union and/or workers from defending their occupational interests in other ways. Only then would the Article 11 freedom be devoid of substance. This invites a broader consideration of the alternatives open to the union where one or more of its collective activities are restricted. For example, where there is a restriction on strike action for civil servants, the legal system could provide other ways for unions to defend the occupational interests of members. This might include participatory rights in relation to legislation affecting the employment conditions of civil servants. A restriction in one domain can be counterbalanced by freedom in another.

The ECtHR has also formulated a list of 'essential' elements of trade union rights under Article 11. This list is non-exhaustive and it is open to further development in line with other international standards and comparative law and practice:

> In line with the aforementioned guiding principles of the Court's approach, the Court has built up, through its case-law, a non-exhaustive list of the essential

[44] *Demir and Baykara v Turkey* [2009] 48 EHRR 54 [144].
[45] Bogg (n 2).

> elements of trade-union freedom, including the right to form and join a trade union, the prohibition of closed-shop agreements, the right for a trade union to seek to persuade the employer to hear what it has to say on behalf of its members and, having regard to developments in labour relations, the right to bargain collectively with the employer, which has, in principle, except in very specific cases, also become one of those essential elements.[46]

It should be noted that the right to strike has not yet been included in this list of essential elements. It would be a mistake to draw the conclusion that the right to strike is of secondary importance. The list is described by the ECtHR itself as non-exhaustive. In certain circumstances, restrictions on the right to strike might render trade union freedoms 'devoid of substance'. In *Hrvatski Lijecnicki Sindikat v Croatia*, for example, a ban on certain public sector strikes for a period of over three years was treated as a disproportionate interference because it disabled the unions from defending the occupational interests of its members.[47] The right to strike is a form of trade union activity. It is also integral to other 'essential' trade union rights such as the right to collective bargaining and the right to seek to persuade the employer and to be heard.[48] Even though it is not expressly listed, there is a respectable argument that the right to strike should be regarded as impliedly contained in those 'essential elements'. Without it, effective trade union action in its 'essential' forms is severely hampered.

The 'totality' and the 'devoid of substance' principles are characteristic of what Leader has described as the 'instrumental' approach. It is the task of the court to ascertain whether the trade union has the general ability, in one way or another, to defend the occupational interests of its members effectively. This is also linked to the 'margin of appreciation' under Article 11, because different legal systems protect this general freedom in a variety of ways.

Interestingly, the 'individual' Article 11 cases do not usually invoke 'totality' or 'devoid of substance' principles. This reflects a basic normative distinction in the jurisprudence, and it is one that has been defended in the early part of the chapter. The individual cases involve intrinsic discrimination wrongs. Any instrumental effects on trade union power are irrelevant to the wrongfulness of the discriminatory acts. The 'collective' cases, by contrast, require the court

[46] *Humpert and others v Germany* Application nos. 59433/18, 59477/18, 59481/18, and 59494/18, 14 December 2023 [100].

[47] No. 36701/09, § 59, 27 November 2014.

[48] *Enerji Yapi-Yol Sen v Turkey* App. No. 68959/01, 21 April 2009, [24].

to consider whether trade unions have the overall capacity to protect members' occupational interests. This depends upon a more general assessment of the 'totality' and whether restrictions leave trade union freedoms 'devoid of substance'. This is aligned with a wide margin of appreciation for states.

C. The individual right to strike

The right to strike was recognised as a protected trade union right under Article 11 in a series of cases concerned with individual sanctions against trade unionists. Most of these cases arose in the Turkish public sector. They often overlapped with freedom of assembly as the disputed measures involved disciplinary responses to the attendance of civil servants at union-organised public protests. Freedom of assembly is an important general freedom under Article 11, and this may have reinforced the ECtHR's strongly protective approach in these 'individual' cases.[49] This has meant that 'margin of appreciation' has a very limited role. It reflects the strict approach of the ECtHR, where sanctions have been imposed on individual workers for trade union reasons. The ECtHR has consistently treated sanctions as having a chilling and dissuasive effect, even where those sanctions are very light.

One of the early cases is *Dilek v Turkey*.[50] Toll booth operators on the Bosphorus Bridge left their posts for three hours to participate in a union-organised strike to protest their working conditions. The public administration brought civil actions for compensatory damages against the workers for the lost toll revenue caused by their unauthorised absence. These sums for compensatory damages were in fact paid by their union, Yapi-Yol Sen. The absence from work was treated by the ECtHR as a 'general collective action in the exercise of trade union rights', and the civil actions against the strikers were an interference with it.[51] The ECtHR went on to consider if the interference was justified, and it held that it was not. While it may have pursued a legitimate aim, ensuring the smooth operation of the public service, it was not proportionate.

A similarly strict approach can be seen in *Karacay v Turkey*.[52] This concerned participation in a union-organised one-day national strike to protest

[49] Interestingly, one of the early cases that considered the chilling and dissuasive effect of sanctions concerned a lawyer's participation in a public protest, and freedom of assembly was integral: see *Ezelin v France* App No. 11800/85, 26 April 1991. *Ezelin* was very influential in the early wave of Turkey strike cases.

[50] App No. 74611/01 and others, 17 July 2007.

[51] Ibid. [57].

[52] App. No. 6615/03, 27 March 2007.

the declining salaries of civil servants. The worker was issued with a disciplinary warning, and there were no other adverse consequences such as financial penalties. The ECtHR found that the sanction, minimal though it was, was not proportionate since it was intended to dissuade members from participating in an official strike concerning working conditions.[53] More recently, in *Guler v Turkey*, the ECtHR considered a disciplinary warning issued to a civil servant for participating in a union-organised May Day public demonstration violated Article 11.[54] According to the Court, the disciplinary sanction, 'although very light, was such as to dissuade trade union members from participation in trade union activities'.[55] There is no consideration of the 'totality' or whether the sanction left Article 11 'devoid of substance'. The 'very light' sanction in *Guler* was 'such as' to dissuade or have a chilling effect on trade union activities. This is effectively treating individual sanctions as intrinsically dissuasive and hence violative of Article 11.

In every case where an individual sanction imposed for participating in a lawful and official strike has been challenged and considered on the merits, the ECtHR has found an Article 11 violation. Indeed, it is unclear if such a sanction could ever be justified under Article 11(2). Other examples include *Kaya & Seyhan v Turkey* (disciplinary warning for participating in a one-day national strike),[56] *Urcan v Turkey* (fines and suspended sentences),[57] and *Enerji Yapi-Yol Sen v Turkey* (advance circular warning workers not to strike and individual disciplinary penalties).[58] In *Danilenkov v Russia*,[59] which involved widespread acts of anti-union discrimination perpetrated in the aftermath of a strike at the Kalingrad seaport, the ECtHR did refer to the 'totality' of measures. It stated that 'the totality of the measures implemented to safeguard the guarantees of art.11 should include protection against discrimination on the ground of trade union membership which, according to the Freedom of Association Committee, constitutes one of the most serious violations of freedom of association, capable of jeopardising the very existence of a trade union'.[60] In other words, the criminal law protections in this case were not adequate, given difficulties of proof of criminal guilt and enforcement. The state was under a positive duty to provide access to an effective and

[53] Ibid. [37].
[54] [2018] IRLR 880.
[55] Ibid. [23].
[56] App. No. 30946/04, 15 December 2009.
[57] App. No. 23019/04 and others, 17 July 2008.
[58] *Enerji Yapi-Yol Sen v Turkey* [2009] ECHR 2251.
[59] (2014) 58 E.H.R.R. 19.
[60] Ibid. [123].

dissuasive civil remedy for acts of trade union discrimination.[61] This was a *necessary* part of the totality; hence, its absence could not be counterbalanced by other supportive legal rules in the 'totality'.

In sum, the individual right is subject to three specific conditions. First, the strike must be lawful under domestic law (or at least the restrictions on the 'collective' aspect must not exceed the state's wide margin of appreciation). Second, the strike must be 'official' and called by a union. Third, the strike must be in defence of occupational or professional interests.

Overall, these cases establish that the state is subject to a positive obligation under Article 11 to prohibit *any* discriminatory sanctions imposed on individuals because of lawful and official strike action in defence of occupational interests. The state must also maintain an accessible legal framework providing for effective and independent judicial protection with dissuasive civil remedies. Margin of appreciation does not have any significant role to play in such cases. The scope for reasonable variation in national laws is limited: there are only so many ways in which different legislators can define a proscribed 'sanction'. There is correspondingly little scope for deference in these 'individual' cases.

This is constitutionally fitting. The robust judicial treatment of sanctions for lawful trade union activities is an aspect of equality under the law. This has nothing at all to do with prioritising an 'individual' over an 'organic' collective right to strike. This concept of constitutional equality is entirely agnostic on this distinction, which varies reasonably across legal systems. Workers should always be protected from discrimination, regardless of the broader national configuration of the right to strike and whether the right is vested in the individual or the trade union. In these individual cases, constitutional norms have strong primacy over ordinary labour legislation.

In the next section, we consider the Article 11 case law on the 'collective' aspects of the right to strike. These do not involve individual discrimination wrongs. In this collective context, there is a markedly different judicial approach. The ECtHR is concerned with the holistic situation in the legal system, as reflected in the 'totality' and 'devoid of substance' principles. The margin of appreciation also plays a very significant role. The ECtHR is justifiably wary of disrupting the political compromises that underlie democratically enacted labour legislation. In this collective sphere, the autonomy of labour law still holds sway.

[61] See also *Tek Gida Is Sendikasi v Turkey* [2017] ECHR 318, [55], emphasising the importance of effective deterrence in remedies and emphasising the narrowness of margin of appreciation.

D. The collective right to strike

We will consider three ECHR cases that exemplify this bifurcation. The first case is *RMT v United Kingdom*, which considered the complex strike ballot notice requirements and the complete ban on secondary action in British labour law.[62] These were long-standing features of UK strike law, which was regulated heavily by statute. The challenge to strike ballot notices was declared inadmissible by the Court. The employer secured an injunction because of alleged errors in the union's description of worker categories in its strike ballot notice. It had been able to take strike action following a fresh attempt to meet the legal requirements, and it was eventually successful in securing a collective agreement. The ECtHR concluded that there was no 'interference' on these facts.[63]

It is in the treatment of secondary action that the ECtHR set out its approach to the margin of appreciation concept. In European comparative terms, the UK ban on secondary action was at the extremely restrictive end of the regulatory spectrum. It had also been subjected to strong criticism by the supervisory bodies of the ILO and ESC.[64] Despite this, the ECtHR concluded that there was no violation because the restriction was within the UK Government's wide margin of appreciation. There is an extensive critical literature on different aspects of the reasoning in the *RMT* judgment.[65] Rather than restate those criticisms, this analysis will consider the contrasting role of margin of appreciation in 'individual' and 'collective' cases. The ECtHR stated that 'It is not to be understood as narrowing decisively and definitively the domestic authorities' margin of appreciation in relation to regulating, *through normal democratic processes,* the exercise of trade union freedom within the social and economic framework of the country concerned.'[66] This emphasises the importance of democratic specification in the sphere of collective matters. This reference to democratic values is not replicated in the individual cases considered in the preceding section. That seems right because it should not matter that the legislature approves of individual workers being victimised. The starting point in *RMT* is therefore that the state has a wide margin in defining the (collective) right to strike.

[62] [2014] IRLR 467.
[63] Ibid. [45].
[64] Ibid. [92]–[98].
[65] Alan Bogg and K.D. Ewing, 'The Implications of the RMT Case' (2014) 43 Industrial Law Journal 221.
[66] *RMT* (n 62) [86] (emphasis added).

The *RMT* approach to the margin enquiry entrenches the primacy and 'autonomy' of the labour law concept of the right to strike. One aspect of this is in the controversial distinction between 'core' and 'accessory' aspects of freedom of association.[67] Where an 'accessory' freedom is subject to restrictions, the state's margin is wider because such freedoms have less importance than those at the normative 'core' of the right. The gradation of importance within a constitutional right is a settled feature of constitutional reasoning. As an example, political expression usually attracts more stringent protection than commercial speech or pornography. In *RMT*, the 'core' of the right to strike is treated as primary strike action, whereas secondary action is treated as 'accessory' or secondary.[68] This treatment of primary strike action as the paradigm case of the right to strike is an example of the constitutional norm tracking the labour law norm. As Chapter 2 demonstrates, the core quality of the primary strike has deep historical roots in British labour law. This is likely to be a more general pattern in many labour law systems: it is the most basic function of the trade union. It may even be implicit in the text of Article 11 itself, which refers to the 'protection of *his* interests'. In *RMT*, the Court does not appear to be deploying a normative theory of the 'core' derived from general human rights law. Its approach to identifying the core takes its cue—implicitly at least—from labour law.

The ECtHR also emphasised the weight to be attached to the deliberations of national-level democratic institutions.[69] This is based upon the value of subsidiarity.[70] These national democratic institutions are often better placed to consider local circumstances and to gather and evaluate relevant information and economic data. These legislative decisions are also intensely *political* in character, in that they involve the conciliation and adjustment of conflicting interests, ideologies, and values. These democratic determinations, crystallised in statutory labour laws, regulated matters that were 'often charged'.[71] This consideration also supported a cautious approach so that the court did not disrupt legislative compromises unless there was a strong case for intervention. While the outcome in *RMT* has been criticised, this judicial recognition of the 'political' nature of labour law embodies a vision of the judicial role that respects the dangers of judicial 'tinkering' in complex labour law systems.[72] It was also a case in which the 'totality' of restrictions was not

[67] Ibid. [87].

[68] Ibid. [82] and [88].

[69] Ibid. [89].

[70] Paulo Carozza, 'Subsidiarity as a Structural Principle of International Human Rights Law' (2003) 97 American Journal of International Law 38.

[71] *RMT* (n 62) [99].

[72] Forde (n 42).

considered very extensively by the ECtHR since it emphasised the need to focus on the concrete factual circumstances of the specific dispute.[73] Since the union had been able to undertake some actions to further the occupational interests of its members, the restrictions did not leave the freedoms 'devoid of substance'. Yet UK strike law is in cumulative terms one of the most restrictive in Europe.[74] The outcome in *RMT* provides some support to Sheldon Leader's concerns that an 'instrumental' approach tends to be aligned with a higher degree of judicial deference. In *RMT*, the deference may have been excessive.

The second case is *Humpert and others v Germany*.[75] This involved a challenge by schoolteachers employed with civil servant status (known as *Beamte*) in Germany to the long-standing ban on striking. The teachers had engaged in unlawful strike action and had been penalised for doing so. This ban was deeply rooted in the constitutional structure of Germany (known as the Basic Law), and its function is to ensure the stability of the public administration by preserving the non-political nature of the *Beamte*. Not all schoolteachers were employed as *Beamte* in Germany, and the ban on strikes for *Beamte*-employed schoolteachers had been criticised under both ILO and the ESC standards.[76] Nevertheless, the ECtHR concluded that the measure was within Germany's margin of appreciation.

It is important to understand *Humpert* from a wider perspective. The German system accords strong employment protections to the *Beamte*, and this is a constitutional *quid pro quo* for the restriction of the right to strike. This totality perspective, which was not prominent in *RMT*, was crucial to the outcome in the *Humpert* case. The *Beamte* enjoy a model of lifelong secure employment, individuals have enforceable rights to adequate maintenance (alimentation), trade unions have participatory rights in respect of legislation affecting the occupational interests of *Beamte*, there are rights of codetermination, and a right to form and join trade unions. Furthermore, this model is deeply rooted in the German constitutional structure, which has itself been shaped by unique political circumstances in the middle decades of the 20th century. Although this case did involve the imposition of individual sanctions on strikers, these sanctions were relatively light. While the lightness of the sanctions is generally irrelevant in cases involving lawful strike action, in *Humpert*, the strike action was unlawful under domestic law. Even here, then, there will still be consideration of the severity of individual

[73] *RMT* (n 62) [98].
[74] Alan Bogg and others, *Human Rights at Work: Reimagining Employment Law* (Hart 2024) 116.
[75] *Humpert* (n 46).
[76] Ibid. [53]–[60].

sanctions. The ECtHR also considered it important that these sanctions were predictable and reasonably foreseeable: the teachers 'could have foreseen, to a degree that was reasonable in the circumstances, that their participation in strikes as teachers with civil servant status would lead to disciplinary measures'.[77]

Although the complete exclusion of the right to strike for the *Beamte* is unusual in comparative terms, the strong protective compensatory norms applying to the *Beamte* mean that this case is also somewhat unique. The reasoning in *Humpert* is strongly 'instrumental'. The ECtHR's enquiry is whether there are adequate substitutes for the right to strike that secure acceptable social and economic outcomes for affected workers. This enabled the ECtHR to avoid a high-noon constitutional confrontation with Germany on a matter that was fundamental to its constitutional structure.

The third case is *Association of Academics v Iceland*, which involved direct state interference through legislation prohibiting a public sector strike and imposing compulsory arbitration following a bargaining impasse.[78] The ECtHR considered that there was no Article 11 violation because the restrictive measure was within the state's margin of appreciation. The Supreme Court in Iceland had scrutinised the presentation of evidence on the ongoing effects of the public sector strike, especially in healthcare. This was based upon documentary and statistical evidence rather than speculative assertions about the impact of the strike. In a strong endorsement of subsidiarity, the ECtHR accepted that this evidence had been considered properly by the Icelandic court. In these circumstances, and where the unions had bargained to an impasse, the ECtHR concluded that the democratically enacted restrictions were necessary in a democratic society. The approach of the ECtHR in this case reveals a wise approach to the limits of judicial expertise in applying instrumental arguments. On the instrumental approach, the court must evaluate whether trade unions enjoy an effective opportunity to defend members' occupational interests. While the ECtHR is not well placed to undertake measurement of the unions' social and economic power directly—it is after all an institution with juridical rather than social science expertise—the ECtHR can ensure that local decision-makers have evaluated the relevant social and economic evidence. This approach supports European supervision of human

[77] Ibid. [117].

[78] App No. 2451/16, 15 May 2018. For an earlier example, see *Federation of Offshore Workers' Trade Unions and Others v Norway* ((dec.), no. 38190/97, ECHR 2002-VI). Although the Article 11 limits are relatively wide in these cases where public authorities intervene to restrict ongoing strikes, those limits were exceeded in *Hrvatski Lijecnicki Sindikat v Croatia* (n 47) where the deprivation of the right to strike for a period of 3 years and 8 months was held to be disproportionate.

rights standards while being sensitive to the epistemic advantages enjoyed by national judicial and legislative institutions.

E. The limits of the individual right to strike

There is a division between intrinsic equality-based arguments and instrumental arguments, and this division tracks the 'individual' and 'collective' aspects of the Article 11 right to strike. This division also explains the limits of the individual right to strike in the ECHR. We shall consider three such limitations. The first limitation is that the individual cases concern *sanctions*. There are disadvantages resulting from strike action that should not be regarded as sanctions, for example, proportionate deductions of pay. This can also have a dissuasive effect, but it is not a sanction or penalty. Proportionate deductions of pay do not raise human rights issues.[79] The task of the legislator is to delimit the category of sanctions so that it permits proportionate deductions from pay.[80]

The second limitation is that Article 11 protections do not apply to the same degree where strike action is not organised by a trade union and fails to meet the stipulated legal conditions provided for in national labour law. This is demonstrated by *Baris v Turkey*, where employees were dismissed because they had engaged in strike action outside of the official union structures.[81] The strike was illegal under Turkish law. According to the ECtHR, this could not be described as protected trade union activity since it was not organised by the trade union. If anything, the strike was organised *against* the trade union. Although this *Baris* restriction is controversial, it reflects coherent limits. The relevant protective principle is equality *before the law*. If strikers are conducting themselves outside the law, their Article 11 protections are attenuated.[82] The law would then be speaking in two voices rather than one: your strike is

[79] See *Compilation of Decisions of the Committee on Freedom of Association* at §§942-944, 953–957. Under the European Social Charter, see, e.g., the ECSR Conclusions XIII-1 France—Article 6(4) and Conclusions 2010—France—Article 6(4), in each case holding that a rule deducting 1/30th of salary for strikes of less than a day was not in conformity with Article 6(4). To the extent the employer deducted wages greater than those which would have been earned during the period of strike, it was a sanction which could dissuade strikers.

[80] It may be that that the touchstone of a proscribed sanction is the *intention* to penalise or deter the strike action. This mental state formulation reflects the general approach to trade union 'detriment' in UK law which focuses on the employer's 'sole or main purpose': see, e.g., Trade Union and Labour Relations (Consolidation) Act 1992 (TULRCA) s. 146.

[81] App No. 66828/16, 27 January 2020.

[82] For another case demonstrating this principle, see *Trofimchuk v Ukraine* App No. 4241/03, 28 October 2010. However, as *Humpert* demonstrates, the Court will still consider the severity of the sanction even in unlawful strikes.

unlawful, but here is your legal protection from its consequences. This has affinities with the public policy doctrine of illegality, where the 'integrity of the legal system' may sometimes support a defence where a claimant is relying on his own illegal activity in a legal claim against a defendant.[83]

It does not follow that unofficial or illegal strikers are always treated as outlaws under Article 11. In *Ognevenko v Russia*,[84] a train driver was dismissed for participating in a strike that was treated as illegal under Russian law because it was deemed an essential service. The ECtHR concluded that there was a violation of Article 11. It was particularly critical of the lack of solid evidence to justify the ban on striking in the railways sector,[85] and this contrasts with the position in *Association of Academics*. Nor were there compensatory guarantees to provide equivalent safeguards for affected workers, such as access to compulsory arbitration.[86] It was also relevant that dismissal was a severe penalty. In *Humpert*, even though the strike by teachers was unlawful, it was relevant to the Court's proportionality assessment that the sanctions were relatively light. *Ognevenko* demonstrates that in relation to collective boundaries on the right to strike, the margin of appreciation has limits. The strongly coercive nature of dismissal will trigger more exacting scrutiny of the collective perimeter, where it leads to severe individual consequences for a striker.

Finally, *Hellgren v Finland* concerned an employer's refusal to accept the partial performance of striking postal workers, who had offered to undertake some employment duties but not others.[87] Following the refusal of partial performance, the employer deducted wages corresponding to the entirety of the performance for the allotted period. The Finnish Supreme Court concluded that this was permissible under Finnish law because the employer was contractually entitled to direct the performance of work (including directing the relevant duties to be performed). English law is like Finnish law in this respect, in that an employer is entitled to refuse partial performance at common law.[88]

The ECtHR did not find a violation on these facts. The ability of employers to refuse partial performance did not render the employees' trade union rights devoid of substance, and the trade union had in fact been able to secure a new collective agreement. As the Court has affirmed on many occasions, the right to strike does not entail a right to prevail. Article 11 did not justify a duty

[83] On the illegality defence generally, see Sarah Green and Alan Bogg (eds), *Illegality after Patel v Mirza* (Hart 2018).
[84] [2019] IRLR 195.
[85] Ibid. [76]–[77].
[86] Ibid. [78].
[87] *Application no. 52977/19*, 17 December 2024.
[88] *Miles v Wakefield* [1987] 1 AC 539.

on the employer to facilitate the union prevailing in an industrial dispute. The 'totality' indicated that trade unions enjoyed a wide range of opportunities to strive for their members' occupational interests. It was also important that 'this was not a situation which exposed trade union members to a real or immediate risk of detriment or of being left defenceless against future attempts to reduce pay or downgrade other work conditions'.[89] Trade union freedom in general had been secured in the Finnish legal system, and there were legal measures protecting trade unionists from dismissal and sanctions because of trade union activities. Where pay deductions are disproportionate, by contrast, this does expose union members to 'a real or immediate risk of detriment' and would risk violation of Article 11.

Hellgren perhaps reflects caution on the part of the ECtHR since the legal characterisation of industrial action short of a full withdrawal of labour is amenable to wide national variations. In some rights-based national systems, it would be regarded as an abuse of right and outside the scope of legal protection,[90] whereas in the UK system, it is treated as protected. *Hellgren* is unusual in that it is an apparently 'individual' case that involves explicit consideration of the 'totality'. The best explanation of this is that the main issue in the case was not concerned with individual sanctions. The treatment of partial performance under Article 11, and whether it counts as a protected strike at all, is a matter on which there is considerable comparative variation.

IV. The Right to Strike in the English Courts: Democracy, Deference, and Detriment

The position of the right to strike in English law flows from its treatment by the ECtHR. The ECHR has a special constitutional status because of its domestic incorporation in the HRA. Like the ECHR, the basic constitutional division between the collective and individual aspects of the right to strike is a feature of the English jurisprudence on the right to strike. There is of course a key difference between the English courts and the ECtHR. The English courts are formulating norms *within* a single national system. Hence, the variety of European models of the right to strike is not a relevant issue because the English courts are not formulating European standards. They are adjudicating on the right to strike in English law. The English courts have nevertheless proceeded cautiously in this context. The primacy of legislation, and respect for

[89] *Hellgren* (n 87) [69].
[90] Bernd Wass (ed), *The Right to Strike: A Comparative View* (Kluwer Law International BV 2014) 53–54.

democracy and parliamentary sovereignty, operate as strong constitutional principles. The one area in which the UK Supreme Court has intervened is in relation to the exposure of individual strikers to detriments for participating in lawful and official strike action. This lacuna in legislative protection led the UK Supreme Court to issue a declaration of incompatibility under the HRA. By contrast, while the collective framework of the right to strike is cumulatively restrictive, the English courts have proceeded more cautiously.

The historical role of the English judiciary has always been particularly controversial in the sphere of industrial action. Indeed, the very notion of a 'right' to strike in English law was contested. Under the judge-made English common law, strikes are (still) unlawful. As set out in Chapter 2, the liberty to strike had been carved out through specific statutory interventions, creating a patchwork of qualified immunities and piecemeal individual protections. At the individual level, withdrawal of labour will usually be a repudiatory breach of contract by the individual striker.[91] This is because the refusal to work goes to the very root of the wage-work bargain. At common law, employers are entitled to dismiss strikers summarily, to refuse offers of partial performance such as selective performance of duties, and even to sue individual strikers for damages for breach of contract.[92]

At the collective level, trade unions and organisers of strike action are engaged in unlawful conduct because persuading workers to breach their contracts is almost invariably a tort. The persuasion will usually amount to inducing breach of contract, but could also involve other wrongs, such as the torts of intimidation or conspiracy to injure. A zone of legality for strike action depended upon Parliament introducing legislation to 'negative' the common law.[93] For trade unions and strike organisers, the negativing legal mechanism is the 'trade dispute' immunity, which provides protection from certain listed torts where they are committed by someone acting 'in contemplation or furtherance of a trade dispute'.[94] Broadly speaking, this immunity covers a primary 'industrial' dispute about working conditions between workers and their own employer. This immunity is hedged with qualifying conditions such as support in a lawful ballot and compliance with complex

[91] *Miles* (n 88). For a recent reconsideration of the common law as it applies to individual strikers, see Jordan English, 'Substantial Performance in Employment Contracts', in Alan Bogg and Paul S. Davies (eds), *Private Law and the Employment Contract* (Hart 2025) chapter 4.

[92] *National Coal Board v Galley* [1958] 1 WLR 16. For an authoritative consideration of the right to strike in the wider context of the English common law, see K.D. Ewing, *The Right to Strike* (OUP 1991).

[93] The classic functional typology of 'negative' statutory intervention to negative common law liabilities is set out in Otto Kahn-Freund, 'Legal Framework', in Allan Flanders and Hugh A. Clegg (eds), *The System of Industrial Relations in Great Britain* (Blackwell 1954) 42, 44.

[94] TULRCA s. 219.

notice requirements. For individual strikers, the principal statutory protection relates to unfair dismissal for participating in 'protected' industrial action.[95] 'Protected' is defined as industrial action that is official and lawful at the collective level.

These statutory immunities were interpreted restrictively for much of the 20th century. For example, in *Express Newspapers v McShane*, Lord Denning observed in the Court of Appeal that 'Parliament granted immunities to the leaders of trade unions, it did not give them any *rights*. It did not give them a right to break the law or to do wrong by inducing people to break contracts. It only gave them immunity if they did'.[96] The point was put even more forcefully by Lord Diplock, who described the immunities as 'intrinsically repugnant to anyone who has spent his life in the practice of the law or the administration of justice'.[97] Certainly, this norm of restrictive statutory interpretation reflected notions of class politics during the fractious industrial relations context of the 1960s and 1970s.[98] It is also tempting to regard these statements as constitutionally subversive, with unelected judges undermining statutory immunities to entrench a conservative approach to civil order and private property. Yet in its own way, this norm of restrictive interpretation was itself a form of purposive statutory interpretation. It was informed by a specific vision of English common law constitutionalism. This was based upon a conception of the rule of law and equality under the law that was embedded in the English common law. We have already encountered A.V. Dicey in Chapter 2. Dicey's account of the rule of law emphasised the primacy of ordinary private law, developed by the judges, with every person (including public officials) subject equally to those ordinary legal rules. The trade dispute immunity was obviously antithetical to this account of the rule of law. For English judges who had imbibed Dicey's *Law of the Constitution* in Middle Temple or Lincoln's Inn, the trade dispute immunity *was* a constitutional aberration that needed to be interpreted restrictively.

Despite some differences of detail, the basic legal structure of strike law has remained remarkably stable. The current Part V of TULRCA would be instantly recognisable to Lord Denning and Lord Diplock. Yet there is now a protected right to strike under Article 11, and the ECHR is incorporated domestically under the HRA. Has this transformed the constitutionalism of the English courts in favour of a rights-based approach? And is such a

[95] TULRCA s. 238A.
[96] [1979] 1 WLR 390, 395H (Lord Denning).
[97] *Duport Steels Ltd. and others v Sirs and others* [1980] 1 WLR 142, 156H.
[98] The exemplar of this view of judicial interpretation as the barometer of middle-class opinion on industrial strength is Lord Wedderburn across the three editions of his classic *The Worker and the Law* text.

transformation even possible, given the persistence of the legal form of the immunity in TULRCA?

The prospects for radical constitutional transformation are inhibited by the HRA itself. There are two main constitutional mechanisms in the HRA. The interpretative obligation in s. 3 requires courts to interpret legislation 'so far as it is possible to do so' to be compatible with Convention rights. This is an obligation of a far-reaching character,[99] but it is subject to limits where the interpretation would contradict a fundamental feature or cut against the grain of the legislation.[100] Beyond this limit, the court is straying from the activity of interpretation into the activity of legislating. Where the legislation cannot be interpreted in accordance with s. 3, the court may issue a declaration of incompatibility under s. 4. Compatibility between ECHR standards and national law is subject to what has been called the 'mirror principle'. This holds that the domestic application of Convention rights by the national courts should reflect but not exceed the level of protection specified in the case law of the ECtHR. It was described in the following way by the UKSC in *Elan-Cane*:

> The [Human Rights Act] . . . defines the Convention rights to which it gives effect in domestic law as the rights which are enforceable against the United Kingdom under international law. It follows that the rights given effect in domestic law have the same content as those which are given effect under international law, although they are enforceable before domestic courts rather than the European court, and against public authorities rather than the United Kingdom as a state. Since the rights have the same content at the domestic level as at the international level, it follows that the relevant articles of the Convention should in principle receive the same interpretation in both contexts.[101]

The fact that there is often a wide margin of appreciation under Article 11 is relevant to the mirror principle. If a restriction falls within the margin of appreciation, there is no violation of a Convention right. If there is no violation of a Convention right, then under the mirror principle, a domestic court cannot decide for its own purposes that there is a violation. The purpose of the HRA is to provide a domestic mode of redress for the victim of a rights violation, but since there is no violation, there is no right to 'bring home' under the HRA.[102] As Lord Sales has explained in an extra-judicial lecture, the question

[99] *Ghaidan v Godin-Mendoza* [2004] 2 AC 557.
[100] *Sheldrake v DPP* [2005] I AC 264, [28].
[101] *R (on the application of Elan-Cane) v Secretary of State for the Home Department* [2021] UKSC 56, [87].
[102] *Rights Brought Home: The Human Rights Bill* (CM 3782, 1997).

of violation is always binary: if the state's actions are within the margin of appreciation, then it follows that there is no violation.[103] The margin of appreciation concept cannot therefore be severed from the interpretation of the Convention rights: it is part and parcel of the exercise of interpretation.[104] According to Lord Reed in *Elan-Cane*,

> When the European court finds that the contracting states should be permitted a margin of appreciation, it does not cede the function of interpreting the Convention to the contracting states, or enable their domestic courts to divide that function between their domestic institutions. Contracting states can of course create rights going beyond those protected by the Convention, but that power exists independently of the Convention and the Human Rights Act, is not dependent on the margin of appreciation doctrine, and is exercisable in accordance with long-established constitutional principles, under which law-making is generally the function of the legislature.[105]

The fundamental distinction between collective and individual elements under the ECHR is largely reflected in the domestic case law. There is however some equivocation on this point in the recent Supreme Court judgment in *Secretary of State for Business and Trade v Mercer*, which is considered below.[106]

A. The right to strike in the UK: collective aspects

The first serious consideration of Article 11 in the context of collective aspects of the right to strike was set out in the judgment of Lloyd LJ in *Metrobus Ltd. v Unite the Union.*[107] It concerned the extensive statutory requirements regulating the timing and content of ballot and strike notices. The union had argued that these provisions, considered cumulatively, were a disproportionate interference. The Court of Appeal concluded that these restrictions were proportionate and so there was no need to read down the legislation under s. 3 HRA.

[103] Lord Sales, 'The Developing Jurisprudence of the Supreme Court on Convention Rights', Scottish Public Law Group Conference, 5 June 2023. [8].
[104] *Elan-Cane* (n 101) [89].
[105] Ibid. [85].
[106] [2024] ICR 814.
[107] [2010] ICR 173.

The judgment is usually remembered for the provocative line of Maurice Kay LJ that 'In this country, the right to strike has never been much more than a slogan or a legal metaphor.'[108] This was really a final flourish of the Diceyan scepticism of immunities as a subversion of equality before the law. Although lacking a memorable aphorism, Lloyd LJ's judgment offered a more serious engagement with the constitutional requirements of the HRA. Lloyd LJ's reasoning is likely to be enduring because it prefigures the general approach in later Article 11 ECHR cases like *Humpert*. This is reflected in four main aspects of his judgment. First, Lloyd LJ recognised that it is necessary to consider 'the present state of the legislation as a whole',[109] which is consistent with the ECHR totality principle. Secondly, he also examines whether the restrictions are so excessively onerous as to be disproportionate,[110] which is consistent with the high threshold set by the ECHR's 'devoid of substance' principle. Thirdly, and in line with the mirror principle, he treats the margin of appreciation in Article 11 cases as highly relevant, observing that, 'The binding effect of article 11 of the European Convention does not restrict the scope for a wide variety of different legislative approaches, other than in a rather general way, at the extremes. Such variety is to be expected and is permitted by the margin of appreciation permitted to member states as regards conformity with the Convention.'[111] Finally, Lloyd LJ noted the democratic pedigree of the statutory provisions and the fact that they had been considered (and reconsidered) by the legislature on different occasions.[112] This had also involved consultation with interested groups. All these factors meant that the legislation should be treated as within the reasonable scope of legislative choice. In light of recent ECHR cases like *Humpert*, it seems unlikely that the ECtHR would take a different view of the merits (or Lloyd LJ's reasoning) in a case like *Metrobus* today.

It would not be correct to say that this has rendered Article 11 superfluous. In a later Court of Appeal judgment that is now rightly regarded as a landmark case, Elias LJ rejected the norm of restrictive statutory interpretation in the following terms:

> The common law's focus on the protection of property and contractual rights is necessarily antithetical to any form of industrial action since the purpose of the action

[108] Ibid. [118].
[109] Ibid. [103].
[110] Ibid. [112].
[111] Ibid. [50].
[112] Ibid. [54]–[56].

> is to interfere with the employer's rights. The statutory immunities are simply the form which the law in this country takes to carve out the ability for unions to take lawful strike action. It is for Parliament to determine how the conflicting interests of employers and unions should be reconciled in the field of industrial relations. But if one starts from the premise that the legislation should be strictly construed against those seeking the benefit of the immunities, the effect is the same as it would be if there were a presumption that Parliament intends that the interests of the employers should hold sway unless the legislation clearly dictates otherwise. I do not think this is now a legitimate approach, if it ever was. In my judgment the legislation should simply be construed in the normal way, without presumptions one way or the other.[113]

This rejection of the restrictive approach to the interpretation of statutory immunities has been followed by the Irish Supreme Court in *H.A. O'Neill Ltd. v Unite the Union and others*.[114] The principle of ordinary interpretation enunciated by Elias LJ emphasises the conflicting economic interests at stake in designing strike laws. These interests ought to be conciliated through politics rather than law, and this supports the primacy of legislation and parliamentary sovereignty. It is democratically legitimate for Parliament to legislate and specify the requirements for a lawful strike. It is incumbent on the courts to interpret these statutory requirements in a workable rather than an obstructive way. While Elias LJ presented his interpretive shift in modest terms, as the retrieval of ordinary statutory interpretation, the real-world consequences have been very significant. Strike injunctions are now much more difficult to secure in practice in the English courts. And as the Irish Supreme Court recognised in *H.A. O'Neill Ltd*, this statutory right to engage in trade union activity promotes equality by responding to the inequality of bargaining power facilitated by the common law and individual freedom of contract.[115] This shift probably now means that the old debates about 'rights versus immunities' are less significant than they once were.[116] And it is unlikely that an alternative semantic formulation in the trade dispute immunity in terms of a 'right' would make any significant difference to statutory interpretation after Elias LJ's judgment. It has wrought a quiet revolution in the best traditions of incremental legal development in common law systems.

[113] *RMT v Serco Ltd; ASLEF v London & Birmingham Railway Ltd* [2011] EWCA Civ 226, [2011] ICR 848, [9] (Elias LJ).
[114] [2024] IESC 8, [2024] 1 ILRM 77 [59].
[115] Ibid.
[116] For a recent reflection on that debate by one of its leading protagonists in the 1980s, see K.D. Ewing, 'Sir Patrick Elias and the Right to Strike' (2025) 54 Industrial Law Journal 954.

UK strike laws are extremely restrictive, and legislative changes have tended to operate in a kind of ratchet effect, with new restrictions added to the existing body of law.[117] This accelerated in the years following the Trade Union Act 2016, a highly restrictive statute which imposed extensive statutory duties on trade unions. In *R (ASLEF) v Secretary of State for Business and Trade*, a group of unions challenged the Conduct of Employment Agencies and Employment Businesses (Amendment) Regulations 2022 through judicial review.[118] These amendments removed the restrictions on agencies providing workers as replacement labour during an official strike. The unions had made submissions on Article 11 and the right to strike, but Linden J focused on the multiple failures of the Secretary of State to comply with the duty to consult. It was relevant to the existence and extent of the Secretary of State's procedural obligations, for example, that the proposal to lift the restrictions in the 2022 Regs was inconsistent with ILO standards on the right to strike.[119] Where there are highly restrictive rules regulating the collective aspects of the right to strike, as in the UK, there is a difficult line between judicial respect for democratic processes and enabling rights violations. Rather than challenging legislation directly, the focus on the quality of consultative processes provides a way for courts to tread that difficult constitutional line.

B. The right to strike in the UK: individual aspects

Under TULRCA s. 238A, there are statutory protections from dismissal for employees engaged in 'protected' (i.e., lawful and official) industrial action, previously restricted to the first 12 weeks of the dispute until the removal of this limit by the Employment Rights Act 2025. There are no parallel statutory protections from detriment for workers engaged in such action. In *Mercer*, the Supreme Court considered whether a worker who (on agreed facts) had been suspended in order to sanction or penalise her for participation in a 'protected' strike—a strike which was lawful under UK law because it complied with all the substantive and procedural rules in Part V of TULRCA—was protected from 'detriment' for her participation in trade union activities under s. 146 TULRCA.[120]

The Supreme Court concluded that this protection was excluded from s. 146, principally because it did not take place 'at an appropriate time'. This

[117] Although there is a prospect of some reversal in statutory restrictions in the Employment Rights Act 2025, which is an unusual legislative trend.
[118] [2023] ICR 1405.
[119] Ibid. [189] (v)–(vi).
[120] *Mercer* (n 106).

meant there was no statutory protection for the claimant on ordinary principles of statutory interpretation. Lady Simler considered that there was a violation of Article 11 because of the absence of *any* protection for individual strikers. The Supreme Court did not think that a s. 3 interpretation was possible because it would amount to 'impermissible judicial legislation'.[121] There were too many controversial policy choices involved in determining which detriments should be proscribed, and in what circumstances. However, the Supreme Court concluded that it was appropriate to issue a declaration of incompatibility under s. 4 HRA. This would require the legislator to consider how best to respond to the incompatibility, which would confer some scope for democratic choice.

The outcome in *Mercer* is surely correct. There cannot be a *right* to strike in circumstances where workers are exposed to penalties for its exercise: the right to strike 'dissolves'.[122] Yet there is some confusion and resulting equivocation in the judgment that undermines its constitutional coherence. This stems from the Supreme Court's treatment of *RMT*.[123] *RMT* is accorded too much significance in *Mercer*, and this is because Lady Simler rejects the bifurcation between individual and collective aspects under Article 11.[124] This leads the Supreme Court to suggest that states have a margin of appreciation in private sector cases involving detriments imposed on individual strikers. The 'individual' ECHR cases on sanctions and penalties have already been considered earlier in this chapter, and the margin of appreciation plays a very limited role. I am aware of no ECHR case where the penalisation of strikers because they were engaged in lawful and official strike action has been found to be justified. And there was no reference at all to margin in another individual detriment case, *Wilson v UK*. Why did the Supreme Court in *Mercer* take the approach that it did? I think there are two main reasons.

The first problem is a confusion between 'core' and 'essential' trade union freedoms, a confusion not helped by the Strasbourg Court itself. Lady Simler suggests that the right to strike is not a 'core' trade union freedom under Article 11. This is based upon her view that 'essential' and 'core' are interchangeable in the ECtHR's reasoning.[125] Since the right to strike is not yet included in the ECtHR's list of 'essential' elements, it follows that it is not a 'core' freedom either. This is a misreading of *RMT*. In that case, the ECtHR drew a distinction between primary (i.e., 'core') strikes and secondary (i.e., 'accessory') strikes.

[121] Ibid. [102].
[122] Ibid. [89].
[123] *RMT* (n 43).
[124] *Mercer* (n 106) [69].
[125] Ibid. [70]–[72].

The margin of appreciation is wider for secondary strikes because it is an 'accessory' rather than a 'core' trade union activity. Yet the strike in *Mercer* was a primary strike. This meant that it was a 'core' rather than an 'accessory' trade union freedom. It was also a lawful and official strike, since it was exercised within the statutory limits determined by the legislature under TULRCA. In these circumstances, the margin of appreciation should be very narrow indeed.

The second problem relates to the permissible scope for employer sanctions in the private sector. For example, Lady Simler observed that 'There may be circumstances where it is permissible to impose a detriment for participating in lawful strike action where employees have necessarily acted in breach of contract, particularly where the manner of the breach is harmful or disruptive.'[126] This is confused because in these circumstances the detriment is not being imposed 'for' participating in lawful strike action. It is being imposed for the wrong that is separable from the lawful protected activity. For example, where a worker is suspended for an assault on a picket line, it is the assault that is being punished, not the strike activity. The separability of the motivating reasons for detriment is the key to addressing this difficulty. The courts are well-used to handling these assessments in discrimination and whistleblowing cases. It is irrelevant to the legal definition of a 'detriment'.

Considerations of democracy were also important in *Mercer*. In particular, the absence of any apparent democratic consideration of this legislative exclusion counted against the Secretary of State's argument that Parliament had struck a fair balance.[127] If there 'had there been legislation addressing action short of dismissal, it might have been possible to say that a fair balance had been struck by Parliament given the wider margin of appreciation to be applied'.[128] While the democratic pedigree of legislation is relevant to the delimitation of the collective freedom, as reflected in *RMT*, *Ognevenko* and *Humpert*, its relevance to individual protection from sanctions is less clear. Even if Parliament *had* authorised the imposition of detriments on lawful and official strikers, it is highly unlikely that the ECtHR would regard that as Article 11 compliant. The full legislative response to *Mercer* is currently being considered in a public consultation following the enactment of the Employment Rights Act 2025. The Act has removed the 12-week period for 'protected' industrial action under the s. 238A dismissal protections to bring UK law into line with Article 11. That must be right, as there is no basis in Article 11 for setting temporal limits on individual protections. The correct

126 Ibid. [83].
127 Ibid. [84]–[90].
128 Ibid. [90].

statutory solution to *Mercer* itself is to ensure that *all* detriments imposed to deter or penalise 'protected' industrial action are unlawful. There is very little role for margin of appreciation to play here.

V. The Right to Strike in Canada: Dignity, Autonomy, and Equality

The right to strike is also recognised as a fundamental constitutional right under s. 2(d) freedom of association in the Canadian Charter. This was established in *Saskatchewan Federation of Labour v Saskatchewan*.[129] The lead judgment was given by Abella J, and there was a strong dissent by Rothstein and Wagner JJ, arguing against constitutional recognition. *Saskatchewan Federation of Labour* arose out of a constitutional challenge to The Public Service Essential Services Act 2008 (PSESA), which prohibited strikes in essential services in Saskatchewan public employment. PSESA did so through a wide definition of 'essential services' and the reservation of broad and unreviewable unilateral powers to public employers in imposing essential work notices. Employees who violated work notices were subject to summary conviction and fines. PSESA made no provision for any substitute mechanisms, such as compulsory arbitration, where the right to strike had been denied. Abella J concluded that there was a substantial interference with freedom of association, and it could not be justified under s. 1.

Saskatchewan Federation of Labour is so interesting because it disrupts some of the assumptions in Sheldon Leader's earlier reflections on 'instrumental' and 'independent' arguments for the right to strike. Recall Leader indicated that a central difficulty with the instrumental argument was its alignment with strong judicial deference. By contrast, the independent argument avoided that problem because it did not depend upon controversial economic arguments about equalising bargaining power. *Saskatchewan Federation of Labour* appears to turn this on its head. Abella J adopted a strongly instrumental approach but was very sceptical about deference. This led the SCC to find that PSESA was unconstitutional under s. 2(d). By contrast, Rothstein and Wagner JJ adopted an independent argument that was coupled with the primacy of statute in collective labour relations. It was thus highly deferential to the Saskatchewan legislator, and it would have insulated PSESA from constitutional challenge.

[129] [2015] 1 SCR 245.

Starting with Abella J, a key paragraph explaining the distinctive core of her instrumental reasoning is set out here:

> The right to strike is essential to realizing these values and objectives through a collective bargaining process because it permits workers to withdraw their labour in concert when collective bargaining reaches an impasse. Through a strike, workers come together to participate directly in the process of determining their wages, working conditions and the rules that will govern their working lives . . . The ability to strike thereby allows workers, through collective action, to refuse to work under imposed terms and conditions. This collective action at the moment of impasse is an affirmation of the dignity and autonomy of employees in their working lives.[130]

Elsewhere, Abella J emphasised that the right to strike was an 'essential part' and 'indispensable component' of the right to a meaningful collective bargaining process.[131] This was supported by reference to the long social history of collective bargaining practices, international standards, and comparative consensus on the essential nature of the right to strike.

A strong theme in Abella J's instrumental reasoning is its orientation to the constitutional values of dignity, autonomy, and equality. This value orientation avoided some of the limitations of Leader's and Langille's freedom of association arguments in respect of their normative thinness. Those accounts could be criticised because they do not explain *why* striking (or any other individual liberty) is especially deserving of constitutional protection. Abella J addresses the issue of why the (individual) withdrawal of labour is a valuable exercise of freedom head-on. This normative argument is necessary to justify its special constitutional protection in *Saskatchewan Federation of Labour*. While judges may not have the social scientific expertise to measure and compare bargaining power, they do have greater expertise to reason on equality, dignity, and autonomy.

This values-based instrumentalism draws a normative connection between the individual and collective counterparts of the right to strike. Dignity and autonomy explain why the right to strike for each employee, exercised collectively with others, is constitutionally fundamental. It enables workers to shape their own working lives and to exercise democratic control through their own actions and endeavours. This provides a distinctive form of worker protection, avoiding passive dependence on benign legislators and employers. Striking and collective bargaining thereby credits workers with agency and

[130] Ibid. [54].
[131] Ibid. [3].

self-respect.[132] It embodies a notion of workers as moral equals in the political community, which is a basis of their human dignity. Its collective exercise empowers workers so that they can bargain with employers in circumstances of substantive equality.[133] Given the constitutional importance of workers' self-directed efforts in workplace democratic participation, the availability of substitute mechanisms needed to be considered under the s. 1 Charter justification rather than s. 2(d). These mechanisms should generally be regarded as a second-best compared with the dignity and autonomy of collective self-help. The absence of any substitute mechanism was a significant factor in holding that PSESA was not a minimal impairment as required by the Charter justification test.

The surprising part of *Saskatchewan Federation of Labour* is that Abella J's instrumental reasoning is aligned with a rejection of strong deference. Sheldon Leader regarded instrumentalism and strong deference as corollaries in the jurisprudence on strikes. The point is put starkly in her judgment: 'If the touchstone of Charter compliance is deference, what is the point of judicial scrutiny?'[134] Of course, there is not a simple binary between deference and scrutiny. It is possible to engage in scrutiny with varying degrees of intensity. Still, the scrutiny in the majority judgment is relatively intensive. This is facilitated by what we described as *autochthony* in fundamental rights jurisprudence discussed earlier in Chapter 4.[135] This term describes a situation where the specific content of rights is shaped by the thick ethical and cultural goods in a national context. The constitutional right to strike in Canada is not identical to the statutory right to strike. Nevertheless, the contours of the constitutional norm are shaped by Canadian social and legal history. For example, the SCC describes the constitutional right to strike as enlivened where there is an *impasse* in collective bargaining. This temporal dimension is not a universal feature of the right to strike—for example, it has no significant role in UK law—but it is a prominent feature of the Canadian approach. Autochthony means there is less of a normative gap between the abstract constitutional standard and the detailed statutory framework under review. Democratic choices as reflected in statute have already shaped the constitutional standard even before the SCC evaluates the

[132] These dignitarian arguments are developed in Alan Bogg, 'Subsidiarity or Freedom of Association? A Perspective from Labor Law' (2016) 61 American Journal of Jurisprudence 143. See also Sergio Gamonal, 'Dignity and the Right to Strike' (2025) 45 Comparative Labor Law and Policy Journal 264.
[133] *Saskatchewan Federation of Labour* (n 129) [56].
[134] Ibid. [76].
[135] Paul Craig, *UK, EU and Global Administrative Law: Foundations and Challenges* (Cambridge UP 2015) 272.

legislation. There is a reflexive interaction between constitutional norm and legislated norm.

The dissenting judgment in *Saskatchewan Federation of Labour* was influenced by Canadian scholars who have articulated a thinner account of freedom of association.[136] As we have already seen in Chapter 4, this approach draws a distinction between freedoms and rights. The common law supports a *freedom* to withdraw labour, but it does not support a *right* to withdraw labour. The right would require the constitutionalisation of 'a duty on employers not to terminate employees who have withdrawn their labour, nor to hire replacement workers'.[137] The constitutionalisation of the right would trespass into the controversial arena of socio-economic policy, which is the province of the legislature.[138] This might ossify these controversial policy judgements and remove them from the democratic process. It reduces the scope for democratic deliberation and the scope for experimentation with different models of labour relations. It also leads judges into areas of adjudication that are ill-suited to their expertise. In many ways, the battery of arguments in the Rothstein/Wagner dissent supports a traditional abstentionist view of the judicial role in labour law. Labour rights and duties must be entrusted to legislation, and the subsidiary task of the court is to interpret and apply that legislation faithfully in accordance with its purpose. Against the arguments of Rothstein and Wagner, I have argued that the protection of individual strikers from detrimental treatment is at the moral core of the right to strike. There is very little scope for variation in defining these rights and duties. And there is a morally compelling case for the judicial recognition of this individual right because it ensures the equal moral standing of workers. This is exactly the kind of task that constitutional courts should be performing.

For now, at least, the distinctive instrumental approach of Abella J holds sway in Canada. Although there are some differences in language, there are similarities to the instrumental approach of the ECtHR. Under s. 1 of the Charter, for example, the absence of a substitute mechanism was treated by the SCC as an important factor in upholding the Charter challenge. To use the language of Strasbourg, this is the court examining the 'totality' of measures' to assess if trade union freedoms are 'devoid of substance'. The major difference between Strasbourg and Ottawa relates to the much stronger emphasis on constitutional values in the SCC. National constitutional courts may feel

[136] See, e.g., *Saskatchewan Federation of Labour* (n 129) [111], referencing the academic work of Brian Langille and Benjamin Oliphant.

[137] Ibid. [112]. It is interesting that the dissent identifies this as the core duty that is correlative to a right to strike and that it relates the situation of the individual striker.

[138] Ibid. [116].

less reticent than supranational courts in affirming thicker constitutional values. This supported the SCC in finding a Charter violation in *Saskatchewan Federation of Labour*. I suspect that the ECtHR would have treated comparable legislation as within the state's wide margin of appreciation under Article 11. This reflects the specific challenges for a supranational court assessing a spectrum of regulatory possibilities across different member states.

VI. The Right to Strike, Deference, and Equal Moral Standing

Twenty years ago, this would have been a radically different chapter. The right to strike was absent from much of the constitutional jurisprudence crafted in Strasbourg, London, and Ottawa. The constitutional landscape has been transformed in the three legal orders we have examined. The right to strike is now constitutionally recognised and protected by the ECtHR, the English courts, and the SCC. Interestingly, the legal reasoning in the landmark cases has not developed in the ways that may have been expected or hoped for by our opening troika of leading scholars. For Sheldon Leader and Keith Ewing, the right to strike as a human right ought to have reconfigured labour law systems in radical ways. This has not happened. While many of the cases examined in this chapter could be described as 'activist' judgments, the courts have proceeded very cautiously in 'collective' cases, sensitive to considerations of democracy and institutional expertise. This has led many scholars to be deflated and disappointed by the constitutional right to strike. Constitutional litigation has often served to entrench rather than subvert the right to strike as it is defined in ordinary legislation. I have argued that when workers appear to enjoy significant compensatory guarantees, as in *Humpert*, this judicial deference to the legislative status quo may be warranted.

There is far less deference in cases involving the discriminatory victimisation of individual strikers. For Brian Langille, the constitutional courts may already have gone too far in their journey from *freedoms* to *rights*. Against that view, I have defended a basic normative distinction between individual and collective counterparts of the right to strike. In cases involving penalties and sanctions imposed on individual strikers, this violates the basic constitutional value of equality before the law. When employers dish out punishment to adult citizens for exercising their human rights lawfully, this demeans their equal moral standing. It is a form of civic disrespect. In such cases, the constitutional *freedom* is not sufficient. Where the legislature fails to protect the individual striker from sanctions and penalties, it is the constitutional responsibility of the court to vindicate equality. It can only do that through recognising and entrenching worker rights and employer duties. This provides a protective perimeter around the basic freedom to withdraw labour. In defining the collective conditions for a lawful strike, such as its purposes and procedures, there continues to be a leading role for legislative delimitation in labour law. The deference of constitutional courts in this collective realm reflects considerations of expertise and democracy. The autonomy of labour law and its statutory categories dominates the approach of courts to the 'collective' boundary in each of these jurisdictions. I have argued that this deference is usually constitutionally fitting.

6

Freedom of Association and the Closed Shop

I. Freedom of Association and the Closed Shop: A Clash between Labour Law and Civil Liberties?

The centrepiece of Wedderburn's critique of the ECHR is his consideration of the fate of the closed shop under Article 11.[1] It is this that really sparks his ire. This protection of the individual's right to disassociate from the union revealed the individualistic foundations of the civil liberty conception of freedom of association. This protection is 'formalistic'.[2] The freedom in Article 11 is a 'false prospectus'.[3] It opens 'yet another avenue for individuals to litigate against trade unions – in the hope, for example, of convincing the English judges to read Article 11(1) (as the six hard-core judges wished in the "Railwaymen's case") to enshrine an absolute "negative" right to disassociate'.[4] This characterisation presupposes a clear divergence between the 'labour law' conception (pro-closed shop) and the 'civil liberty' conception (anti-closed shop), between light and dark. The closed shop represents the clearest case for Wedderburn of the dangers of human rights (and judges in constitutional courts) to the structural integrity of labour law.

In this chapter, I will argue that Wedderburn draws entirely the wrong lesson from the Article 11 closed shop cases. In Section II, we see that the treatment of the closed shop was controversial even within a single labour law tradition, collective laissez-faire. This is reflected in the differences between Wedderburn and Kahn-Freund on the closed shop and union security. There was no single 'labour law' view of the closed shop even between scholars sharing many values and assumptions.

[1] Lord Wedderburn, 'Freedom of Association or Right to Organise? The Common Law and International Sources' in Lord Wedderburn, *Employment Rights in Britain and Europe* (Lawrence & Wishart 1991) 142.
[2] Ibid. 144.
[3] Ibid. 150.
[4] 150–151.

Freedom of Association. Alan Bogg, Oxford University Press. © Alan Bogg 2026. DOI: 10.1093/9780191831690.003.0006

In Section III, the historical development of UK law on the closed shop is examined. This was a dynamic and complex area of law. The common law emphasised the protection of the individual worker from arbitrary treatment. This was not based in a human rights paradigm but drew upon techniques from administrative law such as natural justice. During the 1980s, the statutory framework shifted significantly in favour of restriction of the closed shop. These changes were still justified by wider labour market goals such as reducing trade union power and removing obstructions to efficient labour markets. In this sense, these goals were internal to labour law's statutory development rather than imposed externally by human rights standards. Moreover, these statutory measures were democratically enacted; they were not imposed by unelected judges.

The UK approach favouring legal restriction of the closed shop was not untypical. It reflected a broader convergence in European legal systems that treated the closed shop as normatively suspect. This provides the context to the Article 11 case law examined in Section IV. The Article 11 position is now more hardline than it was when Wedderburn penned his critique. As we shall see, the prohibition of the closed shop is an essential element of trade union rights under Article 11. It would be a serious distortion to present this as the 'civil liberty' approach overriding the 'labour law' approach to the closed shop, however. On the contrary, it reflects an ECtHR sensitive to the autonomy of labour law and conscious of the labour law convergence against the closed shop in European states. It could therefore be understood as human rights judges *deferring* to national labour law practices, not undermining them. The narrow margin of appreciation in closed shop cases is also consistent with other Article 11 cases, for example in the right to strike and right to collective bargaining contexts. The court is vigorous in its protection of the individual from victimisation and discriminatory practices. Those same considerations are relevant to the closed shop.

In this way, the closed shop cases are an element in a broadly coherent approach to Article 11 based on the difference between 'individual' (narrow margin) and 'collective' cases (wide margin). The closed shop engages the 'individual' dimension. The chapter concludes by asking, is there a human right not to be a trade union member? The answer to that is now yes. And is there a human right to the closed shop? The answer is no. In contrast to Wedderburn's critique, I will argue that these were answers developed principally within the domain of labour law. Human rights law simply took its lead from those labour law developments.

II. The Closed Shop and Varieties of Collective Laissez-Faire

The image of a clash between the 'civil liberty' and the 'labour law' conceptions of freedom of association on the closed shop implied that there was a settled and unitary labour law position. This image is very much at odds with contested nature of union security *within* the labour law paradigm. This was true even within the parameters of a single intellectual tradition like British 'collective laissez-faire'. There was no single collective laissez-faire perspective on union security. This can be seen in different approaches to union security and the closed shop in the work of Wedderburn and Kahn-Freund. They were the leading scholars of collective laissez-faire in the post-war period. Naturally enough, as interpreters of an intellectual tradition, they shared many commonalities of method and value, especially on the fundamental societal importance of autonomous trade unionism and collective bargaining.[5] Yet there could still be significant differences between them on specific issues of legal policy.[6] For example, Wedderburn's work was more strongly critical of the English common law and the judiciary as instruments of class oppression.[7] This supported his emphasis on the 'autonomy' of labour law from the English common law, administered by specialist labour courts and based in worker-protective legislation.[8] By contrast, 'autonomy' in Kahn-Freund's work was addressed to the primacy of social norms derived from collective agreements; and his views of the English common law and its judges were less astringent than those of Wedderburn.[9]

These theoretical differences were reflected in significant divergences of normative tone and proposed regulatory approach in relation to union security in British labour law. This registered in the varying uses of 'individualism' in their scholarship.[10] For Wedderburn, 'individualism' undermined solidarity by elevating individual choice over the collective good. Union security was a prime area in which the disruptive social effects of 'individualism'

[5] Ruth Dukes, 'Wedderburn and the Theory of Labour Law: Building on Kahn-Freund' (2015) 44 Industrial Law Journal 357.

[6] This is the fundamental thesis in Alan Bogg, 'The Hero's Journey: Lord Wedderburn and the "Political Constitution" of Labour Law' (2015) 44 Industrial Law Journal 299.

[7] Ibid. 312–315.

[8] The classic work in this vein is Lord Wedderburn, 'Labour Law - From Here to Autonomy? A Franco-British Comparison' in Lord Wedderburn, *Employment Rights in Britain and Europe* (Lawrence & Wishart 1991) 106.

[9] Bogg (n 6) 309, 314–315.

[10] Alan Bogg, '"Individualism" and "Collectivism" in Collective Labour Law' (2017) 46 Industrial Law Journal 72, 78–84.

could be identified. For Kahn-Freund, by contrast, 'individualism' signalled an important residual role for the law in protecting individual workers from oppressive abuse of power in closed shop situations.[11] Overall, Wedderburn's work evinced an attitude of positive support for the closed shop, whereas Kahn-Freund was more agnostic. This demonstrates the contested nature of the social practice even within a specific tradition of labour law.

A. Wedderburn on the closed shop

An early insight into Wedderburn's positive attitude towards the closed shop can be seen in chapter 10 of the first edition of *The Worker and the Law*, 'Members' Rights and Union Security'.[12] It drew extensively upon McCarthy's classic industrial relations treatise on the closed shop which had been published a year earlier and was based upon McCarthy's doctoral thesis.[13] McCarthy's book is an exemplar of the pluralist tradition in its rigorous empiricist assessment of the varieties of union security practices in British industrial relations. It also provided a functionalist justification for the closed shop in terms of its support for joint regulation through collective bargaining. This function depended upon an equilibrium of power, and union security contributed to that, particularly where there was an oversupply of labour in certain labour markets (for example, film extras). McCarthy also considered the need for tailored restrictions to prevent the abuse of powers to exclude or expel workers from union membership. In the final sentence of the book, McCarthy's crystallisation of the arguments in the book were described in the following way: 'In effect this comes to mean no more than that every worker "ought to join his appropriate trade union". This I believe.'[14]

This credo was also evident in Wedderburn's early reflections. For Wedderburn, the common law attitude to legal disputes between the individual dissenter and the trade union in closed shop situations tended to be skewed unduly in favour of the individual member: 'The man "sent to Coventry" by workmates is bound, if no more than that is known, to evoke sympathy in all but the coldest heart. But further investigation so often discloses the less-publicized interests of the individuals with whom he has run into conflict, whose side he chose often to desert.'[15] This characterised the

[11] Ibid. 78–81.
[12] K.W. Wedderburn, *The Worker and the Law* (1st ed, Penguin 1965), 314.
[13] W.E.J. McCarthy, *The Closed Shop in Britain* (Basil Blackwell 1964). McCarthy thanks both Kahn-Freund and Wedderburn in the preface: vii.
[14] Ibid. 281.
[15] Wedderburn (n 12) 314.

issue of union security as a problem of collective solidarity. The maintenance of solidarity through union discipline, especially in closed shop situations, was a critical underpinning to strong trade unions in collective labour relations. The penalty of social and economic ostracism, magnified in closed shop situations, restrained the selfish dispositions of individual workers who took the benefits of collective bargaining without sharing the burdens of collective action.[16] This idea of group solidarity was something that the individualism of the English common law struggled to accommodate. This did not mean that there was no role for the courts. For Wedderburn, however, this role was necessarily limited.

The fundamental legal basis to the courts' jurisdiction was contract. Indeed, the union's (collective) freedom of association was rooted in the common law freedom of contract. This meant that there was limited scope for the courts to challenge exclusionary practices in pre-entry closed shops. Where a union's eligibility rules excluded an individual from membership, there was very little that courts could (or should) do to rectify this.[17] There was no contract to enforce because the parties were unable or unwilling to contract with each other. Without a contract, the basis of the court's jurisdiction was obscure. In relation to post-entry closed shops, the expulsion of trade union members also depended ultimately on the contract and whether the union had a contractual right to sanction the member in this way. This depended upon the legal meaning of the disciplinary 'offence' and any relevant disciplinary procedures in the rule book. While the rules of 'natural justice' were very important in securing fair treatment for union members, Wedderburn regarded these as subject ultimately to the express terms of the contract of membership. These were not mandatory legal norms that overrode the parties' freedom of contract.[18] In this respect, Wedderburn emphasised that the underlying issue here was 'whether, in fact, the courts can themselves single out trade unions (because of their effect on workers' livelihood) for extra regulation'.[19] Wedderburn evidently did not think so, because he was also dismissive of arguments based upon interference with the individual's 'right to work', arguments which he described as 'astonishing'.[20] The 'right to work'

[16] Ibid. 329, while noting the narrow and distinctive position of those with a 'truly conscientious objection' to union membership.

[17] This was at issue in the celebrated case of *Faramus v Film Artistes' Association* [1964] AC 925, HL, discussed below.

[18] This was in response to judicial arguments (especially by Lord Denning) that norms of natural justice were overriding legal duties imposed on trade unions and that could not be excluded by the contract of membership: Wedderburn (n 12) 325.

[19] Ibid. 326.

[20] Ibid. 328.

was concerned with the worker's right to secure employment, the availability of employment opportunities, and restrictions on the employer's dismissal powers. In the context of the closed shop, Wedderburn took the view that the 'right to work' was a misleading normative label for an asserted freedom not to be a trade union member. Overall, it was clear that Wedderburn favoured positive state support to facilitate union security arrangements, with the problems of abuse of union power best resolved through the revision of union rule books.[21] Unsurprisingly, he did not favour an extensive role for the common law and the courts in striking a balance between union security and individual freedoms.

Many years later, Wedderburn's strong critique of the ECHR was motivated primarily by the ECtHR's treatment of 'negative' freedom of association and the closed shop.[22] It contained a battery of criticisms that derived from the precarious legal position of the closed shop under Article 11. In *Young, James and Webster v United Kingdom*, known as the 'Railwaymen's Case', the ECtHR concluded that the law permitting the closed shop arrangements in that case violated Article 11.[23] This judgment was Wedderburn's main target in his more general critique of Article 11. In later cases, of course, the ECtHR's measured approach in the Railwaymen's Case would harden into a full-blown repudiation of the closed shop as inherently violative of Article 11. For Wedderburn, this early judicial attitude reflected an orientation in favour of individual rights protecting the sovereignty of individual choice. It meant that Article 11 was 'skewed towards an individualistic interpretation'.[24] The closed shop jurisprudence also exemplified the undemocratic transfer of political power to an unelected judiciary in evaluating permissible restrictions under Article 11(2). In *Young, James, and Webster*, the ECtHR concluded that the measures failed to achieve an appropriate balance between union members and non-unionists. This proportionality enquiry involved vague and open-textured concepts, and it was a decision of policy masquerading as a decision of law.[25] Such policy judgements ought not to be entrusted to judges who lacked democratic accountability. While recognising that many European countries with social democratic traditions prohibited the closed shop, Wedderburn nevertheless criticised the 'formalism' of the Court's

[21] Wedderburn observed that 'Britain has been fortunately free from obnoxious religious or racial discrimination . . . such as has occurred in the USA': ibid. 330. He would no doubt have regarded this kind of discrimination in membership practices as amenable to statutory prohibition.

[22] Wedderburn (n 1).

[23] *Young, James and Webster v United Kingdom* [1981] ECHR 4.

[24] Wedderburn (n 1) 143.

[25] Ibid. 141.

protection of the individual right to disassociate.[26] It left Article 11 as a 'sham formula' devoid of collective content,[27] more likely to provide free riders with yet another tool to litigate against trade unions. Of course, Wedderburn did not go so far to argue that there was a human right *to* a closed shop. That would be highly disruptive in countries like Italy and France where labour law systems barred the closed shop. This individual right to disassociate was critical in systems like these where unions were divided on ideological or confessional lines.

The problem for Wedderburn was far more fundamental than this. When Wedderburn published this critique in 1987, the statutory restriction of the closed shop in the United Kingdom was already at an advanced stage *within British labour law itself*. This presented a serious dilemma for Wedderburn's democratic arguments against the 'Railwaymen's Case', because the escalating restrictions on the closed shop in the United Kingdom were being implemented through legislative reform. That legislation had been introduced by a democratically elected government as part of its extensive reform of labour market regulation through the restriction of collective trade union power. This could all still be described as 'labour law'. It was just radically different to the kind of labour law defended by Wedderburn. The democratic arguments favouring deference in the Railwaymen's Case presumably also applied to human rights scrutiny of the significant statutory restrictions on the closed shop introduced by parliament during the 1980s. Respect for democracy presumably supported a stance of judicial neutrality on whatever the legislature determined on union security from time to time.

Obviously, there was a chasm between the neoliberal politics of this anti-closed shop legislation and Wedderburn's pro-closed shop arguments.[28] Even within collective laissez-faire, however, there was no agreed intellectual position on the closed shop. While the differences between Wedderburn and Kahn-Freund on union security are not nearly as stark as Wedderburn's disagreements with Thatcherite labour law, they are certainly real differences. This debunks the simple picture even of a 'labour law' conception of freedom of association. The disagreements *within* labour law might be every bit as significant as the disagreements *between* labour law and human rights.

[26] Ibid. 144.

[27] Ibid. 151.

[28] This is set out in Lord Wedderburn, 'Freedom of Association and Philosophies of Labour Law: The Thatcher Ideology' (1989) 18 Industrial Law Journal 1.

B. Kahn-Freund on the closed shop

In Kahn-Freund's famous essay from 1959, 'Labour Law', it is still a surprise to encounter the final section extolling the virtues of the 'individualist tradition' in British labour law.[29] A typical caricature of collective laissez-faire is that it is suspicious of 'individualism', especially as manifested in common law values, because 'individualism' is antithetical to collective values. In fact, Kahn-Freund offered a careful yet positive assessment of the 'individualist tradition', particularly as it had developed in the English common law. This provides a contrast with the general approach of Wedderburn which was hostile to the English common law. This elucidation of the 'individualist tradition' reveals Kahn-Freund's attitude to union security and the closed shop when he crystallised his theory of collective laissez-faire in the 1950s.

Kahn-Freund's praise of the civil libertarian common law begins with a paean to freedom of contract. Again, this seems surprising for a labour lawyer, where freedom of contract is so often the fundamental regulatory problem to be addressed. Yet this was not freedom of contract in the sense of determining the substantive rights and duties in the contract. In 1950s Great Britain, the creative positive freedom in individual employment contracts was typically exercised through trade unions negotiating collective agreements or (in unorganised sectors) the unilateral determination of employers. The most fundamental common law bulwark against oppression was in 'the power to decide whether or not to enter into or to terminate the employment relationship',[30] or 'negative' freedom of contract.[31] This was a vital safeguard against compulsory labour. In 1959, of course, the experience of totalitarianism would still have been vivid for Kahn-Freund, and from this perspective his admiration for the libertarian English common law was natural.[32] Given this context, we can certainly understand the fundamental importance of the worker's freedom to enter or exit the employment relationship. Interestingly, Kahn-Freund was also sceptical that an employer could be compelled to employ a person against its will, and he remarked on the 'futility of attempts to

[29] Otto Kahn-Freund, 'Labour Law', in Otto Kahn-Freund, *Selected Writings* (Stevens & Sons, 1978) 1, 31 (first published in 1959).

[30] Ibid. 31.

[31] On 'positive' and 'negative' freedom of contract, see Nili Cohen, 'Pre-contractual Duties: Two Freedoms and the Contract to Negotiate', in Jack Beatson and Daniel Friedman (eds), *Good Faith and Fault in Contract Law* (OUP 1997) chapter 2.

[32] See Kahn-Freund (n 29) 32, citing Lord Atkin in *Nokes v Doncaster Amalgamated Collieries* [1940] AC 1014. Kahn-Freund also noted Lord Atkin's dissent in *Liversidge v Anderson* [1942] AC 206 and his role 'as one of the champions of civil liberties in our time'.

make people work *or employ* under threats of committal and attachment'.[33] This was written many years before the introduction of statutory unfair dismissal legislation which might encompass legal remedies of reinstatement. Nevertheless, these arguments in 1959 help to explain why the legal focus in protecting individuals from arbitrary exclusion in closed shop situations was on trade union practices rather than employers' dismissal decisions. During the 1980s, with the expansion in *statutory* regulation of the closed shop, this was generally coupled with the wider development of unfair dismissal laws.

The dominance of freedom of contract at common law meant that it was relatively easy for British trade unions and employers to negotiate and enforce closed shop arrangements.[34] Given that dismissal was so lightly regulated in 1959, dismissal of non-unionists provided a powerful sanction for enforcing union security. In the early post-war period, there was little prospect of challenging the employer's dismissal prerogatives entrenched in the common law. This shifted the law's protective focus away from employers and to 'the protection of the individual against superior social forces', reflected in the increased willingness of courts 'to protect minorities inside trade unions'.[35] The intervention of the common law in the internal affairs of trade unions was described as 'an almost necessary corollary of the growing policy of non-interference with labour-management relations, and especially with the operation of 100 percent union and closed-shop practices'.[36] The trade unions' social power of interference in the 'right to work' of workers, facilitated by the law's toleration of closed shop practices, meant that it was necessary for the courts to 'prevent unions from misusing through wrongful expulsion their power of industrial ostracism'.[37] It is interesting to compare Kahn-Freund and Wedderburn on the 'right to work'. As we have seen, Wedderburn was fiercely dismissive of the 'right to work' justification for legal controls over the arbitrary exercise of trade union powers. Yet Kahn-Freund endorses the 'right to work' analysis without any apparent hesitation. This may reflect Kahn-Freund's wider positive view of the common law's virtue in protecting the individual from oppressive action by powerful parties.

Like Wedderburn, however, Kahn-Freund was also sceptical of the common law's capacity to regulate admission to union membership because

[33] Ibid. 34.

[34] The 'collective' freedoms derived from neoclassical liberal freedom of contract are set out in Richard A. Epstein, 'A Common Law for Labor Relations: A Critique of the New Deal Labor Legislation' (1983) 92 Yale Law Journal 1357.

[35] Kahn-Freund (n 29) 36.

[36] Ibid. 37.

[37] Ibid.

there was no contractual relationship between the union and a prospective member.[38] The common law regulation of expulsion to prevent misuse of power was more defensible, and he referred approvingly to Lord Denning's judgment in *Lee v Showmen's Guild of Great Britain*.[39] He did not regard the expansion of legal controls over admissions as a pressing matter because there is not 'in a very homogeneous society, much need for doing so'.[40] The racial homogeneity of British society in the 1950s could be contrasted with the US, where the emergence of a 'duty of fair representation' was a necessary counterpart of exclusive bargaining representation in a racially divided society.[41] It was obviously implicit in this argument that if British society became less homogeneous, the arguments in favour of a more assertive 'individualist tradition' would be strengthened. I would suggest that an understanding of the moral equality of persons, and the law's role in ensuring respect for that value, underpinned Kahn-Freund's early reflections. The arbitrary treatment of individual workers, reflected most strongly in unjustified discrimination because of race, sex, or political viewpoint, violated the moral equality of persons. It was necessary to ensure that the 'superior social forces' did not undermine this moral equality, unchecked by the law. While Kahn-Freund is certainly not hostile to the closed shop in *Labour Law,* his focus is on ensuring the protection of the individual from arbitrary social power. In contrast to Wedderburn, he is less concerned to justify the social practice. He does however accept the closed shop as a social fact of British industrial relations.

Kahn-Freund's final reflections on the closed shop were set out in chapter 7 of his Hamlyn Lectures, *Labour and the Law*.[42] They represent a judicious and learned appraisal of the different varieties of union security, and consideration of the role of the law sensitive to the diverse comparative practices in different labour law systems. The starting point for this analysis is the following arresting observation: 'In many countries the freedom not to organise is put on a par with the freedom to organise . . . The law must also protect people from being in fact constrained or pressed to join.'[43] Kahn-Freund observes that the parity between the right to join and not join a trade union 'appears to be intellectually attractive'.[44] He also recognised that 'the closed shop has

[38] Ibid. Kahn-Freund did refer to the statutory prohibition of discrimination by reason of unwillingness to contribute to the union's political fund in Trade Union Act 1914 s. 3(1)(b).
[39] [1952] 2 Q.B. 329.
[40] Kahn-Freund (n 29) 37.
[41] *Steele v Louisville & Nashville R.R. Co.*, 323 US 192 (1944), cited Kahn-Freund (n 29) 37 n. 57.
[42] Paul L. Davies and Mark Freedland (eds), *Kahn-Freund's Labour and the Law* (3rd ed, Stevens & Sons 1983).
[43] Ibid. 236.
[44] Ibid. 237.

been banned in all or in some of its numerous manifestations in a large part of the world'.[45] He then proceeded to analyse a wide variety of union security arrangements and their legal treatment in different countries. We shall consider two features of Kahn-Freund's approach. The first is in his formidable mastery of comparative law and practice. The second is in the structure of argumentation on the closed shop, which is based upon a principle of ethical neutrality towards union security.

In relation to comparative law and practice, Kahn-Freund identified something approximating to a comparative convergence against closed shop arrangements. This convergence operated across labour law systems with different qualities and characteristics. For example, in the European context, the closed shop was prohibited in France, Italy, Belgium, Switzerland, and Germany. In countries where unions were divided on an ideological or religious basis, as in France or Italy, this prohibition respected the internal logic of the system. However, there was also a prohibition in Germany where unions were organised along more sectoral and occupational lines. In Australia, it was still possible at this time to enforce preferential arrangements for unionists.[46] In the US, 'union security' arrangements might be negotiated whereby non-members provided a fee to the exclusive bargaining agent for its collective bargaining services. While some countries did permit the enforcement of union security—he gives the example of Sweden[47]—the dominant comparative pattern across a diverse mix of legal cultures favoured legal prohibition or restriction. While comparative convergence did not provide an ethical argument against the closed shop, it was likely to be a relevant factor when supranational courts like the European Court of Human Rights were considering the appropriate margin of appreciation in Article 11 cases.

In terms of the structure of argumentation in Chapter 7, Kahn-Freund's point of departure was that 'there are strong arguments in favour of banning or at least restricting the closed shop'.[48] This could be taken to imply that the institution is presumptively illegitimate, so that any scope for legal permission should be narrowly tailored. Wedderburn's argument would never have started from here. Kahn-Freund's *Hamlyn Lecture* arguments echoed many of the considerations elucidated in his 1959 essay. The closed shop interfered with the economic opportunities of workers to pursue their occupational choices. This power could be exercised oppressively. These restrictive

[45] Ibid.
[46] Ibid.
[47] Ibid. 238.
[48] Ibid. 240.

practices could be economically wasteful. In closed shop situations, trade unions were able to impose access restrictions in labour markets when they 'are not publicly responsible' through channels of democratic accountability.[49] The law had an important role in limiting the potential for abuse of power. In terms of the arguments in favour of the closed shop, Kahn-Freund argued that this case 'can only be made in terms of the need for an equilibrium of power. It cannot in the end be sustained or refuted in terms of general ethical sentiments'.[50] The editors of the final edition of the Hamlyn lectures were astute to note that 'many would see the case for toleration as having a greater claim to ethicality than he is prepared to concede here'.[51] This was certainly true of Lord Wedderburn's very different approach. For Kahn-Freund, however, the concern to restrain abuse of power supported a strong role for judicial oversight. For example, Kahn-Freund regarded the rules of natural justice as mandatory legal duties which would override incompatible terms in the contract of membership.[52]

Four decades on, we can see that Kahn-Freund's general arguments on the closed shop were prescient. The comparative trend against the closed shop is now even stronger. For example, one of Kahn-Freund's main examples of a permissive legal regime was Australia. That permissive position has now been reversed. As a result of extensive statutory reforms introduced by neoliberal governments, Stanford concludes that 'Today in Australia there are few legal or institutional supports for union membership. Closed shops, union preference, agency or bargaining fees, and compulsory payroll deductions are all banned.'[53] There are also extensive statutory restrictions on preferential union arrangements in New Zealand.[54]

While agency shop agreements are still permitted under US legislation, requiring the payment of a fee to the bargaining agent in lieu of membership, the screw has been tightening here too. In *Janus v American Federation of State, County, and Municipal Employees, Council 31*, the Supreme Court considered the constitutional position of agency fee arrangements in the Illinois public sector.[55] For the majority, Alito J declared that agency fee arrangements

[49] Ibid.
[50] Ibid. 244.
[51] Ibid. 244 n 31a.
[52] Ibid. 230.
[53] Jim Stanford, 'International Approaches to Solving the "Free Rider" Problem in Industrial Relations' (2021) 31 Labour & Industry 278, 284.
[54] Gordon Anderson and Dawn Duncan, *Employment Law in New Zealand* (3rd ed, Lexis Nexis 2022) 433–437.
[55] 585 US 878 (2018). The Supreme Court of Canada (SCC) has avoided disrupting union security arrangements using the Charter's protection of (negative) freedom of association. This perhaps reflects the sensitivity of the SCC to the existing legislative models that support union security practices. This may be regarded as appropriate judicial deference in a constitutional democracy. See *R v Advance Cutting & Coring*

for employees in the public sector were unconstitutional. By requiring non-members to pay a fee to the bargaining agent without their consent, the constitutional free speech rights of non-members under the First Amendment were violated. The countervailing arguments in favour of agency fees, such as eliminating free riding and promoting labour peace, were not sufficient to outweigh the free speech rights of non-members. While the *Janus* ruling is limited to public sector employment, its robust protection of free speech rights for objecting employees is a barometer of the political and legal milieu for US unions.

Overall, there is now a strong international consensus supporting the legal protection of negative freedom of association and the prohibition of the closed shop. Paradoxically, perhaps, this has been reflected most strongly in European labour law systems aligned with social democratic values. The legal stronghold for union security continues to be the North American systems of enterprise-level collective bargaining, although even here the direction of legal change favours restriction. These constraints on union security have been led predominantly by ordinary labour legislation rather than supervening human rights litigation. In the next section, we will consider the historical development of the closed shop in the UK. The closed shop was regulated as a matter of both common law and statute. All forms of union security are now unenforceable because of restrictive statutory reforms. These legal changes were *internal* to labour law. As with comparative examples, they were not driven externally by human rights judgments.

III. A Brief Legal History of the Closed Shop in the UK

A. Common Law Regulation

Between the 1950s and 1970s, legal regulation of the closed shop was predominantly a matter of common law. This generated many of the leading common law labour cases of the post-war period. Lord Denning was a looming judicial presence throughout.[56] Contrary to popular caricatures of the English common law, this jurisprudence was not antithetical to the closed shop in principle. The courts developed public law-style controls over trade union

[2001] 3 SCR 209 and *Lavigne v. Ontario Public Service Employees Union* [1991] 2 SCR 211. In the Canadian context, constitutional norms defer to legislated norms.

[56] Paul Davies and Mark Freedland, 'Labour Law', in Jeffrey Jowell and Patrick McAuslan (eds), *Lord Denning: The Judge and the Law* (Sweet and Maxwell 1984) 377.

decision-making to ensure that these powers were not abused in depriving people of their right to work and earn a living. The courts also recognised that the closed shop was a legitimate institution, provided that expulsion and admission decisions were fair, reasonable, and in accordance with the rules of natural justice. Notions of equality and non-discrimination shaped the development of the courts' contractual analysis. The human rights analysis of closed shops only emerged in the common law in the early 1980s. Even then, there was no single human rights perspective. Some judges thought that freedom of association supported the fundamental right of a worker to join the union of his choice. Other judges thought that freedom of association supported the union's freedom to disassociate, including individual members whom it did not wish to associate with. Overall, this common law jurisprudence revealed a sophisticated engagement with the closed shop that was internal to labour law. The engagement with human rights came as something of an afterthought.

1. The common law regulation of admission to membership

In the post-war period, the common law regulation of arbitrary exclusion from employment in closed shop arrangements was conceptualised by the courts as a problem of *union* power. At this point, any prospect of common law regulation of the employer's contractual dismissal power was still overshadowed by authorities such as *Addis v Gramophone Co. Ltd.*[57] and *Ridge v Baldwin.*[58] The 'master' could terminate the employment contract for any reason at all, and it also enjoyed a very wide contractual freedom to offer new employment contracts. For this reason, the regulation of abuse of power in closed shop arrangements could not realistically be implemented through the common law regulation of dismissals and job offers. Trade unions were more amenable to judicial supervision, and judges were instinctively far more suspicious of their contractual powers.

The common law regulation of admission to union membership in closed shop situations was considered in the early 1960s in the seminal case of *Faramus v Film Artistes' Association (Faramus).*[59] The conflicting judgments in the Court of Appeal revealed the clash between freedom of contract and freedom of trade. They also revealed an underlying tension between 'private law' and 'public law' modes of analysis. In closed shop arrangements, the trade union's freedom of contract was the legal basis of its freedom to determine its own membership eligibility criteria. Where the trade union had negotiated a closed

[57] [1909] AC 488.
[58] [1964] AC 40.
[59] [1964] AC 925.

shop agreement with the employer through freedom of contract, an individual's freedom to dispose of his labour in the market could be restricted by the trade union rules. During the 19th century, the courts generally favoured the preservation of the individual's freedom to trade his labour on the market over the trade union's 'freedom of contract'.[60] At common law, such rules were likely to be an unreasonable restraint of trade. *Faramus* provided an opportunity for the common law to revisit this old clash in a new social and economic context.

The Film Artistes' Association operated a pre-entry closed shop for film extras. No person could be employed as a film artiste within a fifty-mile radius of Charing Cross unless they were members of the trade union. As Upjohn LJ recognised in the Court of Appeal, the Association had a membership of between 1600 and 1700 members but received between 5000 and 6000 applications per year.[61] The enforcement of restrictive rules meant that employment conditions in the trade continued to be remunerative: 'if the membership was allowed to increase much beyond the present figures, their members would hardly earn a living wage'.[62]

Rule 4(2) provided that no person who had been convicted in a court of law of a criminal offence (other than a motoring offence not punishable by imprisonment) shall be eligible for or retain membership of the association. Tony Faramus had joined the union in 1950 and signed a declaration that he had never been convicted of a criminal offence. In fact, as a young man he had been convicted and imprisoned for criminal offences, some of them during the Nazi occupation of Jersey. This led to his internment in concentration camps in Buchenwald and Mauthausen. He was liberated at the end of the war and weighed just under 6 stone. Shortly afterwards, he lost a lung because of TB. There was no suggestion that his declaration to the union had been deliberatively deceptive. His memory had been affected by harrowing wartime experiences. When his youthful criminal offences were discovered, he lost his membership of the union because he was treated as ineligible for membership. By all accounts, Tony Faramus was a successful film extra and even played the part of a British officer in the celebrated film, *The Colditz Story*, in 1955. He had served on the executive committee of the trade union. There had been no criminality after the war. The disqualification from membership meant in effect that he could no longer work as a film artiste in the British film industry.

The case turned upon the meaning and enforceability of rule 4(2). The union argued that its effect was mandatory and exclusionary. If a prospective

[60] Patrick Atiyah, *The Rise and Fall of Freedom of Contract* (OUP 1979) 528–533.
[61] [1963] 2 Q.B. 527, 544 (Upjohn LJ).
[62] Ibid.

member had in fact been convicted of a relevant criminal offence, the union had no discretion to accept the person into membership because it was prohibited by the contract. Rule 4(2) was an absolute bar. Despite appearances, Tony Faramus had never in fact been a member of the union. A majority in the Court of Appeal, Upjohn LJ and Diplock LJ, supported the union's arguments on rule construction. The terms of the rule were clearly prohibitive. At common law, the rule was certainly an unreasonable restraint of trade because its effect was to prevent the individual from working in his chosen occupation. The statutory rules in the Trade Union Act 1871 meant that an 'agreement' could still be enforceable. In this way, the statutory basis of trade unionism and its exclusion of restraint of trade meant that 'freedom of contract' trumped 'freedom of trade'. This also reflected an endorsement of a 'private law' analysis and the marginalisation of public law approaches to trade union power.

Lord Denning dissented and his judgment echoed the emancipatory language of 'freedom of trade' in the older common law cases on oppressive monopolies.[63] Lord Denning proposed two arguments. The first was an argument of construction, so that the operation of rule 4(2) was directive rather than mandatory. 'Eligible' did not mean legally eligible; it meant suitable, like an 'eligible bachelor'. On this basis, the union still retained an overall discretion to make that judgement of suitability, and hence the contract was voidable rather than void. Since the union had not voided the contract of membership, Tony Faramus retained his membership and could still work as a film extra. On a fair reading of rule 4(2), this construction was linguistically strained and the majority dealt with the construction point in a more satisfactory way. Lord Denning was evidently keen to prevent the rule from barring Tony Faramus from employment.

Lord Denning's second argument was addressed directly to the existence of the closed shop. This meant that the trade union was like the oppressive trade monopolies that had threatened the liberty of the subject in the 18th century:

> The trade union is only the modern equivalent of the medieval guild of craftsmen. A trade union has by statute the power and duty to make rules for its members and to impose fines and forfeitures on them. The old guild had by its charter power to make by-laws for its members and to inflict fines and penalties on them. There is no difference in principle between them.[64]

[63] See the discussion of monopolies in Chapter 2. Lord Denning referred to some of these old monopoly cases in the judgment: 539–540. As outlined in Chapter 2, the challenge to monopoly was a radical political project in the late 18th century, reflected in the political economy of Adam Smith.

[64] *Faramus* (n 61) 539.

It followed that trade union rules were akin to by-laws that could be challenged through public law techniques. These rules were not shielded by the Trade Union Act 1871 because that was concerned with trade union *purposes*, not its discrete *rules*.

Interestingly, the majority judgments in *Faramus* referred to the case of *Kruse v Johnson*,[65] in which Lord Russell CJ considered the legal quality of enacted by-laws that were manifestly discriminatory or partial between different classes of persons.[66] The majority in *Faramus* did not regard *Kruse v Johnson* as relevant to the issue in *Faramus* because it was not possible to apply the public law *ultra vires* doctrine to trade unions. This was because *ultra vires* depended upon a court supervising the legislative authorisation of law-making powers delegated to inferior bodies. This went to the jurisdiction of the inferior body. In *Faramus*, there was no analogous jurisdictional issue because this was treated as an instance of a private contract. Nevertheless, these reflections on *Kruse v Johnson* did provide a glimpse into an alternative way of analysing the trade union's contractual powers. Exclusionary rules could be more or less arbitrary. A rule excluding people who had been convicted of offences of dishonesty might not be arbitrary; yet as Lord Denning observed, what if the union's exclusionary rule had simply referred to the colour of a trade unionist's hair?[67] It was but a short step from this to rules that might exclude a trade unionist because of sex or race. In these circumstances, where union rules barred a person from working in her chosen trade or occupation because of morally wrongful discrimination, the relevance of *Kruse v Johnson* could be more compelling. This public law-style approach would not need to be tethered to a strong idea of *ultra vires* and the delegation of law-making powers to a public body. It would be rooted in the common law's protection of non-discrimination as a fundamental right. This was particularly attractive to common law sensibilities and the judicial fidelity to equality before the law, especially where there was wrongful discrimination in the exercise of power. Abuse of power could occur in private as well as public contexts. It is also important to note that there was an appreciation of the functional justification for the closed shop expressed in the majority Court of Appeal judgments. Even Lord Denning's dissent appears to assume that there could be *reasonable* eligibility rules in closed shop contexts; his objection was to the great width and arbitrary sweep of rule 4(2).[68]

65 Ibid. 546–547, 555–556.
66 [1898] 2 Q.B. 91.
67 *Faramus* (n 61) 539.
68 Ibid.

The House of Lords dismissed the appeal. This represented the highpoint of common law freedom of contract for trade unions, and it underpinned the trade union's freedom of association (especially its internal freedom to determine its own rules, programmes, and activities). Although Lord Evershed declined to reach a conclusion on whether the rule was an unreasonable restraint of trade at common law, their Lordships were unanimous that this point was nugatory because restraint of trade was excluded by the Trade Union Act 1871. Lord Denning's attempt to circumvent the 1871 Act was now closed off, although in retrospect his distinction between rule and purpose seemed like sophistry in the service of a just outcome. Lord Pearce rejected the analogy with judgments like *Kruse v Johnson*, although he recognised that there could be a distinction in terms of public policy (for example, the rules of natural justice) between eligibility cases and expulsion cases. Since *Faramus* was an eligibility case, not an expulsion case, there was no public policy basis for invalidating the contractual rule. There might be more scope for doctrines like natural justice where an existing member was being disciplined and expelled by the trade union. This did not apply to Tony Faramus because he had never been a trade union member in the first place. In effect, *Faramus* confirmed that the statutory framework of immunity from restraint of trade had accorded strong priority to the trade union's freedom of contract. While the judges were universally sympathetic to Tony Faramus' plight, the (private) common law could provide no redress.[69]

The limits of the orthodox private law analysis in *Faramus* were probed in later cases where norms of non-discrimination (and judicial sensibilities) were more acutely engaged. The source of this judicial creativity was none other than Lord Denning himself, who had been the lone dissenting voice in the appellate courts in *Faramus*. The leading example of this was not a trade union case, though it raised many similar issues to closed shop cases and it was clear that trade unions were not far from the judges' minds. *Nagle v Feilden* concerned a challenge to the discriminatory practices of the Jockey Club in issuing licences for trainers.[70] The Jockey Club exercised monopolistic powers for horse racing in Great Britain. It was not possible to pursue one's trade as a horse trainer without a licence. In this respect, it was analogous to the closed

[69] Happily, Tony Faramus and his wife emigrated to the US. He appeared in *King Rat* (1965) and worked as Clark Gable's butler and chauffeur, retiring with his wife to Farnham, Surrey. He even has his own Wikipedia entry (which does not record his legal case against the Film Artistes' Association): Anthony Faramus—Wikipedia. During the final stages of completing this book, I rewatched *The Colditz Story* and was able to spot Tony Faramus in a few of the scenes.

[70] [1966] 2 WLR 1027.

shop in *Faramus*. The Jockey Club issued a licence for Florence Nagle's 'head lad', a man, but it would not issue a licence for Florence Nagle herself because she was a woman. She sought a declaration and injunction against the Jockey Club. Her claim was struck out as unarguable, and she appealed against the striking out. Her appeal was upheld by the Court of Appeal.

The principal legal difficulty was that there was no contract between her and the Jockey Club. Without a contract, did she have any private legal rights at all? And if she had no private legal rights, was there any basis for a declaration or injunction? The Court of Appeal agreed that the contract argument was hopeless. Lord Denning allowed the appeal on the basis that the discriminatory practice of the Jockey Club infringed her 'right to work'. This enlivened a public policy basis where the practice excluded a person from a trade or occupation arbitrarily or capriciously. This would be an abuse of monopolistic power. The exclusion of women trainers was against this public policy. Lord Denning drew a distinction between social clubs, which were free to exclude on any basis, and monopolistic associations wielding power over access to employment, which were within the scope of public policy.[71] Although he did not formulate this public policy as rooted in considerations of equality before the law, I believe that it can be understood in this way. According to Lord Denning, the enquiry for the court was whether the rules and practices were based on differences that were reasonable in respect of access to the occupation.[72] The insistence on Latin for access to the profession of surgery or law might be reasonable, whereas the sex of a trainer was irrelevant to the skills and character necessary to be a successful horse trainer. In this way, it was *unjust* exclusion that offended the public policy. Whether an exclusion was unjust depended upon whether the practice or rule drew relevant distinctions between different classes of person. It was thus rooted in a norm of equality. For Lord Denning, the true legal basis of this public policy was in analogies with *property* rather than *contract*:

> The true ground of jurisdiction in all these cases is a man's right to work. I have said before, and I repeat it now, that a man's right to work at his trade or profession is just as important to him as, perhaps more important than, his rights of property. Just as the courts will intervene to protect his rights of property, they will also intervene to protect his right to work.[73]

[71] Ibid. 1032H.
[72] Ibid. 1033C–E.
[73] Ibid. 1034F–G.

The other judges in *Nagle* formulated the public policy in similar terms, based upon the special function of the courts to protect individuals from oppression and the abuse of monopolistic powers. For example, Salmon LJ drew a distinction between reasonable rules and practices, relevant to the conduct of the trade, and unreasonable exclusions from earning a living.[74] Although the judgments did not refer to *Kruse v Johnson*, similar considerations underlie the reasoning on equality and arbitrariness:

> It follows that the plaintiff may succeed in this action if she can show that the defendants, whilst recognising her good character and long experience and ability as a trainer, have refused her a licence solely on the ground that she is a woman. It would be as capricious to do so as to refuse a man a licence solely because of the colour of his hair.[75]

The practical importance of the common law in regulating admissibility rules and practices has been eclipsed by legislation and the disappearance of the closed shop. *Nagle* tends to be regarded as a wayward judgment today. It straddles public and private law modes of analysis. Many private lawyers regard *Nagle* as aberrant. For example, Stevens has criticised *Nagle* on the basis that there is no common law *right* to work correlative to private law *duties* on other parties.[76] Without the identification of private rights, there was no remedial basis for declarations or injunctions. The 'right to work' is too extravagant in terms of its correlative duties to count as a common law right. On this view, *Nagle* was a distortion of the common law to secure a just outcome that would today be regulated through equality legislation. There may yet be something to say in favour of a private law analysis. In *Nagle*, Lord Denning compared the right to work with property rights, in terms of their relative importance to the person. As we saw in Chapter 2, recent political philosophy has identified the radical roots of 'labour as property'.[77] A person's labour, like her body and her property, represents a critical means through which she can set and pursue her own purposes.[78] For many people, their own labour may be their

[74] Ibid. 1040G.
[75] Ibid. 1042D–E (Salmon LJ).
[76] Robert Stevens, 'Is There a Right to Work?', in Alan Bogg and Paul S. Davies (eds), *Private Law and the Employment Contract* (Hart 2025) 203, 221–222.
[77] Elizabeth Anderson, *Private Government: How Employers Rule Our Lives and Why We Don't Talk about It* (Princeton UP 2017).
[78] For a powerful statement of this internal structure to private wrongs, see Arthur Ripstein, *Private Wrongs* (Harvard UP 2016) 8–9.

most critical means.[79] It is exactly the kind of thing that the law of private wrongs serves to protect.

The legacy of *Nagle* is less tarnished in public law. For example, Dawn Oliver has defended it as an example of how public policy has been used by the courts to subject private power to public law-style constraints.[80] In common with other common law 'monopoly' cases, it imposed constraints on private power based in norms of rationality, reasonableness, and considerate decision-making.[81] These constraints tended to protect the dignity and security of citizens by ensuring that they were not unfairly excluded from access to a job and the ability to earn a living. As we shall see in the next section, these public law values were very important in the great trade union 'expulsion' cases during the era of the closed shop.

In closing, it is important to recognise that *Faramus* and *Nagle* were both regarded as 'labour law cases' albeit developed through common law reasoning. It is also misleading to portray these judgments as categorically hostile to trade unions and the closed shop. The reasoning was far more nuanced. *Nagle* was a sophisticated common law attempt to ensure that private power was exercised in accordance with norms of rationality. Where rules and practices were based upon *reasonable* distinctions between classes of person, and avoided wrongful discrimination, closed shop practices could be compatible with common law public policy. This is quite different to the vigorous protection of individual 'choices' to disassociate from the trade union. Indeed, these cases were not analysed by the judges as 'freedom of association' cases at all, or in terms of 'choice' or individual autonomy. Instead, they drew upon public law ideas of equality, non-discrimination, and abuse of power.

2. The common law regulation of expulsion

The legal basis of the court's jurisdiction in disciplinary expulsion cases was at least clearer than in the exclusion cases. It was based in contract. The imposition of the disciplinary sanction had to be in accordance with the union rule-book. This meant that the sanction needed to be authorised by the relevant disciplinary rule as defined in the contract of membership. It also required the union to comply with any contractually binding disciplinary procedures. As with the exclusion cases, however, this private law contract analysis was shaped by public law values. These public law values were justified by the common law right to work, and this generated a body of case law that was very

[79] For a broad discussion of these issues, see the range of rich essays in Virginia Mantouvalou (ed), *The Right to Work* (Hart 2017).
[80] Dawn Oliver, *Common Values and the Public-Private Divide* (Butterworths 1999) 208–209.
[81] Ibid. 216–218.

difficult to rationalise from the perspective of orthodox contract law. Indeed, some of this case law would have been scarcely recognisable to a scholar of English contract law while being very familiar to a scholar of English administrative law. The context of the closed shop was integral to this fusion of public and private law in common law reasoning.

The starting point for this fusion approach is *Lee v The Showmen's Guild of Great Britain.*[82] This involved a dispute between two members of the Guild over the allocation of a fairground site. The plaintiff was charged with a disciplinary offence of 'unfair competition' and fined by the committee. He refused to pay the fine and was expelled from the union. This expulsion also meant that he was deprived of the opportunity to work at fairgrounds controlled by the Guild. He was granted a declaration and an injunction on the basis that his expulsion was *ultra vires*, because his conduct did not constitute 'unfair competition'. The disciplinary committee had misconstrued the relevant offence. The Court of Appeal found in favour of the plaintiff. Of the three separate judgments, Lord Denning provided the strongest statement of the public law approach to contract interpretation in trade union disciplinary cases. However, recognition of the serious consequences for the plaintiff's trade and livelihood was a feature of all three judgments.

Lord Denning's judgment proceeded on the basis that the union's power to discipline a member must be based in contract. He drew a distinction between social clubs and associations (like trade unions) wielding power over a person's livelihood and trade. This deprivation of livelihood, reflected in an interference with the right to work, justified a distinctive judicial approach to the contract of membership:

> Is such a tribunal to be treated by these courts on the same footing as a social club? I say no. A man's right to work is just as important to him as, if not more important than, his rights of property. These courts intervene every day to protect rights of property. They must also intervene to protect the right to work.[83]

This right to work generated limits on freedom of contract, and it meant that the parties were 'not free to make any contract they like'.[84] These limitations were rooted in public policy. First, this meant that the procedural rules of natural justice (such as the right to notice of the charge, an opportunity to be heard, an unbiased tribunal) were compulsory legal duties that could not be

[82] [1952] 2 Q.B. 329.
[83] Ibid. 343.
[84] Ibid. 342.

waived by the parties. While this was controversial as a matter of general contract law, Kahn-Freund later described the rules of natural justice as 'mandatory', either as compulsory implied terms or as a matter of 'higher law' rooted in overriding public policy.[85] Second, the judges were especially wary of any attempt to oust the jurisdiction of the court in right to work cases. Where there was a dispute between the parties about the meaning of a legal rule, questions of legal interpretation were matters to be determined by a court. The legal construction of a rule was a matter that was within the expertise of the reviewing court, and this justified more stringent review compared with purely ethical determinations by a domestic committee. Although this was not yet formulated in terms of a fundamental common law right of access to a court, Denning LJ's judgment in *Lee* can certainly be understood in these terms.[86] Finally, the right to work was relevant to remedies. While declarations were available in breach of contract cases involving social clubs, injunctions were also available in trade union cases. This was because of the analogies between the right to earn a living and rights of private property.[87] In *Lee*, the function of the reviewing court was to ensure that the domestic tribunal did not exceed the jurisdiction conferred upon it by the contract. This language of jurisdiction and *ultra vires* was redolent of public law judicial review. For Denning LJ, the domestic tribunal would remain within its jurisdiction only where the facts were reasonably capable of supporting the finding that the rule had been breached.[88]

The highpoint of the interventionist common law approach is *Edwards v Society of Graphical and Allied Trades (SOGAT)*.[89] This concerned the automatic expulsion of Beresford Edwards from SOGAT, and the subsequent refusal to readmit him to the union. The expulsion occurred under a rule authorising expulsion for non-payment of union dues, though it was accepted that the failure to collect the dues was attributable to the fault of the trade union. This had a serious impact on his ability to earn a living in his chosen occupation as a printer because of union security practices in the industry. Beresford Edwards would later become a community leader and an activist on behalf of the black community in Manchester.[90] While there was

[85] Kahn-Freund (n 42) 230. See also Patrick Elias and K.D. Ewing writing in 1987 that this was 'little doubt' that this was now the common law approach: Patrick Elias and K.D. Ewing, *Trade Union Democracy, Members' Rights and the Law* (Mansell 1987) 217.

[86] Romer LJ's judgment articulated this right of access to a court in particularly strong terms: *Lee* (n 82) 354.

[87] Ibid. 342–343.

[88] Ibid. 345.

[89] [1971] Ch. 354.

[90] Tribute to hero of black history gets £50k cash boost—Manchester Evening News (https://www.manchestereveningnews.co.uk/news/greater-manchester-news/tribute-heroblack-history-gets-4020828k).

no substantive allegation of racism in *Edwards*, four other members who had been expelled unfairly under the same rule were readmitted back unto membership. Beresford Edwards was not. As Lord Denning observed, 'Mr. Edwards did not suggest that this was due to the colour of his skin. He only said: "Being black doesn't make it any easier." '[91] In certain respects, *Edwards* and *Nagle* can be understood as common law responses to arbitrary and unfair treatment where that treatment may have been tainted by wrongful discrimination, for example because of race or sex. Indeed, in his judgment in *Edwards*, Lord Denning drew a specific analogy with *Nagle*.[92]

Much of the judgment in *Edwards* was concerned with the assessment of contract damages where an individual had been deprived of work opportunities because of an unlawful expulsion. It also contained some important reflections on the role of public policy as a basis for striking down unreasonable union rules. This would include rules that made provision for automatic expulsion as in the circumstances of *Edwards*. Lord Denning explained the basis of the court's jurisdiction to declare the rule invalid in the following way:

> I do not think this trade union, or any other trade union, can give itself by its rules an unfettered discretion to expel a man or to withdraw his membership. The reason lies in the man's right to work. This is now fully recognised by law. It is a right which is of especial importance when a trade union operates a "closed shop" or "100 per cent, membership": for that means that no man can become employed or remain in employment with a firm unless he is a member of the union. If his union card is withdrawn, he has to leave the employment. He is deprived of his livelihood. The courts of this country will not allow so great a power to be exercised arbitrarily or capriciously or with unfair discrimination, neither in the making of rules, nor in the enforcement of them.[93]

This precluded a rule that led to expulsion without a hearing, as in this case. It also provided a common law mechanism to ensure that such rules were not applied arbitrarily. This included situations where decisions were based upon unjustified discrimination between classes of persons: 'They could discriminate in favour of some and against others as they liked (as indeed Mr. Edwards thought happened to him). They could turn him out of his work without any good or sufficient cause. Such cannot be permitted. It is ultra vires.'[94] Although

[91] *Edwards* (n 89) 373D.
[92] Ibid. 377D–E.
[93] Ibid. 376 C–D.
[94] Ibid. 377B–C.

the union's disciplinary rules were contractual in nature, they could be supervised by the courts based upon common law values of equality and non-discrimination. In short, trade unions in closed shop situations were obliged to respect the equality of persons under the law, and to ensure that their rules were defined and applied consistently and fairly. The common law would not tolerate wrongful discrimination. Sachs LJ also pointed to the oppressive dangers of arbitrary power, and the availability of common law techniques to ensure that trade union power was not wielded on an arbitrary basis.[95]

By the 1980s, the practical importance of common law litigation reduced in significance as statutory regulation of the closed shop expanded. The final great common law case on trade union expulsion was decided in 1983 in *Cheall v Association of Professional Executive Clerical and Computer Staff*.[96] The House of Lords considered a legal challenge by a union member where his expulsion had been ordered by the TUC Disputes Committee. This TUC Committee enforced the 'Bridlington Principles' which were designed to coordinate the organisational activities of affiliated trade unions and to limit the scope for 'poaching' union members. Organisational poaching was an important source of inter-union conflict. What is particularly striking in *Cheall* is the explicit consideration of Article 11 freedom of association arguments by the English courts. This represented an important shift from the dominant administrative law paradigm, reflected in cases like *Lee* and *Edwards*, to an emerging human rights paradigm. It also revealed that there was no single 'human rights' perspective on conflicts between individual members and the trade union. In the Court of Appeal in *Cheall*, Lord Denning considered that Article 11 supported the expelled member's legal arguments.[97] In the House of Lords, Lord Diplock arrived at the opposite view. In this way, the issue of union security was as contested *within* the human rights paradigm as it was between labour law and human rights perspectives. The conflicts between norms and values were far messier than the simple picture of 'labour law' versus 'human rights' which was this chapter's point of departure.

In the Court of Appeal, Lord Denning used language that would be echoed many years later in justifying the Human Rights Act 1998. It was important that the relevant Convention rights should be brought home and domesticated, so that they were accessible in the national courts rather than requiring claimants to embark on a lengthy and expensive trip to Strasbourg. According

95 Ibid. 383E.
96 [1983] 2 AC 180.
97 [1983] QB 126.

to Lord Denning, there was a common law right of every person to join a union of his choice for the protection of his interests.[98] It followed that:

> By being vindicated in this way, we reach the conclusion that article 11 (1) of the Convention is part of the law of England or at any rate the same as the law of England. The courts of England should themselves give effect to it rather than put a citizen to all the trouble and expense of going to the European Court of Human Rights at Strasbourg. Our courts should themselves uphold the right of every man to join a trade union of his choice for the protection of his interests.[99]

This fundamental common law right could be implemented through public policy, by requiring reasonable cause for expulsion and observance of the rules of natural justice. Once again, Lord Denning linked these principles to equality and non-discrimination: 'The rule itself must be confined to cases where there is reasonable cause for expulsion or termination. If the rule authorised the committee to expel a man because he had red hair or a woman because she wore trousers, it would be invalid.'[100] It would be invalid because the differentiation between classes of persons was not relevant to the justification for the rule. Lord Denning concluded that the expulsion was unlawful because it violated his fundamental common law right to join a trade union of his choice.

The House of Lords upheld the union's appeal. On the freedom of association and public policy point, Lord Diplock rejected Lord Denning's analysis with this pithy and enduring statement: 'My Lords, freedom of association can only be mutual; there can be no right of an individual to associate with other individuals who are not willing to associate with him.'[101] Lord Diplock's judgment was prescient in terms of the future development of Article 11 in Strasbourg. He emphasised that the trade union itself enjoyed a right to freedom of association. That would require a measure of respect for 'trade union autonomy' in determining its own rules, constitution, and activities. While the deprivation of livelihood in a closed shop situation might justify proportionate restrictions on the trade union's 'negative' freedom to disassociate, those considerations were not engaged on the facts in this case. Accordingly, freedom of association supported the union rather than the disgruntled member. This was also aligned with the orthodox contractual

[98] Ibid. 137B.
[99] Ibid. 137C–D.
[100] Ibid. 138E–F.
[101] *Cheall* (n 96) 191C.

analysis of the relevant union rules in the case. Mr Cheall's attempt to pursue his case in Strasbourg was unsuccessful because it was declared inadmissible by the Commission.[102] The *Cheall* episode demonstrated that the 'human rights' paradigm, like the 'labour law' paradigm, each encompassed a range of positions and disagreements on union security. At this point, neither paradigm was intrinsically pro- or anti- the closed shop.

B. Statutory Regulation

By the 1970s, the common law was starting to be eclipsed by statutory regulation of the closed shop. This reflected the expanding significance of legislative intervention and an increasing sense that governments had public responsibilities for regulating labour markets to ensure efficient and decent outcomes. The two leading treatises on legislative history in labour law during this period were Paul Davies and Mark Freedland's *Labour Legislation and Public Policy*[103] and Simon Auerbach's *Legislating for Conflict*.[104] Both works examined the various statutory reforms of closed shops in the wider context of labour law reform. During periods of intensive legislative activity, which often encompassed the statutory regulation of closed shops, this legislation was not prompted by considerations of workers' (or trade unions') human rights. Statutory reforms were justified by reference to regulatory goals that were internal to labour law, and they were continuous with broader statutory reforms to other areas such as strike laws, unfair dismissal, and trade union recognition. These justifications included (at various times) the balance of industrial power, controlling inflation, promoting labour market efficiency, promoting collective bargaining, and encouraging responsible collective bargaining practices. In fact, these two legislative histories reveal how marginal human rights arguments often were to the statutory development of labour law throughout the 1970s and 1980s. While there were some attempts to use human rights arguments in the courts, these were unsuccessful until the early 2000s and *Wilson v United Kingdom*.[105] By this time, the closed shop was completely unenforceable anyway as a result of incremental statutory reforms. This is now a settled part of the industrial relations context. There have been

[102] *Cheall v UK* App no. 10550/83, 13 May 1985.
[103] Paul Davies and Mark Freedland, *Labour Legislation and Public Policy* (OUP 1993).
[104] Simon Auerbach, *Legislating for Conflict* (OUP 1990).
[105] [2002] 35 EHRR 20 (*Wilson*). For an account of this litigation, in the wider context of human rights argumentation, see Alan Bogg, 'Wilson and Palmer: A Biographical Portrait of a Landmark Case', in Jeremias Adams-Prassl and others, *Landmark Cases in Labour Law* (Hart 2022) chapter 10.

no legislative proposals to reverse the position and promote union security since the mid-1970s.

This section will not provide a complete legislative history of the closed shop in the UK. That would require its own monograph. Its aim is more modest, which is to demonstrate that statutory reforms of the closed shop were connected to broader programmes of legislative reform in labour law. This was true both in terms of justification and implementation. These changes were internal to labour law, and they were not shaped by 'external' human rights arguments in any significant way.

1. From the Industrial Relations Act 1971 to the Employment Act 1990

The Industrial Relations Act 1971 (IRA) was a gargantuan piece of legislation, an attempt to reconstitute the totality of British labour law in a single step. It sought to do this through comprehensive statutory regulation which depended upon union registration. Registration would facilitate tighter control of trade union practices implemented through statutory juridification. In this respect, it represented a significant breach with the voluntarist values of collective laissez-faire and the underlying political consensus on those values. In Lord Wedderburn's memorable contemporary assessment, the IRA appeared to be the work of two phantom drafters: the 'organization-man' seeking to bring order through law to untidy collective bargaining practices and structures; and a 'Conservative lawyer' guided by a concern to protect individual rights.[106] A significant portion of Wedderburn's critique considered the closed shop aspects of the IRA and the broader consequences of what he described as its 'extreme individualism'. However, the legislation also sought to regulate and control unofficial industrial action, the legal enforcement of collective agreements, restrict secondary strike activity, introduce unfair dismissal protections, and promote an orderly legal procedure for union recognition.[107] The virtue of Davies and Freedland's analysis is that it situates the closed shop reforms in that broader legislative context.

The right not to join a trade union was enshrined in s. 5(1)(b) IRA as a necessary counterpart of the positive right to join a trade union. It reflected the individualistic concerns of Wedderburn's 'Conservative lawyer'. While I have suggested that human rights arguments were marginal to the IRA's broader goals, they were not completely irrelevant. For example, in Simpson and Wood's extensive analysis of IRA, they suggest that the Universal Declaration

[106] K.W. Wedderburn, 'Labour Law and Labour Relations in Britain' (1972) 10 British Journal of Industrial Relations 270, 282.
[107] Davies and Freedland (n 103) 282–301.

of Human Rights was used to justify the statutory protection of the right not to join.[108] However, the hostility to the closed shop in IRA probably reflected broader concerns about excessive union power and the irresponsible use of that power. This was reflected in the different approaches to the pre-entry and post-entry closed shops. Section 7 declared pre-entry closed shop agreements to be void. For Davies and Freedland, this was because pre-entry closed shops were a greater encroachment on managerial hiring prerogatives and were more likely to lead to inefficient working practices.[109] The post-entry closed shop was also subject to more stringent legal regulation. The IRA's preferred model was based upon a US-style agency shop. This arrangement required a non-member to pay a contribution to the union in lieu of membership, and the IRA also permitted conscientious objectors to pay that sum to a charity. Where there was a dispute between the union and the employer about entering an agency shop agreement, the IRA provided for a ballot procedure to authorise the arrangement. This could be satisfied by the support of a majority of those eligible to vote or two-thirds of those voting.[110] The IRA also provided for a model of 'approved closed shop agreements' which limited the scope for workers to pay a fee in lieu of membership.[111] Overall, these provisions authorised much tighter public legal control over the closed shop, and the use of law to formalise and regularise industrial practices. The use of balloting procedures was typical of this technique. According to Davies and Freedland, the legal conceptualisation of the closed shop also 'sought to combine legal restructuring of industrial relations with legal control of industrial action, and to make that restructuring and that control reinforce each other'.[112] This was reflected in restrictions on industrial action where that action was aimed at subverting the statutory model. These legal provisions on the closed shop were part of a complex web of legal rules aimed at promoting order and responsibility in collective bargaining.

The failure of the IRA and its replacement by the 'social contract' legislation of the mid-1970s led to a significant reversal of legal policy on the closed shop. It was not sufficient to repeal the collective aspects of the IRA. The continuation of individual unfair dismissal protections required the legislation to specify the circumstances in which 'closed shop' dismissals were fair. The configuration of dismissal law was central to the redefinition of labour law's post-IRA objectives. The Labour Government reversed the IRA policy by limiting

108 R.C. Simpson and John Wood, *Industrial Relations* (Pitman 1973) 104.
109 Davies and Freedland (n 103) 292–293.
110 IRA s. 13(1).
111 Simpson and Wood (n 108) 123–125.
112 Davies and Freedland (n 103) 293–294.

unfairness to situations where an employee objected on religious grounds to trade union membership. According to Davies and Freedland, 'where the new individual rights clashed with collective freedoms, it was the former that were to give way'.[113] This was a restoration of collective laissez-faire which accorded primacy to promoting collective bargaining and supporting union bargaining power. Another change of government in 1979 led to further changes to closed shop regulation in the Employment Act 1980. This was the first step in a sequenced programme of reducing trade union power,[114] and this narrowed the scope for fair dismissals. It imposed formal balloting requirements to approve closed shop arrangements, and it extended protections for those who had a conscientious objection to union membership.[115] It would be a mistake to view the Employment Act 1980 as a human rights intervention, however. In Auerbach's assessment, the 1980 Act 'was much influenced by the balance of political calculations of different wings of the Conservative Government concerning the most appropriate posture to strike towards the union movement'.[116]

In the late 1980s, there was a ratcheting of the legal restrictions on closed shops. The Employment Act 1988 removed the scope for any ballot authorisation of closed shops, and it removed the statutory immunity for any industrial action aimed at enforcing preferential practices for union members.[117] It also introduced a statutory right against unjustifiable discipline by a trade union, which included a refusal to participate or to support industrial action.[118] Section 1 of the Employment Act 1990 introduced a right not to be refused employment because of union membership. This measure was targeted at the pre-entry closed shop, and the Government justifications focused on the negative labour market effects of union security in terms of reduced employment, higher labour costs, and damage to profitability.[119] These were labour market reform justifications rather than human rights justifications. It is undoubtedly true that the overall pattern of statutory restraints on the closed shop deviated from the 'traditional analysis' based upon the protection of workers through trade unions and voluntary collective bargaining.[120] For Wedderburn, the neoliberal hostility to the closed shop flowed from the fact that 'the trade union

[113] Ibid. 374.
[114] Ibid. chapter 9.
[115] Ibid. 450–454.
[116] Auerbach (n 104) 65.
[117] Ibid.186.
[118] Employment Act 1988 s. 3.
[119] Davies and Freedland (n 103) 510.
[120] Lord Wedderburn, 'Freedom of Association and Philosophies of Labour Law', in Lord Wedderburn, *Employment Rights in Britain and Europe* (Lawrence & Wishart 1991) 198, 199–201.

is seen as the obstacle to the competitive market and a threat alike to individuals and to private property'.[121] This ideological reading of statutory developments continues to be persuasive. Yet these arguments are still *internal* to labour law, and hence labour law arguments. The radical legislative changes to the closed shop during this period reflected profound shifts in the ideological foundations of the discipline, and what counted as a 'labour law argument'. Human rights were marginal to this legislative story.

IV. Article 11 and the Freedom to Disassociate

A. The Railwaymen's Case

The legislative framework on the closed shop in the UK was in considerable flux after 1971. This provided the backdrop to the first Article 11 challenge to the closed shop in *Young, James and Webster v United Kingdom*.[122] This involved three applicants who had been employed at British Rail and who were then subject to a post-entry closed shop agreement from 1975. This coincided with the repeal of the restrictive IRA regime. The closed shop agreement required employees to join one of three specified unions unless a specific religious exemption applied. As a post-entry closed shop, the failure to comply with this requirement would lead to dismissal. Each of the applicants objected to membership of trade unions and/or the specific trade union, but in no case was this attributable to a religious conscientious objection. The applicants were dismissed, and these dismissals were fair under the 'social contract' unfair dismissal legislation in force at the time. This was an unusual situation because by the time the case was being argued in Strasbourg, there had been a change of government. Unsurprisingly, perhaps, the new Conservative Government did not pursue the arguments on justification under Article 11(2) as originally pleaded by the Labour Government. This is likely to have undermined the overall strength of the United Kingdom's case. The TUC submitted a document as a memorial which set out the general functional justifications for the closed shop, and Lord Wedderburn was heard on behalf of the TUC for the purposes of information at the oral hearing.

The applicants succeeded in their Article 11 claims. The majority avoided basing this decision on general propositions about the position and weight of the negative freedom to disassociate in Article 11. It was sufficient to resolve

[121] Ibid. 218.
[122] *Young, James and Webster v United Kingdom* [1981] ECHR 4.

the case for the Court to find that the negative aspect did not fall 'completely outside the ambit of Article 11'.[123] It was therefore left open whether the negative freedom was 'on the same footing' as the positive freedom.[124] Instead, the judgment focused carefully on the specific interference on the facts in the claims. This encompassed a range of relevant considerations.

First, the compulsion entailed by a dismissal and the loss of livelihood was a 'serious form of compulsion' and constituted an interference with the applicants' Article 11 rights.[125] This implied that other forms of compulsion, such as detriments short of dismissal or refusal of employment in pre-entry closed shops, might be permissible under Article 11. Second, it was relevant that they were *already* employees before the closed shop agreement was introduced and enforced.[126] This suggested that the enforcement of closed shop agreements where the employee was engaged after the arrangement had been agreed would be easier to reconcile with Article 11. Third, the restriction on a free choice of which union to join meant that the compulsion entailed an interference. The Government argued that the applicants could have formed their own union and so their freedom was not compromised. The Court considered that there would be an interference where 'the freedom of action or choice which remains available to him is either non-existent or so reduced as to be of no practical value'.[127] This approach was focused on the reality of the freedom in practice. Where the freedom was theoretical but practically illusory, that would not be sufficient. And it was fanciful to think that the applicants would form their own trade union. Finally, the Court noted that two of the applicants objected based on their conscientious convictions. The failure to provide for conscientious exemption meant that the compulsion struck at the very substance of the freedom.[128] This suggested that there may be greater latitude for compulsion where a refusal was based in a simple choice or preference for free riding on collective benefits.

Having established an interference, the Court then considered justification under Article 11(2). It declined to consider the general functional justifications for the closed shop, which had presumably been set out in the TUC's memorial.[129] This was because the Court's task was to consider the specific closed shop agreement on the facts rather than the closed shop in general. On proportionality, the Court was particularly concerned by the fact that many

[123] Ibid. [52].
[124] Ibid. [55].
[125] Ibid.
[126] Ibid.
[127] Ibid.
[128] Ibid. [57].
[129] Ibid. [61].

closed shop agreements did not require existing non-union members to join and that the Donovan Commission had proposed special safeguards for existing employees.[130] Furthermore, the organisational strength of trade unions in the railway sector meant that 'the railway unions would in no way have been prevented from striving for the protection of their members' interests . . . through the operation of the agreement with British Rail'.[131] The threshold of 'prevention' was of course a high one. However, this did leave open the possibility that in other situations the absence of strong union security might 'prevent' a union from protecting its members' interests.

There was a strong dissenting opinion of Judges Sorensen, Thor Vilhjalmsson, and Lagergren. These judges were from Denmark, Iceland, and Sweden, countries with laws and industrial relations systems that were (unusually in European terms) more accommodating of union security arrangements. They rejected the logical correlativity of positive and negative freedom of association.[132] These rights pursued different functions which did not stand or fall together. Positive freedom of association supported social activities, solidarity, and the shared pursuit of common goals. Negative freedom of association could be a constraint on the abuse of collective power by facilitating individual exit from the group. The appropriate balance between these competing functions was a matter to be determined by member states. That balance might also be affected by different industrial relations contexts. For example, compulsion to join a trade union in a system where unions are divided on ideological or religious lines has a different quality to compulsion where unions are organised on an industrial or occupational basis. The dissenting judgment considered that Article 11 should be neutral on the closed shop, neither required nor prohibited.

As an early Article 11 judgment, it is difficult to identify clear principles on negative freedom of association. The majority's reasoning was highly particularised and focused on the specific compulsion on the facts of the case. This no doubt reflected caution about their constitutional legitimacy given the national sensitivities in these early industrial relations cases. In an important analysis and critique, Forde offered the following observations:

> A general issue arising out of the case is the appropriateness of judges, many of them with relatively little industrial relations expertise, laying down common

[130] Ibid. [64]. Report of the Royal Commission on Trade Unions and Employers' Associations (1965–1968) (Cmnd. 3623), known as the 'Donovan Commission' because the Chair was Lord Donovan.
[131] Ibid.
[132] Ibid. [6].

> standards for collective bargaining systems of great complexity that often differ fundamentally from each other. The closed shop question itself may fall outside the specifically industrial relations realm and more within that of civil liberties. Nevertheless, and especially at the international level, there is a grave danger of amateurs, no matter how eminent they may be as jurists, tinkering with arrangements they do not fully understand.[133]

This touches upon the fundamental issue of this book. Is *Young, James and Webster* an example of the civil liberty undermining the labour law conception of freedom of association? There is little doubt that Wedderburn himself was sympathetic to Forde's analysis. Against Forde, I think that *Young, James and Webster* points in the opposite direction. There can be little doubt that the dissenting judges had brought their own national industrial relations knowledge to bear in crafting their opinion. For different reasons, I think the majority were also guided by labour law considerations in reaching their conclusions.

First, we have already encountered the incommensurability argument in Chapter 4 on the right to collective bargaining. There are wide comparative variations in the legislative definition of the right to collective bargaining. That is not the case for the closed shop in Europe. Even by the early 1980s, closed shop practices were either prohibited or severely restricted in many European countries. In this way, the restrictive approach in *Young, James and Webster* was integrating an emerging European *labour law consensus* that the closed shop was fundamentally suspect. This was not an example of amateur judicial tinkering or the clumsy elevation of a civil liberty conception. On the contrary, the Court appears to have been sensitive to its expertise deficit in treating the closed shop arrangement as suspect, given the clarity on the comparative law position in Europe. It was a clarity that was highly unusual in comparative labour law in Europe.

Second, the applicants had been subjected to strong compulsion in the form of dismissal that (in two cases) interfered with deeply held conscientious convictions. Given the Court's observations on justification, there was no good reason for the law to permit their dismissal in these circumstances. This case is therefore aligned with the strong protection of individual workers from discriminatory treatment in the 'right to organise' and 'right to strike' case law examined in Chapters 4 and 5. The dismissals constituted an abuse of private power, with severe social and economic consequences for the individual workers. *Young, James and Webster* is fully aligned with the strong

[133] Michael Forde, 'The "Closed Shop" Case' (1982) 11 Industrial Law Journal 1, 13.

protection of individuals from discriminatory treatment in 'positive' freedom of association cases like *Wilson v UK* and *Danilenkov v Russia*.[134] In the terminology of Chapters 4 and 5, these closed shop cases should be understood as 'individual' rather than 'collective' cases. Finally, the Court was evidently aware of the legislative changes in the UK. The closed shop was in the process of being restricted by democratically enacted legislation. In this way, the majority judgment respected democratic values and the freedom of member states to legislate on industrial relations matters. This demonstrates respect for subsidiarity, which is particularly important in the industrial relations context.

When *Young, James and Webster* was decided, there still seemed to be scope for argument that closed shop arrangements could be justified under Article 11 in particular circumstances. The later cases pursued a tougher line on the closed shop and fuller recognition of negative freedom of association.

B. Article 11 and negative freedom of association

Today, most ECHR judgments on trade union rights set out the 'essential' elements in the following terms:

> the Court has built up, through its case-law, a non-exhaustive list of the essential elements of trade-union freedom, including the right to form and join a trade union, the prohibition of closed-shop agreements, the right for a trade union to seek to persuade the employer to hear what it has to say on behalf of its members and, having regard to developments in labour relations, the right to bargain collectively with the employer, which has, in principle, except in very specific cases, also become one of those essential elements.[135]

There are two aspects to this paragraph that indicate something unusual about the treatment of the closed shop. The first is that the other elements are described as 'rights', such as the right to form and join a trade union or the right to bargain collectively with the employer. By contrast, there is no reference to a *right* not to join a trade union. Instead, it is formulated as the *prohibition* of closed shop arrangements. The second is that the formulation of this as prohibitive implies that closed shop agreements can no longer be justified

[134] [2009] ECHR 1243.

[135] *Humpert and others v Germany* Applications nos. 59433/18, 59477/18, 59481/18, and 59494/18, 14 December 2023 [100].

under Article 11(2). If justification was possible, it would be misleading to describe closed shop as prohibited. The proportionality enquiry would be facilitated by describing the relevant entitlement as a right not to join a trade union, but it is not characterised as a right, unlike the other listed essential elements.

After *Young, James and Webster*, the closed shop has been considered again in several later cases, the most important of which was *Sorensen and Rasmussen v Denmark*.[136] The Court in *Sorensen* considered the position in relevant comparative and international law and practice. There were two features of significance. The first was the comparative position and the convergence of national legal norms in Europe to prohibit or restrict the closed shop: 'It appears that among the member states of the Council of Europe, only a very limited number of States, including Denmark and Iceland, permit by law pre-entry closed shop agreements in general or in certain sectors.'[137] The second was the position under the European Social Charter (ESC) which treated the closed shop as a violation of Article 5 and the right to organise.[138] The relevance of these factors went to the position of the ECtHR as a non-specialist court in respect of labour issues. Where national labour laws and practices and socio-economic rights instruments like the ESC converged on treating closed shops as illegitimate, this meant that an Article 11 interpretation supporting the closed shop was more likely to be normatively suspect. This case demonstrates that the civil liberty was sensitive to widely shared labour law understandings of the relevant freedoms. The Court also indicated that it was important to take account 'of changing perceptions of the relevance of closed shop agreements for securing the effective enjoyment of trade union freedom.'[139]

This led the Court to be more explicit in its recognition of negative freedom of association: 'the notion of personal autonomy is an important principle underlying the interpretation of the Convention guarantees. This notion must therefore be seen as an essential corollary of the individual's freedom of choice implicit in Article 11 and confirmation of the importance of the negative aspect of that provision.'[140] It also followed that, unlike in other contexts of trade union freedoms, there was a reduced margin of appreciation for states in respect of closed shop agreements.[141] This was because of the threats posed to individuals and minorities by closed shop arrangements, and the risk of abuse

[136] [2008] 46 EHRR 29.
[137] Ibid. [34].
[138] Ibid. [35]–[36].
[139] Ibid. [58].
[140] Ibid. [54].
[141] Ibid. [58].

of a dominant position by the union.[142] This mirrored the justifications for a narrower margin of appreciation in cases involving risks of employer abuse of dominant position as in trade union victimisation cases. This applied to all forms of closed shop, whether pre- or post-entry. In Denmark itself, there had been various attempts to legislate against the closed shop, and closed shops only applied to a minority of employees in the Danish labour market. The Court regarded this as further evidence that closed shops were not an essential means for securing the interests of workers and trade unions.[143] After *Sorensen*, it was but a short step to the current position that the prohibition of the closed shop is an essential element of Article 11.

Other decisions demonstrate the far-reaching consequences of the ECtHR's protection of negative freedom of association. For example, *Vordur Olafsson v Iceland* (*Vordur Olafsson*) involved an Article 11 challenge to a compulsory levy (the 'Industry Charge') imposed on certain private sector enterprises, collected by the State Treasury in the manner of a special tax and then distributed to the Federation of Icelandic Industries (FII).[144] The FII was a private law organisation and its objective was to promote Icelandic industry and a competitive working environment for Icelandic businesses. The applicant was a member of the Master Builders' Association which was not affiliated to the FII. While it was possible for him to be a member of the FII, the applicant did not join it. He also objected to its positive stance on accession to the European Union. In fact, more than 10,000 persons were subject to the mandatory Industry Charge, whereas the FII only had approximately 1100–1200 members. There were special benefits for members of the FII, although its policy work was undertaken on behalf of Icelandic businesses more generally. The claimant alleged that this compulsory levy violated his Article 11 right, specifically the negative right to freedom of association. The Court concluded that there had been a violation of Article 11.

It is surprising that the Court treated this as engaging trade union freedoms at all under Article 11 because the FII was engaged in advocacy on behalf of Icelandic businesses. It was not engaged in collective bargaining activities, and it did not represent workers' interests. The levy corresponded to a modest statutory rate of only 0.08% of annual turnover, and he was under no compulsion to join it. The Court nevertheless concluded that the arrangement interfered with his negative freedom of association. The compulsory contributions supported an association that espoused views on Europe that were incompatible

142 Ibid.
143 Ibid. [70].
144 Application no. 20161/06, *Vordur Olafsson v Iceland*, judgment of 27 April 2010.

with his own. His preferred association, the Master Builders' Association, was disadvantaged in connection with membership fees, and this was an interference with the claimant's right to join an organisation of his own choosing.[145] Given this judgment, it is now highly unlikely that even modest agency shop agreements—paying a fee in lieu of membership—would be compatible with Article 11. It is still possible for member states to organise their collective bargaining frameworks to give preferential treatment to representative trade unions.[146]

Another expansive negative freedom case is *Sigurjonsson v Iceland (Sigurjonsson).*[147] The litigation arose out of a challenge to the regulation of taxi services in the Reykjavik area in Iceland. Under the 1989 Law on Motor Vehicle for Public Hire and Regulation no. 208/1989, taxi services in the Reykjavik area were subject to restrictions placed on the number of vehicles available for private hire. A Committee for Taxicab Supervision exercised regulatory supervision and control of taxi services in the area subject to these restrictions. The Committee had three members, one of which was nominated by the relevant trade union. In the Reykjavík area, the relevant trade union was 'Frami', an organisation which existed to protect and represent the professional interests of drivers. While Frami did not undertake collective bargaining on behalf of its members, it was concerned with the fixing of rates for services, monitored the suitability of vehicles and the observance of licence conditions, and other regulatory tasks. The 1989 Law provided for compulsory union membership within an area where restrictions on taxicabs were in force. This meant that the holding of an operating licence was dependent upon membership of Frami in the Reykjavík area. In *Sigurjonsson*, a self-employed driver used negative freedom of association under Article 11 to challenge these restrictions based in compulsory membership. The Court upheld the Article 11 challenge to the 1989 Law.

The threshold issue was whether Frami was an 'association' at all under Article 11. The Court considered that Frami was an autonomous organisation with the freedom to set its own internal rules and objectives. On that basis, it was a private law association. The Court did not decide whether Frami was a 'trade union' because it was not necessary to do so 'since the right to form and join trade unions in that provision is an aspect of the wider right to freedom of association, rather than a separate right'.[148] Yet the Court also

[145] Ibid. [53]. The Court went on to conclude that the interference was not justified under Art 11 (2), so that there was a violation of Art 11.

[146] See the discussion in Chapter 4.

[147] *Sigurdur Sigurjónsson v Iceland* (1993) 16 EHRR 462.

[148] Ibid. [32].

referred to relevant international material on trade unions and the right to organise, including the Committee of Independent Experts under the ESC. This supported its conclusion that there had been an interference with his negative freedom of association.[149] The interference was not justified because the Government had not demonstrated that compulsory membership was necessary to the performance of Frami's supervisory functions.[150] The Court's formulation of the legal issue was crystallised as a matter of individual conscientious objection: '[he] objected to being a member of the association in question partly because he disagreed with its policy in favour of limiting the number of taxicabs and, thus, access to the occupation; in his opinion the interests of the country were better served by extensive personal freedoms, including freedom of occupation, than State regulation.'[151] This is a controversial position. Many business owners no doubt have strong beliefs in unregulated labour markets, but it is doubtful that this belief in free markets is an argument in favour of dismantling or opting out of schemes of public economic regulation.

There are often important differences between trade unions and, say, churches and political parties, where disagreement over values and beliefs means that forced membership is repugnant to values that affirm individual conscience.[152] The deregulation of private taxi hire has facilitated the growth of platform work, which has had significant consequences for working conditions in the sector.[153] *Sigurjonsson* is a striking example of how challenges to union security can have broader deregulatory consequences. In this way, the Court's robust approach to negative freedom of association has tended to reinforce deregulatory approaches to labour law. Nevertheless, human rights law can hardly be singled out as a significant causal factor in this regard. Most labour law systems have tended towards deregulation, in varying degrees, through their own internal legislative developments. The most that can be said is that human rights law (and courts) have not operated as a brake on deregulation.

Before concluding this analysis of negative freedom of association, we would do well to remember that this freedom is also enjoyed by trade unions.

[149] Ibid. [35].
[150] Ibid. [41].
[151] Ibid. [37].
[152] See Stuart White, 'Trade Unionism in a Liberal State', in Amy Gutmann (ed), *Freedom of Association* (Princeton UP 1998) chapter 12. Compelled association in a church or a political party engages the right to conscientious objection in a stronger way than compulsion in respect of schemes of economic regulation. The distinctiveness of trade unions in this regard is weaker where trade unions are religiously or ideologically oriented as in pluralistic systems like France.
[153] Veena Dubal, 'The Drive to Precarity: A Political History of Work, Regulation and Labor Advocacy in San Francisco's Taxi and Uber Economies' (2017) 38 Berkeley Journal of Employment and Labor Law 73.

Indeed, this was recognised by Lord Diplock in *Cheall*. For this reason, the negative freedom is both individual *and* collective. The leading judgment on the trade union's negative freedom of association is *ASLEF v UK*.[154] The ECtHR considered the scope of the trade union's freedom to determine its own membership criteria under UK law by reference to Article 11. The case arose out of the union's attempts to expel Mr Lee from the trade union because of his association with a far-right political party, the British National Party (BNP). This was based in the union's view that Mr Lee's political association was antithetical to its anti-fascist values as an organisation. These values were specified in the constitutional objects of ASLEF which included a commitment to socialist principles and anti-racism. The union's ability to determine its membership criteria was extensively regulated and restricted by statute.

The Court found that UK law violated Article 11. The Court in *ASLEF* referred to ILO materials in support of its reasoning.[155] Trade union autonomy is a fundamental principle under ILO Convention 87 Article 2, which provides that 'Workers and employers, without distinction whatsoever, shall have the right to establish and, subject only to the rules of the organisation concerned, to join organisations of their own choosing without previous authorisation'. This is subject to Article 8 which requires organisations to respect the general law of the land in exercising their rights under Convention 87. The Court also referred to the ESC, and the ECSR's criticisms of the statutory rules under consideration in the *ASLEF* case itself.[156] These statutory rules were held to infringe Article 5 of the ESC.

The Court drew an explicit parallel with the individual's negative freedom:

> As an employee or worker should be free to join, or not join a trade union without being sanctioned or subject to disincentives (*e.g. Young, James and Webster v. the United Kingdom*, judgment of 13 August 1981, Series A no. 44, *mutatis mutandis, Wilson & the National Union of Journalists and Others*, cited above), so should the trade union be equally free to choose its members. Article 11 cannot be interpreted as imposing an obligation on associations or organisations to admit whosoever wishes to join. Where associations are formed by people, who, espousing particular values or ideals, intend to pursue common goals, it would run counter to the very effectiveness of the freedom at stake if they had no control over their membership.[157]

[154] [2007] ECHR 184.
[155] Ibid. [25].
[156] Ibid. [22]–[24].
[157] Ibid. [39].

The limits to this collective negative freedom were circumscribed by the protection of individuals from the potential for abuse of a dominant position by the union:

> the State must nonetheless protect the individual against any abuse of a dominant position by trade unions (see *Young, James and Webster* judgment, cited above, § 63). Such abuse might occur, for example, where exclusion or expulsion from a trade union was not in accordance with union rules or where the rules were wholly unreasonable or arbitrary or where the consequences of exclusion or expulsion resulted in exceptional hardship (see *Cheall*, cited above, *Johanssen v. Norway*, no. 13537/88, Comm. Dec. 7.5.90).[158]

This reinforces the foundational importance of the protection of individuals from abuse of power and arbitrary treatment. It is a thread that not only connects the justifications for protecting individual and collective 'negative' freedom of association. It runs through the entire body of judge-made law on freedom of association, including the right to organise and the right to strike. Even as the Court was protecting collective rights in *ASLEF*, it did not lose sight of equality, non-discrimination, and the curtailment of arbitrary power.

V. Is There a Human Right Not to Be a Trade Union Member?

Reflecting on the closed shop from a human rights perspective, Virginia Mantouvalou asked if there is a human right not to be a trade union member?[159] She examined this question using Kahn-Freund's now familiar distinction between the 'civil liberty' and the 'labour law' conceptions of freedom of association. Mantouvalou rejected the idea that these two conceptions are necessarily in conflict with each other. She envisaged a mutually supportive relation based in the realisation of real freedom in the workplace. This meant that there was no human right not to be a trade union member. Provided that the closed shop respected principled limits, such as the avoidance of arbitrary power and non-encroachment on the conscientious political

[158] Ibid. [43].

[159] Virginia Mantouvalou, 'Is There a Human Right Not to Be a Union Member? Labour Rights under the European Convention on Human Rights', in Colin Fenwick and Tonia Novitz (eds), *Human Rights at Work* (Hart 2010) chapter 15.

commitments of the individual worker, closed shops were compatible with human rights. In contributing to effective trade union action in the workplace, by consolidating bargaining strength, it supported rather than eroded workers' real freedom.

It is worth reflecting further on the nature of the distinction between the civil liberty and labour law conceptions in the context of negative freedom of association. This chapter has demonstrated that the closed shop was controversial even within the single intellectual tradition of collective laissez-faire. The case study of the UK also revealed a complex pattern of legal regulation. The common law was relatively permissive of the closed shop while developing public law controls to protect individuals from abuse of power by trade unions. Statutory interventions were shaped by the wider justifications for labour law which underwent significant changes from the 1970s onwards. By the beginning of the 1990s, the restriction of closed shops was justified by a mixture of justifications emphasising worker free choice, reduction of trade union power, and the removal of obstructions to efficient labour markets. The legislative justifications owed little to human rights. Unusually, perhaps, the UK was not an outlier in terms of its restrictiveness. There was a developing consensus in European countries that closed shops were suspect labour market institutions and should be restricted or even prohibited. In this way, the restrictive approach of the ECtHR was aligned with convergent social conventions and legal practices in European labour law systems. In no sense was this a civil liberty conception disrupting the labour law conception of negative freedom of association.

This narrow margin of appreciation in the Article 11 closed shop cases was consistent with the reduced margin in other 'individual' Article 11 cases where individual workers are exposed to the risk of abuse of power through trade union victimisation. These cases have been considered in Chapters 4 and 5. Even if one disagrees with the ECtHR's repudiation of closed shops, it is at least internally coherent with its broader approach to other trade union rights.

Is there a human right not to be a trade union member? The answer today under Article 11 is almost certainly yes. Against Wedderburn's views, this does not reflect the unwieldy intervention of an overbearing human rights court disrupting national labour law systems in pursuit of an alien civil liberty agenda. It has flowed from the Court's respect for subsidiarity and the autonomy of national labour law systems which have converged on protection for negative freedom of association. It has also flowed from the judicial concern to protect individuals from arbitrary treatment, discrimination, and abuse of power.

The more pertinent question now is, is there a human right to the closed shop (and against labour law developments)? The answer to that is now tolerably clear: the prohibition of the closed shop is an essential element of trade union rights under Article 11. This has been led by democratically enacted legislation and evolving social practices. It owes very little to abstract philosophical arguments about freedom or judicial tinkering by well-meaning amateurs in remote human rights courts.

7
The Enduring Autonomy of Labour Law

This book started with Sir Otto Kahn-Freund's famous quotation on the two legal lives of freedom of association:

> Freedom to organise has two social and therefore two legal functions. It is a civil liberty, a human right, an aspect of freedom of association . . . its existence and adequate guarantees for its exercise are, however, also indispensable conditions for the operation of collective labour relations.[1]

This bifurcation has been explored through the legal history of freedom of association; the determination of personal scope; and the rights to bargain collectively, to strike, and to disassociate. The focus has been on jurisdictions where there has been a reflexive interaction between general constitutional standards and the (usually statutory) legal rules and institutions of collective labour relations. The arguments inevitably have less relevance to legal systems where there is limited constitutional interaction between freedom of association and labour legislation. The exemplar of this case is the US legal system, where constitutional interactions with labour law have been minimal, which has contributed to the 'ossification' of federal labour laws.[2] Indeed, given the current ideological orientation of the US Supreme Court, minimal interaction may be the safest bet for organised labour.

In broad terms, I have argued that there is a basic distinction between the 'collective' and 'individual' aspects of freedom of association. When courts have considered the 'collective' aspects of freedom of association—for example, the protection of secondary strike action, the legal criteria of 'representative' trade unions, and the procedural preconditions of a lawful strike—they

[1] Kahn-Freund, cited in Lord Wedderburn, 'Freedom of Association or Right to Organise? The Common Law and International Sources', in Lord Wedderburn, *Employment Rights in Britain and Europe* (Lawrence & Wishart 1991) 142.

[2] I am grateful to Cindy Estlund for emphasising this point to me. See Cynthia Estlund, 'The Ossification of American Labor Law' (2002) 102 Columbia Law Review 1527. It is also important to recognise that the US Supreme Court should not be regarded as the central case of a flourishing set of constitutional arrangements for the purposes of comparative enquiry. See further Peter Cane, *The Distorting Lens of Convergent Constitutional Theory* (Hart 2025).

Freedom of Association. Alan Bogg, Oxford University Press. © Alan Bogg 2026. DOI: 10.1093/9780191831690.003.0007

have proceeded with due restraint. The courts have deferred to legislatures, sensitive to considerations of democracy and their own limited judicial expertise. This has been aligned with a style of reasoning that is instrumental in character. Typically, the threshold for judicial intervention is triggered when the collective norms in the legal framework have prevented the trade union from representing the occupational interests of its members. Often, adjudication in this collective sphere has depended upon the identification of core elements of trade union activity. Typically, this core has consisted of primary collective bargaining (and primary strikes) between an employer and its own workers. Other forms of trade union activity, such as secondary or political strikes, receive more attenuated legal protection. This determination of the core by human rights courts reflects deeply embedded categories and understandings of legitimate trade union activity that can be traced back into the 19th- and early 20th-century development of labour law: see Chapter 2. In this 'collective' domain, the autonomy of labour law is alive and well in the human rights courts. This vitality flows from the theory of judicial deference elaborated in Chapter 1.

By contrast, where 'individual' aspects of freedom of association are engaged, the courts have proceeded with less deference. This reflects the fundamental importance to the judicial role of equality, non-discrimination, and restraining abuse of power. Equality before the law is a multifaceted ideal, and it has been relevant in a range of different contexts. Chapter 3 considered the role of equality arguments in evaluating the allocation of statutory protections to different groups of workers. Where occupational groups are excluded from legislation, the court must assess whether the exclusion can be justified by relevant reasons. Where occupational groups experience significant disadvantages, the court must assess whether substantive equality demands tailored protections that ensure a level associational playing field. Chapters 4 and 5 considered the distinctive importance of equal moral standing as a basis for constitutional protections against discrimination and victimisation. The exposure of workers to risks of private punishment for exercising their trade union rights is demeaning to them. The closed shop also operates as a potential threat to the equal moral standing of workers, and this was considered in Chapter 6. The closed shop should therefore be treated as an 'individual' issue on the typology defended here.

The constitutional elaboration of duties not to dismiss or otherwise victimise workers for exercising their rights at work is a basic requirement of equal moral standing. Here, instrumental arguments are less important. It does not matter if individual victimisation impedes the achievement of collective goals in the workplace. Discriminatory victimisation is intrinsically wrongful, quite apart from any consequential effects on trade union organisational strength in the workplace.

Does it follow that human rights challenges to 'collective' freedom of association measures are inevitably destined to fail? Or that human rights have nothing to add to whatever the labour legislation happens to say? While human rights challenges will always face significant deference hurdles, there will be circumstances where the autonomy of legislated labour law can be overcome. Sometimes, where a legal restriction has the effect of negating the union's ability to protect the occupational interests of workers, the legal framework may violate human rights unless the restriction can be justified in accordance with a strict proportionality standard. As an example, take the recent situation in P&O Ferries where nearly 800 seafarers were dismissed with immediate effect. It was impossible to organise any effective countervailing industrial pressure on the employer because of the restrictions on secondary and political strikes.[3] There could be no primary dispute because there were no longer any seafarers employed on the relevant routes: they had been replaced by non-unionised agency workers. Unlike the *RMT* case, where the union had been able to defend its members' occupational interests despite the legal restrictions,[4] the facts in P&O Ferries were more propitious for an effective Article 11 challenge. Other examples include where legislation was enacted based on inadequate consultation or flawed democratic processes, or where collective restrictions are particularly invasive of primary collective bargaining and have been subject to criticism by expert international bodies such as the ILO or ESC committees. While there are wide democratic limits for the 'collective' elements of freedom of association, these are still *limits*, and constitutional courts have an important role to play in supervising them.

What of the role of courts more generally? Does this study have anything to contribute to wider debates about judicial power? Labour law represents an excellent case study because the democratic sensitivities around judicial intervention are so acute, even for constituencies that might be thought to welcome it (such as trade unions). The pages of law journals are often peppered with the language of frustration and disappointment when courts fail to vindicate workers' human rights. This reaches back into a venerable critical tradition that identified courts as aligned with and supportive of the social and economic status quo. Courts and judges should always be evaluated by the cogency of their reasoning, and by reference to constitutional values such as

[3] See Alan Bogg, 'Rhetoric and Reality: The P&O Ferries Scandal and the Right to Strike' (2025) 45 Comparative Labor Law and Policy Journal 398.
[4] *RMT v UK* [2014] IRLR 467.

democracy and the separation of powers. To criticise courts for aligning with the (democratically endorsed) economic status quo is like criticising water for being wet. The role of courts is to decide disputes based upon the authoritative legal sources. Legal reasoning is meant to be conservative because it is inevitably tethered to those norms and established legal and political institutions. Legal change in courts is incremental. This does not mean that radical scholars and activists should give up on transformative structural change. It does mean that this is best pursued through legislation and democratic participation. The most appropriate contribution of the courts is to be guided by relevant deference considerations and to facilitate transformative democratic change within wide constitutional limits.

Contrary to some popular caricatures of Strasbourg, there is very little evidence of rogue human rights courts applying human rights principles willy-nilly in ways that are disruptive of labour legislation. The courts have generally deferred to legislation when they ought to have deferred (especially in 'collective' cases), and they have intervened when they ought to have intervened (especially in 'individual' cases). Under Article 11, subsidiarity has been a living legal and political value. It is not something that the judges merely pay lip service to.

The ECtHR has been especially mindful of the diversity of labour law systems in Europe. This raises interesting questions about the distinction between supranational and national constitutional standards. The ECtHR has deployed the margin of appreciation concept to ensure there is appropriate respect for cultural and legal diversity in collective labour relations. The adherence of English courts to the mirror principle has generated strict limits on what can be achieved through Article 11 in domestic litigation. The mirror principle holds that if there is no violation in the eyes of the Strasbourg court, the English court must defer to that European norm. That is because if there is no rights violation, there is no right to bring home under the HRA. The contrast with the position of the Supreme Court of Canada (SCC) is striking. The SCC is interpreting a Canadian constitutional text in accordance with Canadian constitutional values and Canadian labour history. It has been able to develop contextualised principles and a Canadian right to collective bargaining, to strike, and so forth. The mechanics of the HRA, in domesticating ECHR Convention rights, imposes stronger limits on the constitutional creativity of English courts. It is for the reader to decide if the gains of the ECHR outweigh these costs. For what it is worth, I think that the gains do outweigh the costs, and the mirror principle has instilled a healthy sense of caution on the part of our judges in collective labour relations.

In terms of methodology, the book has pursued an internal interpretive approach. It has sought to understand and apply the legal and constitutional principles immanent in the existing fabric of legal systems. In Chapter 1, I acknowledged that there were certain risks in this enterprise. The most significant risk is the lack of critical distance between lawmaker and scholar. It could mean that a study of this kind might have been written by Dr Pangloss, so that whatever the courts happen to decide is the best of all possible worlds because the judges are the best and wisest among us. I hope the content of this book persuades the reader that an internal approach can be suitably critical. At many points in this book, the reasoning of the courts has been criticised, for example, *Deliveroo* in Chapter 4 and *Mercer* in Chapter 5. Critique is not anathema to the internal method. This method simply dictates the form that critique should take. It is not sufficient to wave a pet political or economic theory at judges and shout at them. That kind of external critique is easy. It is also less likely to achieve positive changes in the case law because most judges will just react with a shrug. The internalist critic must expose the ways in which the reasoning is defective *as legal reasoning*, how it deviates from norms and values that ought to have influenced that reasoning. That is harder to do because it requires the critic to take the law seriously in its own terms. While this book certainly contains errors and flaws, eulogising judges (whether living or dead) is not one of them.

The book started with Sir Otto Kahn-Freund. It is fitting that it should finish with him too. Kahn-Freund was right. The human right to freedom of association is indispensable to the operation of collective labour relations. It is a vision of human rights that is both modest and radical.

Index

For the benefit of digital users, indexed terms that span two pages (e.g., 52–53) may, on occasion, appear on only one of those pages.